ATTEWELL, Paul A. Radical political economy since the sixties; a sociology of knowledge analysis. Rutgers, 1984. 306p bibl index 83-24650. 30.00 ISBN 0-8135-1053-8. CIP

Attewell examines the nature and fate of Western Marxist scholarship. These are concerns also addressed by Perry Anderson's *Considerations on Western Marxism* (CH, Apr '77) and Alvin Gouldner's *The Two Marxisms* (CH, Jul '80). Using a sociology of knowledge approach oriented toward Thomas Kuhn's notion of paradigm (see *The Structure of Scientific Revolutions*, 2nd ed., CH, Jul '70), Attewell explores radical scholarship in terms of "the type of work chosen, its style and its conclusions" (p. 5) and how academic life affects such work. In a highly informative survey of literature, he examines a variety of topics radical scholars address: industrial segmentation (Bluestone, Wachtel, Hudson); the dual labor market (Gordon, Edwards, Reich, Beck, Horan, Tolbert); the labor process (Braverman, Kusterer, Coombs); the firm (Marglin, Noble, Stone); various forms of crisis theory—disproportionality, underconsumption (Bleaney); rising organic composition of capital, rising wage, the fiscal crisis of the state (O'Connor); imperialism (Baran, ECLA); dependency (Frank); and unequal exchange (Emmanuel, Amin). Attewell detects a tendency in radical scholarship to select questions of a moral philosophic nature (e.g., poverty). In addition, he notes a tendency to modify the major paradigm (Marxism) to meet unfolding conditions, to orient work so that it challenges orthodox formulations, and to embrace dominant modes of Western scholarship methodologies such as positivism. This is an excellent introduction to the ideas, networks, and personalities of a growing presence in the Western academy. Index; bibliography; well produced. For upper-division undergraduates.—*A.S. Wilke, Auburn University*

RADICAL

POLITICAL ECONOMY

SINCE THE SIXTIES

Radical

Political Economy

Since the Sixties

A Sociology of Knowledge Analysis

PAUL A. ATTEWELL

RUTGERS UNIVERSITY PRESS

New Brunswick, New Jersey

Library of Congress Cataloging in Publication Data
Attewell, Paul A., 1949–
  Radical political economy since the sixties.

  Bibliography: p.
  Includes index.
  1. Marxian economics. I. Title.
HB97.5.A88 1984   335.4   83–24650
ISBN 0–8135–1053–8

CONTENTS

ACKNOWLEDGMENTS

THIS BOOK HAS BEEN several years in the making and reflects the benefits of my association with numerous teachers, colleagues, students, and steadfast friends. It is a pleasure to acknowledge them here.

The members of my doctoral dissertation committee read the earliest version and provided useful suggestions for its improvement. My thanks go to Stanley Aronowitz, Bennett Berger, Randall Collins, Roy D'Andrade, and Joseph Gusfield.

I was fortunate to have a year as a postdoctoral fellow at the University of California, Berkeley, where I spent many hours discussing political economy with Michael Burawoy, Bob Fitzgerald, and Jim Stockinger. My intellectual debt to them is considerable.

I am grateful to my colleagues and students at the University of California, Santa Cruz, most especially Bob Marotto, Jr., and William Friedland. They have their own views about the issues treated in this book and did me the honor of debating our differences.

Marlie Wasserman, my editor at Rutgers University Press, was unfailing in her support of this book. She guided it through the painful process of review and revision with patience and determination. I am grateful for all of her efforts.

My wife and colleague, Katherine Newman, was involved in every stage of producing this manuscript, offering substantive criticisms, improving my grammar, and convincing me that if a book is worth writing, it is worth rewriting. I am greatly in her debt.

Finally, I would like to thank my parents, Reginald and Zara Attewell. They encouraged me in the pursuit of the academic life; but more important, they introduced me to the theory and practice of socialism, a family tradition for several generations.

RADICAL

POLITICAL ECONOMY

SINCE THE SIXTIES

INTRODUCTION

IT IS VERY DIFFICULT for the younger generation of left-wing academics in America to come to terms with scholars like Daniel Bell and his collaborators. If history had taken a slightly different course, his generation would have constituted the leading group of left intellectuals of the post–World War II era, for they are among the most important intellectual remnants of the last great upsurge of American leftism. They experienced the political turmoil of the thirties and forties and emerged from it as a left intelligentsia whose knowledge of socialist intellectual history, along with the practical concerns of political organization, has yet to be equaled in this country.

However, the forties and fifties saw the destruction of this American left, the result, in part, of internal and external repression and, in part, of its own failures as a political movement. Some members were crushed by McCarthyism; some were purged by the Party. Others were so appalled by the effects of Stalinism at home or in the USSR that they quit the left in disillusionment. Those who had become supporters of the Trotskyist parties found themselves occupying an increasingly marginal position on the political spectrum, and some began to move slowly rightward.

Thus we have the irony that many of those who might have become the senior figures of today's Marxist intelligentsia are instead ensconced in universities and prestigious research institutes, many having become solidly anticommunist and anti-Marxist. A remarkable proportion of the neo-conservative intellectuals of the 1980s New

Right are aging ex-leftists who received a Marxist political education in the forties. Many other leftists of the forties and fifties simply withdrew from the political arena, not changing their personal politics, but ceasing to pass on their knowledge and values to future generations.

As a result, the left in America suffers from a generation gap that is more profound, I suspect, even than that which the ravages of fascism inflicted upon European leftism. In much of Europe a decimated left emerged from the rubble of World War II too weakened to rule but strong in moral stature, having gained a legitimacy in the antifascist struggle that even Stalinism has been unable to discredit. And the fruition of that movement may well dictate the European politics of the 1980s.

In contrast, the American left intelligentsia, with a few important exceptions, failed to survive its crisis. It is in this sense, I think, that we should understand Bell's *End of Ideology* (1964). What that thesis really represents is the realization that Bell's generation was unable to produce a successor. Having quit the socialist left, he and his colleagues found that there was no one remaining to debate with and apparently no new left intelligentsia in the making. Their response, in most cases, was to announce that the debate itself—or ideology as they saw it—had ended. And in that sense, it had.

But in making this pronouncement, those Old Leftists who had become the New Right were interpreting their own personal development with left political thought as a general historical phenomenon, as a statement by Bell makes clear:

> A number of sociologists—Raymond Aron, Edward Shills, S. M. Lipset, and myself—thus came to view the 1950s as characterized by "an end to ideology." By this we meant that the older political ideas of the radical movement had become exhausted and no longer had the power to compel allegiance or passion among the intelligentsia. (Bell and Kristol 1971: 24)

Here Bell is projecting his own disillusionment, his own shift in allegiance and passion.[1] He also neglects the extent to which the wave of

---

1 John Laslett puts the matter rather well: "Bell's oversimplifications here, as elsewhere in this book, result from his confusing the demise of the Old Left of the 1930s, and particularly the death of the old CP (i.e. the End of Ideology, or the end of the dominant radical impulse for Bell's own particular generation), with the death of socialist idealism generally, which as the rise of the New Left has effectively demonstrated is still very much alive" (Laslett and Lipset 1974: 117).

repression of the 1950s contributed to the apparent "exhaustion" of radical ideas (Caute 1978). Bell and his colleagues chose to see the quiescence of the radical movement among intellectuals as an expression of the bankruptcy of Marxian ideology rather than as a manifestation of the organizational impotence of the Left.[2]

This interpretation led to some backpedaling in the sixties, as social and ideological conflict reached new heights. Bell was moved to elaborate his position: "I should point out that the 'end of ideology' did *not* assume that all social conflict had ended and that the intelligentsia would forswear the search for new ideologies" (Bell and Kristol 1971: 24). Nevertheless, because Bell and many of his collaborators chose not to propagate the Marxist culture in which they themselves were formed, believing it to be dead, they tended to overlook the beginnings of a new left intelligentsia that was returning to the "old" ideology. Instead they tended to view the sixties as a cultural phenomenon rather than as a political one. They emphasized the "counter-culture" as a "psychedelic bazaar" and stressed the new Left's anti-intellectualism. A reading of Bell's *Cultural Contradictions of Capitalism* (1976) might have one believe that the barrenness of the end of the Marxist ideology had extended, for the intelligentsia, right through the sixties.

In fact, a left intelligentsia was re-forming around the few threads of continuity with the thirties and forties. The work of Paul Baran and Paul Sweezy of *Monthly Review*, of Herbert Marcuse, C. Wright Mills, the *Dissent* group, and others, inspired the creation of a new radical consciousness. When Lewis Feuer wrote in 1969, in his "set of post-ideological essays," that "in this history of thought the last decade might well be called the Age of New-Marxism" (Feuer 1969: 1), he had in mind a vulgar, anti-intellectual, "neo-primitivist" Marxism. In truth, however, the late sixties and early seventies saw the formation of radical and/or Marxist journals of philosophy, history, geography, sociology, and political economy in American universities, as well as the establishment of publications in applied fields such as criminology,

---

2 Of course, McCarthyism was not the sole reason for the exhaustion of the left. The failures of the left as a political movement contributed to the burn-out of its members. The revelations concerning Stalinism in the USSR and the endless debates over the character of the Soviet Union took their toll. The left's extraordinary degree of organizational factionalism also contributed to its failure as a political movement and to the exhaustion of its members, as did the practical difficulties of organizing in America. As Bill Friedland has pointed out, the early promise of industrial unionism and the CIO began to fade by the fifties, leaving those involved in working-class activism fighting an ever more difficult battle.

social work, and clinical psychology. A new Marxist intelligentsia was forming in and around the universities, and it was far from anti-intellectual in its approach.

This is not to say that there was a return to the mass Marxist left of the prewar years. The new movement was much smaller, and, so-ciologically speaking, it had a class and organizational base very different from that of its predecessor. In crucial ways it had lost almost all of its intellectual heritage: it suffered from a "generation gap," a lack of continuity with the left of the thirties and forties. Nonetheless, the newly emerging academic left survived and grew through the late six-ties and the seventies while producing a large and distinctive body of scholarship.

The purpose of this book is to describe and comment upon this intel-lectual movement and its work. I shall focus on two theoretical tasks. The first involves a description of the intellectual works of this move-ment. As I mentioned above, the sixties and seventies produced new radical journals in a wide range of disciplines. However, the impact of radical thought was most strongly felt in the academic disciplines of economics, history, political science, and sociology, and especially in their area of overlap, once known as "political economy." My goal, therefore, is to provide a review and analysis of several major theories and discoveries that constitute the new political economy.

Radical political economy is a complex and often jargon-ridden lit-erature. I shall try to order it and make it accessible to the nonspecialist by showing how the different pieces relate to one another, by demon-strating the emergence of arguments and counter-arguments, and by giving my own assessment of the strengths and weaknesses of various analyses. I have chosen to limit my discussion to four major areas: the theory of economic and labor market segmentation; theories of the la-bor process and the firm; analyses of economic crises; and the litera-ture on imperialism and economic dependency. In my opinion these are core topics of radical political economy. Explicating them is a large undertaking, and by limiting my analysis to these areas, I must neces-sarily neglect other important left-wing literatures. Most notably, theo-ries of the state, radical history, class analysis, left analyses of ideol-ogy and culture, and radical feminist analyses of the interrelation of gender and political economy are not dealt with here.

The second intellectual task of this book involves what is known as the "sociology of knowledge." By this I mean the analysis of a body of intellectual work in terms of the social context in which it was produced. I shall seek answers to two questions: How is the political orientation of the theorists manifested in the type of work chosen, its style, and its conclusions? And how does the academic setting of these radical intellectuals further affect the nature of their work?

With these general intellectual tasks understood, I can now outline the structure of this book. The first chapter deals with the sociology of knowledge aspect of the new political economy. It briefly reviews the historical origins of the journals in which most of the work is published and then builds a theoretical model of what characterizes left intellectual work or what is distinctive about a piece of radical scholarship. The impact of institutional surroundings upon left scholarship is also discussed, in part by contrasting the new American political economy with its counterpart in Great Britain.

Subsequent chapters present substantive materials from the new political economy. Chapter Two discusses the theory of segmented labor markets and its application to the analysis of poverty in America. Chapter Three reviews research on the historical development of the labor process and on changes in the structure of the business enterprise. Chapter Four analyzes Marxist and neo-Marxist theories of economic crises, the business cycle, inflation, and so forth. Chapter Five examines theories of imperialism and economic dependency. The last chapter summarizes the issues raised throughout this work, discusses the directions that this body of radical scholarship may take in the future, and provides an overall assessment of the importance of the new political economy.

Chapter One

RADICAL ACADEMIA

THE NEW POLITICAL ECONOMY is not a body of ideas created in a vacuum. On the contrary, in terms of topics, style of exposition, and methodology, this body of work has distinctive characteristics. These derive in part from the structural situation that radical academics face in America and in part from tensions inherent in radical scholarship itself. I shall therefore begin by discussing the origins and subsequent contexts in which radical scholarship develops and how these are related to the goals of radical scholarship. Once these links have been made, the reader will have a sense of the agenda underlying the new political economy.

Origins

Mere remnants of an American left emerged from the 1950s. The Communist Party had been decimated, and the Trotskyist left was fragmented into numerous small parties. Within the solidly anticommunist trade union movement, socialist activists had to adopt a guarded stance. Intellectual survivors of the left were scattered in small numbers throughout academia, but they lacked organizational coherence. Indeed, most were still on the defensive from McCarthyist attempts to expel them from the universities (cf. Caute 1978).

One of the few exceptions to this general state of disorganization was a group of intellectuals centered around *Monthly Review*, an independent socialist journal. *Monthly Review* provided the most distinctive and coherent school of radical analysis in postwar America. Over the years, it elaborated a theory of stagnation crises in the U.S. economy, it developed a critique of the military-industrial complex and of waste in consumerist America, and it analyzed the economic doldrums of Third War countries from a perspective that came to be known as "underdevelopment theory."

Perhaps the most noteworthy competitor of *Monthly Review* was the journal *Dissent*. Here too a group of scholars provided ongoing critical analyses of domestic and foreign affairs while espousing a democratic-socialist alternative. Less successful than *Monthly Review* in developing a distinctive school of thought, *Dissent* was less Marxist in its perspective and much more vehement in criticizing the Soviet bloc. Its theoretical eclecticism probably blunted its influence. There were also individual intellectuals, such as C. Wright Mills and Herbert Marcuse, who continued the traditions of radical scholarship and succeeded to some extent in reaching beyond the audience of the already converted.

Yet, despite the obvious merits of these journals and individuals, they were too few in number and too small in influence to constitute a socialist movement in the United States, or to transmit successfully the lessons of the thirties to the generation of the sixties. As a result, the movements of the sixties were born into a political vacuum, and the absence of an organized left led to a chaotic pluralism of political philosophies.

As almost all chroniclers of the sixties note, the decade first produced a massive and potent social movement that only *later* gave rise to (or, rather, adopted) a socio-political philosophy. Indeed, the history of Students for a Democratic Society, the largest organized body to arise from the antiwar movement, is frequently portrayed in three stages: first, a period of pacifism, protest, and reform during which participants espoused an ill-formed ideology that owed more to Camus than to Marx (Flacks 1971); second, a phase of increasing radicalization and confrontation in which the movement searched for a political ideology; and finally, a time of fragmentation into several vying Marxist-Leninist groups and a disoriented non-Leninist rump (Flacks 1971; Ericson 1975). Thus the sixties movements came to Marxism only on their deathbed, so to speak.

Pre-1960 radical intellectuals frequently found themselves trailing in the rear of these movements, attempting to come to terms with a student activism whose aims they applauded but whose lack of discipline and occasional nihilism strained their loyalties. The upheavals of the sixties nevertheless revitalized left academics in a variety of organizational contexts. Academic trade unions and associations cohered, expanded, and took a more combative role toward university administrations and war research on campus. More important for our purposes were several attempts at creating interdisciplinary organizations of left academics: namely, the New University Conference, the Socialist Scholars Conference, and the Movement for a Democratic Society.

The Socialist Scholars Conference (SSC), founded in 1964, represents one response of the more established left scholars toward the sixties movements.[1] The organization originated with a group of historians—John M. Cammett, Lloyd Gardiner, Eugene D. Genovese, and Warren Susman—who called for a conference of socialist scholars in December 1964. It is a testament to the enduring fear of McCarthyism that these left academics were seriously worried about the use of the term "socialist" in the conference title.

The original intention of the conference founders was to create a forum for socialist intellectual work. Presumably in anticipation of sectarian strife, the conference itself was declared open to all radicals, but the organization was to eschew "taking positions on any political issue" (Fischer et al. 1971: vii). It held a series of successful annual conferences: in 1965, one thousand persons attended; in 1966, over two thousand; in 1967, three thousand; in 1968, six hundred; in 1969, eight hundred; and in 1970, six hundred. Yet by 1971 the organization was defunct.

In many ways the SSC experience epitomized the dilemma of established left intellectuals in the sixties. The organization desperately wanted to avoid sectarianism and to institute a common forum for left scholarship, a first step toward building a left intellectual community in the United States. But its role proved contradictory. The notion of scholarship was confronted with the aspiration of political relevance, and pressure mounted year by year to move from scholarship in general to scholarship applied to the needs of the student and antiwar

---

1 My description of the history of the Socialist Scholars Conference is based upon an essay written by several of its founders, printed as the preface to George Fischer, Alan Block, John M. Cammett, and Richard Friedman (eds.), *The Revival of American Socialism: Selected Papers of the Socialist Scholars Conference*. See Fischer et al. 1971.

movements. Beginning in 1967, the conference attempted to address such relevant issues, only to find that the "agents of change" themselves objected to being studied. Abbie Hoffman became incensed at a participant's work on Yippies, and a Student Non-Violent Coordinating Committee member took exception to a presentation on Black Power.

Unable to reconcile such contradictory demands—scholarship versus relevance, research versus involvement—the organization folded in late 1970. Its key figures went on to combine politics and scholarship on a more individual basis. Almost all presently combine scholarly research, often on left topics, with separate political activism via journals, newspapers, and political parties.[2]

Other organizations of professionals, academics, and nonstudents also formed at this time, often as offshoots of Students for a Democratic Society (SDS). Among others, these included the New University Conference (NUC), Teachers for a Democratic Society, the Movement for a Democratic Society, and Radicals in the Professions. Although typically oriented more toward activism than SSC had been, these organizations faced many of the same dilemmas, especially the problem of combining radical politics with work in specific professions or other workplaces (cf. Sale 1974; Ericson 1975).

A clear pattern emerges from the histories of these multidisciplinary left organizations.[3] Unable to gain a wide consensus concerning their goals, they were racked by internal struggles. Not surprisingly, the major splits occurred between advocates of left scholarship and teaching within the universities or professions and those whose major orientation was working-class organizing and extra-professional activities.

In retrospect, such divisions are predictable. In any period during which revolutionary political action seems plausible, activists feel that they should use any and all organizations of the left as recruiting grounds for party membership. They tend to decry parochial concerns such as university reform and left scholarship while insisting on party political activism. What sets the sixties apart is that in the absence of acceptable left parties outside academia, Leninist and other revolutionaries repeatedly attempted to turn these gatherings of liberal-left pro-

---

2 Professor George Fischer, personal communication.

3 Here I depend upon a detailed, but unfriendly, history provided by Edward E. Ericson in *Radicals in the University* (1975).

fessionals and academics into surrogates for political parties. The result, as Edward Ericson (1975) points out, was to burden such organizations with an impossible range of objectives. A trade union of academics is not a political party; nor is a forum for left scholarship or a pressure group for university reform. Yet SSC, NUC, and other such organizations were all destroyed by conflicts between those who accepted the limited functions of academic and professional organizations and those who either saw these organizations as potential political parties or denied the validity of left organizations with limited functions. Having lost the ability to achieve realistic goals, the organizations became mired down in debate over wider political issues over which they had little real control (Ericson 1975). Indeed, the push for ultimate ends destroyed the moral basis for more limited (hence epithetically "reformist") concerns.

One can only speculate about what would have happened had there been credible political parties in existence. Academic organizations might have successfully defined more limited intellectual, trade union, and scholarly roles as complementary to those of political parties. However, lacking such a party or parties, they became recruiting forums for every political splinter group, their members demoralized by their inability to pursue "relevance," political activism, and scholarship simultaneously and by the constant conflict and confrontation.

By contrast, certain organizations with more limited goals *did* succeed (in terms of longevity) where these interdisciplinary unions of professionals and academics failed. These organizations were notably limited to specific academic disciplines, such as economics, history, and sociology. Lacking the grandiosity (or size) to consider themselves major political actors, they worked to achieve more limited intellectual and university-oriented goals. Thus the late sixties and early seventies saw the appearance of left caucuses in many of the academic disciplines, particularly in the social sciences.

Yet even these caucuses could not remain immune to the dilemmas of scholarship versus relevance and limited political activism versus "turn to the working class" organizing. They also faced invasion from recruiting splinter groups. However, united by their common intellectual concerns and general political stance, these academic caucuses were better able to stave off such assaults. Also, as the sixties receded, the prospects for political activism declined and the rhetorical demands for commitment to a revolutionary party appeared more dubious.

Organizationally, these caucuses adopted formats similar to those of the apolitical professional associations that dominate American academia. Paralleling the American Economics Association was the Union for Radical Political Economics; alongside the American Political Science Association there formed a group called the Caucus for a New Political Science—and so on for sociology, English, and history. Most of these caucuses sponsored journals for the publication of radical scholarship.

During the height of activism in the sixties, radical caucuses in several disciplines attempted more wide-reaching actions. Moves to gain power in the apolitical disciplinary associations were sometimes successful in the short term.[4] But over time there has been a retrenchment. Radical caucuses typically meet yearly, often in the same city and at the same time as their discipline's nonpolitical association. In those fields with the smallest numbers of radicals the organizations have sometimes become moribund while the left journals continue. In disciplines most akin to Marxism—economics, political science, and sociology—the radical paradigm has proven most successful, and the left caucuses have larger memberships, produce research journals with considerable readerships, and so on.

From the perspective of the more activist participants in the sixties movements, this activity is a far cry from (and for some a betrayal of) the hopes of yesteryear. From a larger standpoint, it is indeed a rather pitiable legacy, given the drama of the sixties events. But within academia the radical cause is by no means trivial. Despite much disparagement from orthodox foes, the left position has made its mark in terms of force of scholarship and recruitment of students and faculty. In several academic disciplines left-wing alternatives to orthodoxy have attained recognized size and prestige.

It is worth noting the contrast between this outcome of sixties radicalism, with its academic caucuses and journals of left scholarship, and that of an earlier period in the United States. The 1920s and 1930s saw the last upheavals of socialist movements in the United States. Although the social movements of that era were pre-eminently those of working people, various intellectuals of the period also rallied to so-

---

4 Alan Wolfe (1971) details the attempts by radicals in political science; Edward Ericson (1975) describes radicalism in the Modern Language Association; and Martin Nicolaus (1973) describes radical activism in the American Sociological Association.

cialist and communist parties in that act of identification with the proletariat that Marx and Engels described as a prelude to all great class
conflicts.

However, the universities of the period were comparatively small
and generally conservative. Indeed, most of the intellectuals who
turned leftward came from journalism, the arts, and especially the literary world, rather than from academia. Professors who did join the
left movements generally subsumed their particular specialist interests
in favor of general political activism. Thus, while left literary journals
flourished, the various academic disciplines did not contribute *as such*
to the movements of the thirties. Radical academia did not produce a
bevy of disciplinary journals. The nearest equivalents were *Science
and Society*, an interdisciplinary journal, and the literary *Partisan Review*. T. B. Bottomore, in reviewing this earlier era, concluded:

> This decade of the 1930's has sometimes been portrayed as a
> "Marxist" period in American intellectual life, but the judgment
> calls for many qualifications. Certainly, Marxism was more fre-
> quently and extensively discussed in such liberal journals as *The
> Nation* and *The New Republic*. Yet it was not widely accepted; and
> above all, there was not created any significant body of Marxist
> social thought applied directly to American society and culture.
> (Bottomore 1967: 38)

By contrast, the sixties and early seventies saw a proliferation of journals designed to disseminate left-oriented theory and research within
the boundaries of established university disciplines. Much of this work
was specifically oriented toward American society and culture.[5]

To the best of my knowledge, this flowering of academicized left
scholarship is peculiar to the generation of the 1960s. It has been
mirrored on an international scale across Western Europe and North
America. For better or worse, mass higher education has shifted the

---

5 One should add that Bottomore's view of the lack of social analysis in the thirties
is not shared by everyone. Although the left in academia was small then, some say that
it produced important intellectual works. For example, Richard Schlatter, writing of
left historians, cites F. O. Matthiessen's *American Renaissance* (1941) and Arthur
Schlesinger's *Age of Jackson* (1946) as important products of thirties academic radicalism. See Schlatter 1977: 605–615. Nevertheless Bottomore's basic point is well
taken. By contrast, the sixties and seventies have produced a much larger body of left
social and cultural analysis of American society. See Stanley Aronowitz, *False Promises* (1974), as a good example.

locus and style of radical political protest in the advanced capitalist countries, giving it a distinctly academic tinge. Hal Draper may be partially correct in his dour prediction concerning most of the sixties student radicals:

> Ten years from now most of them will be rising in the world and in income, living in the suburbs from Terra Linda to Atherton, raising two or three babies, voting Democratic, and wondering what on earth they were doing in Sproul Hall—trying to remember and failing. (Draper 1965: 169)

Nevertheless, the aftermath of that era *is* still present within academia in the form of the various left academic caucuses, their journals, and the impact that their scholarship has had upon the orthodox social sciences. I shall characterize these journals and the institutional context of left academicians before proceeding to describe the theories they have produced.

The Journals

Looking at the journals listed in Table 1, one is struck by their diverse organizational affiliations. Some are organs of left academic associations (e.g., *The Review of Radical Political Economics*); some are produced by intellectual collectives (*Socialist Review, Kapitalistate*); and some explicitly abjure organizational affiliation (*Monthly Review, Dissent*). For a number of reasons I consider that the specific organizational base of these journals is fairly unimportant.

First, each journal accepts articles from a wider range of individuals than the organizational collectives or editorial boards attached to them. With perhaps one exception, these publications declare their commitment to accept serious contributions regardless of the author's political affiliation so long as the contribution falls within some general rubric such as left, Marxist, or radical. Hence both the contributorship and the readership of the journals are decentralized. In this sense they are relatively open forums.

Second, these publications do not espouse a "party line." They are journals of intellectual debate rather than popular propaganda.[6] Arti-

---

6 The journal *Monthly Review* is a partial exception. Although not a propaganda magazine in the sense described above, it does have a distinctive theoretical and politi-

TABLE I. *Left Theoretical Journals Since the 1960s*

Discipline	Journal(s)	Organization
Anthropology	*Dialectical Anthropology*	
Clinical Psychology	*Radical Therapist*	
Criminology	*Crime and Social Justice*	Union of Radical Criminologists
Economics	*Review of Radical Political Economics*	Union for Radical Political Economics
English	*Radical Teacher*	Radical Caucus in English
Geography	*Antipode*	
German	*New German Critique*	
History	*Radical History Review*	Mid-Atlantic Radical Historians Organization
Philosophy	*Telos*	
Political Science	*Politics and Society*	Caucus for a New Political Science
Psychology	*Dialectical Psychology Newsletter*	
Social Work	*Catalyst*	
Sociology	*Insurgent Sociologist*	Union of Marxist Social Scientists
	Berkeley Journal of Sociology	
Cross-Disciplinary	*Bulletin of Concerned Asian Scholars* *Kapitalistate* *Latin American Perspectives* *Marxist Perspectives* *Left Curve* *Social Text* *Theory and Society* *Contemporary Crises* *Socialist Review* *Radical America*	

cles in one journal are frequently referenced in others. Debates between opposed (or simply different) opinions also go on *within* individual journals.

Another aspect of these journals that distinguishes them from the propaganda organs of political parties is the unresolved attitude they take toward political and theoretical issues. Party organs typically apply a framework like Marxist-Leninism to a particular situation. The small, organized group of contributors that runs the party journal then seeks to transmit the completed analysis to a larger audience. By contrast, the intellectual journals are *seeking* an analysis as much as transmitting one, allowing alternative perspectives to debate, refute, and test one another, and leaving numerous questions open.

The relatively open character of these journals is also to be seen in their nationwide and often international contributors and readerships. For example, *Kapitalistate* is an international journal that shifted its editorial base from Europe to the United States, and its articles are drawn from numerous countries. This internationalism is true, though to a lesser extent, of the other journals. Many have international subscribers and accept contributions from various countries, some specially translated.

This internationalism reflects an additional and very important feature of the American left: the conceptual sophistication of current English-language Marxism is immeasurably indebted to foreign theorists. Wave after wave of new discoveries has transformed "traditional" Marxism. Translations of Antonio Gramsci, Karl Korsch, Georg Lukács, Lucio Colletti, Louis Althusser, Nicos Poulantzas, Ernest Mandel, Arghiri Emmanuel, Samir Amin, Jurgen Habermas, Claus Offe, and others have enabled American theory to leapfrog forward. American journals such as *Telos* and *New German Critique* have specialized in the translation and analysis of foreign texts and the introduction of European theorists. Certain British journals, especially *New Left Review* and *Capital and Class* (originally *Bulletin of the Conference of Socialist Economists*), have also become part of the American left scene.

---

cal position to which it adheres in most of its articles. The journal clearly is a medium for disseminating the views of the editors rather than a journal of debate and research. Nevertheless, it too is a relatively open forum. It publishes manuscripts submitted by non-editorial board authors, and over the years it has seemed to broaden the range of published analyses. It stands somewhere between the party journals of the prewar era and the contemporary research journals in terms of its purposes and organization.

The relative openness of these American journals, their focus on debate, and the decentralization of their contributorship as well as readership pull them away from parochialism and/or a tendency to develop into party-line propaganda journals. Although each journal has its specific area of expertise and its own distinctive style, there is sufficient overlap of issues, general orientation, readership, and contributorship to suggest that they are developing a shared body of knowledge, a common marketplace for ideas, and, ultimately, a left intellectual community. But who constitutes the community? Who writes for these journals, and who reads them? Although it is hard to obtain an objective answer to these questions, the available information suggests that these journals are published overwhelmingly by and for academicians—if one understands this term in its widest sense as including faculty, students, and others engaged in intellectual labor. This conclusion comes from examining journals that give biographical data or institutional affiliations of contributors. With a few exceptions, the contributors are academics.

Again, *Monthly Review* is something of an exception. Of its core group of editors (Baran, Sweezy, Harry Braverman, and Harry Magdoff), only two are/were academics. The *Monthly Review* consciously attempts to be nontechnical in order to reach a lay audience, whereas the other journals tolerate technical jargon, academic writing styles, and occasionally mathematical notation. *Monthly Review* probably spans, more than any other publication, the non-academic (and aging) members of the Old Left and the younger academically oriented New Left.

In any event, the intellectual community we are talking about is quite small—a tiny and atypical group in this country of 200 million. *Monthly Review* sells about 13,000 copies; the *Review of Radical Political Economics* goes to 3,000 persons; *Telos* and *New German Critique* to 3,000; and *The Insurgent Sociologist* to 1,500. By comparison, the *American Economic Review* has a circulation of 26,000; the *American Political Science Review*, 20,000; and the *American Sociological Review*, 15,000. Each of the latter publications is sponsored by the professional association of its respective discipline. But in the world of ideas, numbers are less important than elsewhere. The left has made a disproportionate impact in several disciplines. As will be seen, it has generated numerous theoretical innovations, and its theories have stimulated much debate within the nonradical academic world. According to Ladd and Lipset (1975), the left is also overrepresented in the "heights" of academia—in the research universities and prestige colleges—which may explain its disproportionate influence.

Nevertheless, the academic left is in a rather anomalous position within academia. Left-wing intellectuals, by their own choosing, adopt a different stance toward their professional enterprise than do their apolitical colleagues. And, not of their own choosing, they evoke a variety of responses from their more orthodox colleagues, some of which are quite negative. To understand the background of the new political economy, we therefore need to consider the role of left-wing academics, to gain a sense of their goals and of the institutional context in which they work.

The Left Academic

The following remarks are limited to left-wing academicians in the social sciences and liberal arts faculties of American universities. For the left-wing scholar in these disciplines, political commitment and scholarship intertwine in complex ways. There are political implications in the topic of one's research, one's methodology, one's style of analysis, and so on. To understand this, we begin at the most abstract level by constructing a *homunculus*—a hypothetical left-wing academic. Three fundamental goals or concerns may be ascribed to our homunculus. Each sets off the left scholar from his/her apolitical colleagues; each manifests itself to some degree in any piece of work that the academic produces.

The first goal consists of an interest in maintaining, extending, and applying Marxism as a theoretical paradigm.[7] I do not mean by this that left academics are "orthodox" Marxists, Leninists, or whatever. On the contrary, they are a heterodox group spanning the spectrum from liberal democrats through resolute Stalinists. But almost all draw upon a general theoretical orientation laid down by Marx: historical

---

7 Kuhn's (1962) concept of a paradigm refers to a school of thought, a particular theoretical approach that provides its adherents with a distinct conceptual framework and methodological techniques for research. But behind this abstract notion are real people. A paradigm is constituted by a community of scholars who share a certain training, use the same terminology, agree on a conceptual approach to the world, and have similar methodological skills.

change is dominated by class conflicts; material/economic structures mold the rest of society; property systems are methods for expropriating the labor power of the lower classes.

Very few left intellectuals feel bold or confident enough to jettison Marxism totally in favor of a personal system. As revisionist or eclectic as they are, most see themselves as working within a tradition, as sharing a common project with like-minded colleagues. Hence I shall call this first goal "paradigm maintenance," by which I mean that one protects the continuity of certain analytic categories and concepts, modes of analysis and exposition, and terminology. It also involves maintaining the *coherence* of theory, avoiding contradictory positions while assimilating new data into the paradigm. Left scholars strive for a consensual framework within which to work and for methodologies to implement that framework, but they nevertheless disagree considerably over what exactly the Marxist paradigm is or should consist of. So I should qualify my initial statement: one goal of the left academic involves an ongoing attempt to define, maintain, and extend a Marxist or radical paradigm. I should add that this first goal of our left homunculus is equivalent to that of any other social scientist, save that his/her particular paradigm is Marxist rather than functionalist, symbolic interactionist, neoclassical, or institutionalist.

A second goal involves taking a moral and evaluatory stance toward social phenomena and events. Left intellectuals are moralists: they view the social and intellectual world in terms of social values derived from a socialist world-view. The impetus to this evaluatory attitude is complex. At the simplest level, the moralistic, often condemnatory, position of leftists stems from their belief that the world does not have to be the way it is. They believe that many present human sufferings are unnecessary. Without this basic belief, a moral/evaluatory position would be absurd.

In contrast to the evaluatory position stands an apolitical orientation, which Marxists call "false naturalism." Marx and Lukács both castigated bourgeois intellectuals for falling into the conceptual trap of viewing existing social relations as permanent rather than transitory. Apolitical intellectuals regard the present not just as a temporary set of social relations that will change but as "natural," as "bound to be that way," as "functional" or "optimally efficient." The apolitical intellectual's equivalent of the leftist's moralism is therefore a *Realpolitik*, or cynical fatalism that asserts that "this is the way things are bound to be whether or not we like it." But to reiterate our central point, as one part of his/her project, the contemporary left intellectual is involved in the articulation of a moral/evaluatory analysis of the phenomenon under study.

A third goal of our hypothetical academic is to analyze emerging social events, to act as an intellectual commentator on contemporary affairs. Even left historians seem drawn to analyze the present, and among left sociologists and economists this emphasis is very strong. Why this special interest in contemporary events as they unfold? In one sense, this attitude generally demarcates policy sciences from theoretical sciences. The policy scientist is involved with the contemporary situation, what is special and new in it, and how to manipulate it. The theorist is more interested in generalizing from any situation and integrating it into a cumulative body of knowledge or established models. The present has *no special status* for the theoretical scientist. In contrast, the present is of paramount importance to the policy scientist since it is the present, not the past, that must be grasped and changed. These considerations hold true for all types of policy scientists, and in important ways Marxist intellectuals are like policy scientists—policy scientists *manqués*, if you will, or policy scientists out of power but policy scientists nevertheless.

This interest in the present also derives from a pressing dilemma for the left intellectual, the problem of *praxis*. It is far from clear how radical studies of the lineages of the absolutist state, of popular culture, or even of the world economy translate into a form of political action. Yet left academics try to be scholars and simultaneously to make a contribution to social change. I suggest that one partial and unsatisfactory attempt to resolve this dilemma occurs when left scholars theorize about contemporary social issues. To the extent that the scholar's work has relevance for analyzing contemporary events, s/he feels a partial resolution of the "praxis problem," a sense that s/he is contributing to political discourse and hence indirectly to social change.

Other factors strengthen this interest in the present. One is the millennialist or future-orientation of much Marxist theory, which it shares with other evolutionary perspectives. Present-day events are the gauge of whether posited historical changes are unfolding, of whether one's evolutionary model is correct.

Finally, the study of the contemporary scene affords the left intellectual an opportunity to demonstrate the efficacy, and implicitly the superiority, of the radical world-view or analysis. If the left intellectual can explain the latest events on the basis of a Marxist theoretical schema while "orthodox" science looks on in confusion, the superiority of the radical paradigm over the latter is demonstrated. This view is explicitly stated, in almost ritualistic fashion, in much of the literature we shall discuss.

To summarize, I argue that the left intellectual is involved in the pursuit of three goals. S/he attempts to be both an analyst and a moral evaluator. S/he shares with other scientists the problem of maintaining a paradigm while assimilating new data into it. Moreover, left theorists put special emphasis upon explaining current events, a concern that is not necessarily salient for apolitical theoretical scholars but is similar to the orientation of policy scientists.

It may seem overly abstract or even simplistic to characterize left intellectuals in terms of these three elements. However, the value of this formulation lies in its capacity to anticipate a series of potential strains among these goals. Left scholars often find it difficult to achieve the three goals simultaneously. For example, there can be conflicts between paradigm maintenance and moral evaluation, or between paradigm maintenance and analysis of contemporary events. In a later section I intend to show how these tensions can be used to analyze the evolution of particular theories over time, but first I want to consider some further problems besetting our hypothetical left academic.

Tensions and Paradoxes

In his book *Radical Paradoxes* (1973), Peter Clecak advanced the useful notion that a series of books or articles may express an ongoing but unresolved effort to solve some intellectual problem. This "paradox," as he calls it, provides an agenda for an intellectual's work. The agenda may not be stated explicitly in any one work; indeed, the writer may not be aware of it. Nevertheless, an outside analyst who reads a whole corpus of work can recognize that there is such an agenda, that each work represents a fresh attempt to resolve or attack the intellectual paradox in question.

I want to suggest something similar for the body of work I have called the new political economy. Even though it has been produced by many scholars and addresses numerous substantive issues, this work has certain stylistic and topical regularities. These common features are not accidental, in my opinion. Rather, they stem from the authors' shared position as left academics *or* from certain characteristics intrinsic to Marxist theory itself. The former sociological factors I call "tensions from outside the theory," the latter, "tensions within the theory." Once again, my purpose is to show how these external and internal tensions mold the content and style of contemporary political economy.

Tensions from Outside the Theory

The first tension I wish to discuss is an external one: the tension between a radical intellectual's commitment to a Marxist approach and his or her professional role as a university academic. Historically, the pioneering Marxist intellectuals maintained only marginal institutional affiliations. They could not easily find positions in which they could make a living. Marx suffered extreme hardships; Lenin led a financially troubled life during his exile; Rosa Luxemburg precariously held on to various positions in the German socialist movement. But even though there were few paid positions for Marxist intellectuals in the pre-World War II era, they found emotional and intellectual vindication and support in the large-scale working-class political movements of their time.

Since World War II the situation has reversed, at least in the United States and Britain. An increasing number of left intellectuals can be found in paid academic positions, yet they lack a "reference group" in the form of a sizable Marxist political movement. These academicians can be characterized as less marginal institutionally but much more marginal in terms of emotional support and identity, compared to their predecessors.

Although more professional positions are filled by left intellectuals, radical scholars have not necessarily achieved institutional security in America. On the contrary, American Marxists often find themselves in a difficult professional position. They cannot enjoy the emotional security of a dominant or generally accepted paradigm. Instead, they are viewed with considerable skepticism, if not outright hostility, by many of their nonradical colleagues.

In part, this situation occurs because there are multiple paradigms within most contemporary social science disciplines, unlike the physical sciences, which tend to have only one or at most two paradigms at any one time. In some social science disciplines—for example, economics—one clearly dominant or orthodox paradigm far outstrips its competitors; in other disciplines, such as sociology, there are several approaches or paradigms, each contending for approval, each seeking converts, each convinced that it is the correct one. Behind this intellectual competition, of course, there is the competition of real people striving for fame and fortune or simply for a job at a prestigious university. The result, as Thomas Kuhn (1962) points out, is that paradigms conflict—not just over their differences in ideas, but also over jobs, research funds, and the like. Individuals believe in the superiority of their approach and are likely to favor their fellow paradigm members. At times interparadigmatic rivalry will be amicable, the mood tolerant and generous. At other times it will be bitter and hostile, with each paradigm's adherents viewing the other paradigms as invalid or second-rate.

Supporters of rival paradigms may disparage one another's approaches in various ways, but by far the most typical is the claim that one's rivals are not truly "scientific." This criticism arises because the social sciences in America are quite insecure about their status. Many social scientists have something of an inferiority complex over their inability to reach the levels of predictive accuracy and explanatory power of the natural sciences. Thus, if one wishes to hit a rival paradigm in a painful spot, accusing it of being unscientific, nonrigorous, or "impressionistic" is particularly damning.

To some extent, this kind of paradigm conflict and disparagement befalls other minority paradigms or schools of thought in the same way it does Marxism. So, for example, some neoclassical economists disparage the relevance, validity, and rigor of the minority paradigm called institutional economics. Symbolic interactionism and ethnomethodology, two sociological schools, are often considered unscientific or "soft" by quantitative sociologists.

However, Marxist social science evokes even greater interparadigmatic hostility than other minority paradigms. In my opinion the most important reason is that Marxism's adherence to an explicitly moral/evaluatory framework clashes with a widely accepted cultural image of the scientist as a dispassionate observer/measurer. Scientists are not meant to be moralists; having a moral stance toward the phenomenon one studies is supposed to compromise one's ability to describe it objectively and fairly.

In any event, I believe it is accurate to say that the Marxist paradigm is singularly distrusted by many members of the other schools in economics, sociology, and political science. Many nonradical academics believe that Marxism is out of date and erroneous and that if it were not for leftist scholars' adherence to a political value system they would not hold to Marxist theory. This criticism amounts to stating that Marxism is not tenable as a science, that the Marxist academic is not really a serious scholar or scientist but a political activist.

Interparadigmatic hostility can go beyond name-calling and have material consequences for left intellectuals, owing to certain organizational features of American universities, especially the tenure process. American universities usually hire junior faculty on short-term contracts for perhaps the first eight years of their teaching careers. During this time, contract renewals depend heavily on favorable review by an academic's senior departmental colleagues. After seven or eight years the junior faculty member is judged for tenure, also a decision strongly influenced by senior colleagues. Tenure review ostensibly depends on proving that the candidate has a strong record of scholarly research and is a competent teacher. In actuality, both scholarship and personality factors tend to be involved. Of much import are the scholarly or scientific rigor and significance of a candidate's academic work—precisely the topics over which paradigm conflicts are likely to occur. The junior scholar is therefore in a peculiarly dependent position. He or she must produce work that impresses senior colleagues, who typically represent other paradigms.[8]

I would argue that this dependency generates a structural situation in which young American academics are pressured toward intellectual conformity. Of course, this does not mean that young scholars uncritically adopt their senior colleagues' views. It does mean that junior academics are aware of the need to present their work in such a way that it meets professional standards of quality and that contentious aspects of their work are, as far as possible, protected from attack. It also forces them at least to take into account the alternative paradigms'

8 The high degree of dependency of junior academics upon the long-term approval of a substantial number of their senior colleagues has been a peculiarity of American universities. By contrast, in Britain until the mid-1970s, tenure was usually given after a few years of teaching and was granted on a relatively routine basis. Since the mid-1970s, however, the British system has been shifting closer to the American model.

findings or analyses. In terms of left-wing scholarship, as I detail below, this pressure shows itself as an attempt to adopt academic style and to "scientize" Marxist scholarship. The result is a less polemical, more empirical radical research in constant dialogue with the orthodox paradigm. In Britain, left research can be and is more polemical, more concerned with debates internal to Marxism, and much less oriented toward nonradical scholarship. It is also more theoretical and less empirical (or epithetically "empiricist") than its American counterpart.

Two possible consequences can follow from a situation of academic dependency. On the one hand, paradigm conflicts and political antipathy toward Marxists may lead to the purging of left scholars via the denial of contract renewals and tenure. Various commentators on the left have claimed that this has been the case, and they cite examples.[9] On the other hand, radical scholars may be judged fairly and tolerantly. If so, many will get tenure. It is probably impossible to determine the relative frequency of these two outcomes, and undoubtedly there is considerable variation from department to department, institution to institution. However, for my analysis it is sufficient to point out that left scholars *believe* their work may be dismissed as ideology and not taken seriously as scholarship or science. Many junior academics experience this potential delegitimation of their work as an ongoing tension and a threat to their careers. Radical academics respond to this situation in a variety of ways, some of which are sufficiently common that they generate distinct genres of left research.

Perhaps the most common response is to adopt a style of exposition that is very close to standard academic discourse and has little in common with traditional Marxist-Leninist style. The standard epithets in Marxist writing (e.g., "bourgeois-reactionary") are relatively infrequent in contemporary left scholarship. Rather, technical Marxist terms appear—"mode of production," "organic composition," and the like—which are carefully defined in academic fashion. The withering *ad hominem* attacks so characteristic of Marxist-Leninism are also rare. Instead, left scholarship is replete with footnotes, citations, and other hallmarks of academic style.

This sensitivity to style carries over to the places where radical scholarship is published. Certain journals and publishing houses have

---

9 See Lifschultz (1974), Colfax (1973), and Walsh (1978) for descriptions of the career and tenure problems of radicals in American universities.

emerged as leading forums for the new political economy. They combine a sober intellectual style with a scholarly elitism in that they publish only articles that they view as intellectually sound and innovative. Gone is the old concern with a political line; instead, we have peer review of submitted manuscripts. If these left journals simply wanted to promote political debate, review of manuscripts would be unnecessary. But if the journals are trying to build an image of intellectual quality and rigor for themselves, it becomes very important. (It is also relevant to note changes and choices of journal names. In the mid-1970s *Socialist Revolution* became the *Socialist Review*. Perhaps the *Insurgent Sociologist* will someday become the *Critical Sociologist*? At any rate, the tendency is toward nonstrident titles.)

As socialist scholarship becomes more successful, one hears complaints from the editors of radical journals that they are losing manuscripts to the established (nonpolitical) academic journals. The more widely recognized radical academicians sometimes choose to publish with professional periodicals and university presses in order to address a wider audience and to gain prestige in the eyes of apolitical colleagues.

Beyond these relatively superficial issues of style are more significant responses to the potential delegitimation of partisan scholarship as ideology. Some leftists accept the notion of science-versus-ideology and use it as a reverse weapon against the dominant paradigms. Thus, neoclassical and marginalist economics are lambasted repeatedly for operating with a model whose assumptions are clearly contradicted by the real world. If the assumptions of orthodox economics are invalidated by the facts, it follows that the dominant paradigm is unscientific; the proponents of these assumptions—free competition, harmony of interests, optimal efficiency—must therefore be ideologically motivated. In sociology, similar attacks have been made against the functionalist paradigm. Ironically, the radical paradigm is said to be more realistic and therefore more scientific in its assumptions.

A second approach is to recast the nature of political critique. The notion that one is doing proletarian science versus bourgeois science brings both politics and class warfare into academia. The present generation avoids this approach. A much easier method of maintaining the politics-science combination is to transform one's political position into a moral critique. This tactic has become so widespread among contemporary radicals that I have identified it as one of the three goals of left scholarship: namely, the integration of a moral-evaluatory position into one's analyses. To do this convincingly, one must demonstrate scientifically that various phenomena generally accepted as blameworthy or evil are systematic outcomes of capitalism. This approach raises the hackles of apolitical social scientists, double-binding them because it relies upon accepted "scientific" methods to point to politically potent conclusions. Much of the radical analysis in the areas of poverty, unemployment, racism, sexism, poor health care, and so on can be understood as "systematizing" the evils of capitalism. To some degree, the effectiveness of systematizing explains the relative concentration of left economists and sociologists in the field of "social problems" (cf. Edwards, Reich, and Weisskopf 1972). It has led an exasperated non-Marxist researcher on poverty to complain that caring about the poor is not the monopoly of any one political persuasion (Cain 1975).

A third response to potential delegitimation is apparent in the methodological orientation of radical scholarship. Researchers have become very concerned with empirical documentation and are increasingly dependent upon sophisticated quantitative methods of analysis. This orientation is not surprising when one considers that the contemporary generation of radical scholars was university-trained in the standard approaches to academic disciplines. Marxist economists were schooled in Keynes, Friedman, and Samuelson, just as radical sociologists learned structural functionalism, symbolic interactionism, the Chicago school, and survey methodologies. Thus the contemporary Marxist intellectual possesses the technical capacity to reform himself or herself into a more standard academic or, for that matter, to co-opt the standard paradigm or methodology for Marxist purposes.

Nonradicals may find it easy to dismiss left scholarship as mere ideology when the work in question is purely theoretical. But when radical research emphasizes empirical data, using the most up-to-date quantitative techniques, such criticisms have a hollow ring, for in the contemporary social sciences, quantification has come to be equated with scientific rigor. Many left scholars have chosen to adopt these methodologies and have thereby succeeded in gaining greater respect in the eyes of their nonradical colleagues. Thus several areas of the new political economy do battle with academic orthodoxy by using multiple regression, factor analysis, econometrics, and the like. Even left scholars who do not use these techniques take considerable care to document their arguments with empirical evidence. A certain irony rests in the fact that much left political economy is based upon statistics drawn from the U.S. Departments of Labor and Commerce. Moreover, the work of orthodox economists and sociologists often serves as the analytic substratum for left analyses. Thus William Nordhaus is used on the falling rate of profit, Thor Hultgren on the business cycle, and John Blair on monopoly price behavior.

In summary, the tension between the left academic's political identities and his or her role as an academic centers on the scholarly legitimacy of his or her research and writing. Left theorists resolve that tension in several ways. Most legitimate their work by adopting a scholarly style, by publishing in respected journals, and by emphasizing the rigorous empirical foundations of their arguments, which often use quantitative techniques of analysis. On the other hand, these scholars assert their political commitment partly by choice of topic, partly by adherence to a Marxist conceptual paradigm, and often by adopting a research program that focuses on the evils of capitalism. They are therefore simultaneously politically committed and professionalized.

The tension or conflict described above is different from that presented by Peter Clecak in *Radical Paradoxes: Dilemmas of the Left, 1945 to 1970* (1973). Clecak interviewed several leading American leftists of the older generation: Paul Baran, Paul Sweezy, Herbert Marcuse, and C. Wright Mills. He argues that they faced a paradox because they believed in a socialist revolution during a period when the proletariat was clearly nonrevolutionary. Baran, Sweezy, and Marcuse responded to this paradox by searching for a revolutionary agent in their writings: ethnic minorities, youth, women, the Third World, and national independence movements. An additional paradox, according to Clecak, emerged from the theorists' commitment to a democratic vision of a socialist or communist community in the face of the undemocratic behavior of so-called socialist countries. Again, a search for the socialist role model was evidence in their work, as their initial enthusiasm for various socialist countries turned to disillusionment.

Clecak calls these radical dilemmas paradoxes because he believes that an underlying and inherent contradiction exists between the socialist ideal of the communistic society and the commitment to democratic forms of social change. He doubts that one can have both. Thus the search for democratic communism amounted to an impossible quest.

Clecak makes a convincing case regarding some of the intellectual dilemmas of the older generation of leftists, but I believe that there has been a relative diminution of these paradoxes for the younger generation of academic Marxists at the forefront of the new political economy. I do not mean that debates over the policies of China, Cuba, or the Soviet Union have ceased; nor has the issue of a revolutionary agent been resolved. But the dilemmas of politics and intellectual work have been addressed, in part, by separating the two spheres institutionally. Theoretical work has become more and more scientific and is found in journals that publish research contributions from a wide variety of political factions. Politics is done in whatever party one belongs to, and in party journals the debates over the errors of the Soviet Union, Cuba, and China continue unabated. Theoretical work and practical politics, which an earlier generation fused within its writing, have generally become separated for the contemporary academic left into two distinct spheres.

Several influences converge to enforce this separation. Perhaps the most important factor is the present generation's fear of political factionalism and its disastrous consequences for the left. The left intellectual community in America realizes that it cannot afford to allow factionalism to take over in the theoretical journals: the community is simply too small. Participation by all positions is seen as necessary for the continuation of a viable contributorship and readership. The left community could not sustain several faction-specific theoretical journals.

A particularly clear example of the fear of sectarian bias—of aiding one political position or stifling another—was provided by a conflict in the British political economy journal *Bulletin of the Conference of Socialist Economists*. One board member accused the editorial board of refusing an article on factional grounds and resigned in protest. The editorial board insisted that it had no intention of judging the correctness of an article's politics. It had merely asked for partial rewriting to respond to peer reviewers' comments. Nevertheless, the board felt obliged to recant, to offer immediate publication of the disputed article, and to request the disaffected member to rejoin. That is how strong the aversion to factionalism is.

In addition to aversion to sectarian strife, institutional separation has been encouraged by the growth of Marxism as a scientific discourse (as economics or sociology), which allows theoretical journals to separate understanding capitalism from doing anything about it. Thus a flood of explanatory articles and books will appear when a recession occurs, regardless of the level of political activity of the proletariat. Marxist scholarship provides a surrogate for political activity, a way of sustaining a socialist identity in the absence of a socialist movement.

The response of academic radicals to the present enervation of Marxism as practical politics has therefore been to turn to Marxism as science and knowledge (cf. Korsch 1970; Korsch 1974; Gramsci 1971: 336). To the extent that Marxism offers a powerful explanation of capitalism and its socio-economic consequences, it becomes viable for this constituency of professionalized economists and sociologists, independent of practical politics. A politics of sorts continues in left journals, but not the tactical politics that threatens factionalism. Politics takes the form of elaboration and extension of a moral-evaluative critique of capitalism (as it did for the Frankfurt school) and scientific studies of capitalism and its dynamics.

Tensions and Change Within the Theory

Having considered the impact of external institutional forces on radical scholarship, we turn to the ways in which internal problems shape the work of left academics. Earlier I characterized Marxist scholarship in terms of three goals and suggested that strains between them influence the path of left research. I shall begin here with the tensions between maintaining a paradigm that articulates the traditional concepts, methods, and findings of Marxism and developing analyses of the contemporary economy. Thomas Kuhn provides us with a point of entry for considering this problem.

Change in Theory: Physical and Historical Sciences

Thomas Kuhn wrote his *Structure of Scientific Revolutions* (1962) as a contribution to the sociology or philosophy of the natural sciences. His widely applauded effort consisted in the main of debunking the prevalent notion that scientific theory develops in a constant dialogue between theory and data, by which theory is continuously updated to account for new discoveries. Kuhn offered a view of scientific advance as a discontinuous, rather jerky process. Various historical stages in scientific theory are constituted by different paradigms, world-views, or "disciplinary matrices." Each paradigm provides a method of approaching scientific work quite different from that which came before.

One of the most distinctive aspects of Kuhn's model was his reformulation of the status of the "anomalous" result—that is, a phenomenon that cannot be explained by current theory, or one that contradicts what current theory leads a researcher to expect. Prior to Kuhn, the orthodox position maintained that such anomalies cause scientists to revise their theories immediately in order to re-establish harmony between theory and observation. Kuhn argued that, on the contrary, anomalies tend to accumulate and are ignored by most scientists intent on pursuing the positive explanatory power of prevailing theory to its utmost.

Kuhn therefore advanced a two-stage theory of scientific progress. In the first phase anomalies are ignored in favor of the pursuit of "normal science." Researchers follow the accepted paradigm to exhaust its positive possibilities for explanation, leaving the anomalies to one side. In a second, "crisis stage" a different group of scientists orients research toward the accumulated anomalous phenomena and reformulates theory to create a new paradigm that successfully accounts for the previously anomalous observations. What is common to both Kuhn and his predecessors' views of physical science is an acceptance of anomalies as "real," in the sense that they represent a genuine aspect of the physical world. The existence of anomalous phenomena therefore proves that the present theoretical framework is flawed.

I believe that the social and historical sciences have a different option when confronted with anomaly. Whereas anomalies represent some aspect of an unchanging natural order for the physical sciences, social science anomalies appear in a historical and social order that is itself constantly changing. Consequently, the discovery of an anomaly in social science indicates not that present theoretical knowledge is *wrong* but merely that *reality has changed*. Two implications follow. An anomaly still signals that the old theory needs to be updated. But the old theory may still be correct for an earlier historical epoch.

This distinction is critical for Marxism, where the theorist's identity is wrapped up in an intellectual identification with earlier writers like Marx and Engels. Political economic theory can be revised without imputing error to Marx by arguing that the emergence of a new reality requires a new explanation, a new focus of enquiry. Such an outlook enables a historical-social science to avoid or diffuse some of the confrontation implicit in paradigm conflict. It helps to maintain the coherence of a community of scholars who identify themselves as working within one paradigm, even when they use somewhat different theoretical constructs.

This process manifests itself in the left literature as a preoccupation with *periodization*. From Lenin on, theorists have invoked the notion of a "newer" or "higher" phase of capitalism to justify departure from the traditional analysis and introduction of new ideas. The most successful example is the now widely accepted formulation of capitalism as monopolistic. By embracing the idea that monopoly is dominant in present-day capitalism, monopoly-capital theorists can ignore large sections of *Capital* (and its faults) while still remaining faithful Marxists.

Periodization permits a broader spectrum of radical analyses to co-exist than would otherwise be the case. Some theorists, while accepting the existence of monopoly, prefer nevertheless to consider it a secondary factor, and they operate from Marx's competitive models (e.g., Boddy and Crotty 1976b). Others (e.g., Howard Sherman 1976b) use the monopoly notion and work in a modernized context, thus avoiding various problems in *Capital* (the falling rate of profit, the transformation problem, productive versus unproductive labor). Baran and Sweezy (1966) took the more perilous course, both noting the emergence of monopoly as a new phase and pointing out the failure of certain features of Marx's earlier model. Orthodox Marxists took umbrage, and a spirited clash followed.

A good example of the way in which periodization acts to legitimate two logically incompatible positions is seen in an article by Erik Wright (1975). In surveying theories of the economic crisis of capitalism, Wright identified both the traditional organic composition/falling rate of profit position and the monopoly capital position, which stresses overproduction, relative to investment opportunities (see Chapter Four). Rather than view the two theories as embodiments of contrasting and conflicting assumptions, Wright chose to treat each of them as an acceptable analysis of a *different period*. He therefore set up a historical sequence whereby capitalism moved from a period where rising organic composition led to crises of unprofitability (falling rate of profit) to a period where the crises were due to underconsumption and lack of investment opportunities.

I am not suggesting that periodization is deliberately used to avoid confrontations between old and new frameworks. Those who argue for a stage theory of capitalism are undoubtedly sincere in their belief. I am simply noting that periodization has certain consequences, one of which is to soften the paradigm conflict that results from altering a framework to account for anomalies. Periodization also encourages the conceptual eclecticism of American Marxism, its tendency to borrow bits and pieces of theory from various sources while maintaining its emotional and political identification with Marxism.

Within radical scholarship there is a constant tension between those who wish to explain any observation in terms of an established "exemplar" (to use Kuhn's term) and those who use it as an occasion to generate and legitimate a new theoretical approach. This is the tension between the dual goals of paradigm maintenance and analysis of contemporary events. However, we do not see in intellectual Marxism the enormous theoretical inertia that Kuhn says characterizes the natural sciences. Anomalies do not pile up unnoticed in theoretical Marxism. On the contrary, as we shall see in subsequent chapters, revisionism is and always has been rampant in radical scholarship, as theorists insist that new circumstances demand a revamping of theory. Perhaps it is because Marxism has the option of periodization that change within Marxist theory is evolutionary and less likely to produce conflict. Ironically, it is within the natural sciences, according to Kuhn, that theoretical change is extremely contentious and requires "revolutions" before a new perspective can be accommodated.

The tension within Marxism between the dual goals of paradigm maintenance and the analysis of current events is not completely eradicated by periodization. Traditionalist and revisionist wings still debate one another. There are also real difficulties in explaining some new events in terms of the traditional paradigm. Some theorists struggle to absorb new phenomena without distorting the basic paradigm. Others view certain new phenomena as so important that they make enormous changes in the traditional paradigm. In this sense, then, the tension between the goals of maintaining a paradigm and explaining new events is continuous.

The Metaphoricality of Marxism

The next tension within Marxist theory involves the goal of paradigm maintenance and that of moral critique. Here it will be useful to begin with Alvin Gouldner's article, "The Metaphoricality of Marxism and the Context-Free Grammar of Socialism" (1974), in which Gouldner adopts Noam Chomsky's terminology of surface and deep structure to analyze Marxist theory. Gouldner asks how Marxism can have gained such popularity among a wide variety of nations and classes at various historical periods. The reason cannot simply be the validity of Marxism's analyses of particular situations (which Gouldner compares to "surface structures"). Rather, it must be because Marxism appeals to a deeper level of belief and feeling common to many people in many societies. This, says Gouldner, is the "deep structure" of Marxism. It consists of a basic metaphor—slavery—and a call to the oppressed to overthrow slavery. This is the core message that makes Marxism so appealing in divergent cultures and classes. Gouldner also argues that this Marxist metaphor is "context free," by which he seems to mean that it can be articulated independently of the context in which it is used.

Gouldner's approach is insightful in that it suggests a separation between the substance of a Marxist analysis of a particular situation and the underlying moral message that appeals to the listener. It implies a dual analytical-moral message within Marxist analysis. (I have offered a related formulation, that Marxist research includes a moral-evaluatory component.) However, I would suggest that Marxism draws upon several moral metaphors, not one as Gouldner suggests. For example, the metaphor of capitalism as "theft" of the workers' product looms large in much of political economy.

Second, I do not accept Gouldner's contention that metaphors are context free. Indeed, it seems to me that it is not easy to articulate a moral critique in every situation and that theorists continually face the problem of matching moral critique and theoretical analysis to various contexts. The analyst's desire to articulate a moral-evaluatory metaphor in a certain situation may well clash with the need to maintain a traditional logic of analysis. (I described this conflict earlier as the strain between the moral-evaluatory goal and the paradigm maintenance goal.)

The outward expression of such a strain is often seen in situations where traditional left theory does not appear to assign "systematic" blame to capitalism. That is, left theory inadequately links a particular "evil" to the nature of capitalist relations. Here is a case where the need to direct blame in the particular systematic scientized manner described earlier is out of step with the need to maintain a consistent body of Marxist theory and method. The effect of such a tension is frequently to spur innovation in theory in order to produce a more effective moral critique.

Marx himself faced these problems. His own analysis of exploitation was based on a comparatively nonmoralistic notion of *equal exchange*: the laborer was paid the value of his/her labor (not less). Even in Marx's own day, socialists sought to strengthen the moral message at the cost of negating the theoretical framework. They did so by claiming that the labor theory of value showed that employers steal surplus value from its rightful owners, the laborers. Marx (1972) inveighed against this misinterpretation of his work, as did Engels (1970: vi).

The theory of imperialism and underdevelopment (discussed in Chapter Five) shows a similar effect of the tension between moral evaluation and paradigm maintenance. Paul Baran's (1957) contribution to this theory advanced the moral critique of imperialism by showing how the West appropriated the Third World's economic surplus. To do so, however, he had to define "surplus" in ways incompatible with orthodox Marxist theory. He did violence to the traditional framework in order to ground his new critique.

Arghiri Emmanuel (1972) continued this process by advancing a theory of unequal exchange, whereby Third World countries are impoverished not only by loss of actual and potential profits to multinational corporations but also by unfavorable terms of trade for products produced in the Third World. Again, this formula advanced the moral critique of imperialism, but only at the cost of scrambling the Marxian theory of wage determination.

For Pierre Jalee (1968) and others, the impetus to critique overwhelms paradigm maintenance. From wealth being a product of someone's labor, Jalee returns to a nationalist definition: wealth belongs to the natural owner by right of residence. Thus he indicts the West for stealing the mineral wealth of the Third World. The theoretical paradigm yields in order to provide new bases for systematizing blame. The moral metaphor is that imperialism is theft. But theft implies a theory of property and value, and Marxism already has such a theory. For better or worse, the Marxist theory does not fit certain critiques. Critique wins out over paradigm maintenance, and we see the theft metaphor applied nonetheless, taking on successively Marxist, petit-bourgeois, and nationalist definitions of property.

My point here is that we must conceptualize the developments in radical economic theory as stemming from changes not just in the analytic or theoretical framework but also in the moral-evaluatory stance, and especially from the tension between the two goals. It is in this sense that Gouldner erred in his notion of "context-free" Marxist metaphors, for he saw the imposition of such metaphors as unproblematic and the content of the metaphors as unchanging. In his example of "slavery," he may be correct. However, once we allow for similar metaphors in theoretical Marxism we see that the application of a moral metaphor to a particular situation may violate the traditional theoretical framework. The difficulty of attaining a satisfactory dual political-economic and moral-evaluatory stance toward unfolding events produces a dynamic, a tendency toward *innovation* in the theory.

The theory of monopoly capitalism presented by Baran and Sweezy (1966) can also be understood in this way (see Chapter Four). Though their theoretical advance was comparatively small, its power lay elsewhere. First, they persuasively argued that the dominant position of monopolies in the economy demands a reorientation and an updated version of Marxist theory (cf. the earlier discussion of periodization). More important for our present discussion, Baran and Sweezy succeeded in systematically incorporating into their new economic theory a notion of monopoly capitalism's inherent need to produce "waste" in order to combat economic stagnation. Rising surplus leads to the necessity of military spending, massive advertising, and frivolous consumerism. The major achievement of Baran and Sweezy's *Monopoly Capital* is that it updated Marxist political economy to mesh with a powerful Frankfurt school moral-evaluatory critique of 1950s America. A position that indicted capitalism for its wastefulness, consumerism, and dehumanization was clearly superior to the traditional moral critique grounded in the theory of the immiseration or impoverishment of the proletariat, the expansion of the army of the unemployed, and the anarchy of unplanned production. By 1950, the time for a change in moral critique had come. Baran and Sweezy provided the economic analysis that allowed systematic application of the new moral-evaluatory position.

This is not to suggest that Baran and Sweezy consciously strove to build a new moral critique of capitalism, nor should my description be read as evidence that moralizing comes first in Marxist writing and that theory is secondary. To reiterate: a major goal of most left theorizing is the *dual accomplishment* of a political-economic analysis and a moral critique in which the economic analysis shows that an "evil" is systematically and necessarily produced by capitalism. Baran and Sweezy's efforts were a tour de force in this respect. Their ability to justify the shift in analytic structure on the basis of a historical change in capitalism helped to rationalize the innovation to fellow leftists.

The interpenetration of the two spheres of political-economic analysis and moral evaluation in no way invalidates the force, the logic, or the scientific status of left scholarship. One cannot dismiss a Marxist political economic work simply because it fuses evaluatory and analytic elements. Indeed, its artfulness lies in showing that if one accepts the economic analysis as scientifically correct, one cannot evade the moral conclusion, since it follows logically. That is the double-bind that Marxism attempts to spin around apolitical social science!

Genres and Idioms

In the sections above I have argued for a model of tensions, strains, and multiple goals as a device for explaining the structure, style, and dynamics of the new political economy. In this final section I shall pull these threads together and give an overview of this body of research in terms of its genres and idioms. Later chapters will provide descriptions of specific areas of theory and research. My purpose here is to show the thematic coherence of this material.

Reading the journal articles, books, and manuscripts of the new political economy, one's initial impression is of extraordinary eclecticism in terms of topic and method. Reviews of contemporary political developments in various geographical areas are juxtaposed with historical descriptions of social institutions. Theoretical articles on the labor theory of value, descriptions of the technocratic working class, or critiques of neoclassical economics accompany discussions of the latest economic indicators or commentary on current political events. This multiplicity of topics is mirrored by a plurality of methods. One finds historical description based on documentary research; statistical analyses of census, labor, and commerce statistics; journalistic reportage; and exegesis of texts. Mathematical expositions follow erudite polemics; quotations from Marx are interspersed with ones from *Business*

Week. Behind this bewildering variety there is a pattern, understandable in terms of our three-goal schema.

One large part of the literature consists of articles on contemporary events. This differs from newspaper reportage in that events are analyzed in terms of larger processes, as instances of underlying structures rather than as surface happenings. Thus, for example, the *Monthly Review* regarded Felix Rohatyn's remarks concerning a new federal investment corporation as finance capital's latest strategy for coping with endemic stagflation, while the *New York Times* treated it as a case of an influential financier's personal brainstorm. The left journals comb the various profit and unemployment statistics as closely as the *Wall Street Journal* or the *Economist*. But whereas the latter journals use such data to argue whether market prospects are improving, the former see them as a cipher to be cracked. One of Paul Sweezy's favorite formats in the "Review of the Month" is a shadow "dialogue" with *Business Week*, in which government statistics are remolded to show what is really going on and how *Business Week* simply does not look far enough.

This genre fulfills two functions within our earlier framework. On the one hand, the analysis of contemporary events provides a test for left theory: can the theory anticipate and explain unfolding events? On the other hand, this genre offers a forum for interparadigmatic rivalries. If *Monthly Review* can understand stagflation while the *Wall Street Journal* scratches its head, doesn't this demonstrate the superiority of Marxist theory?

A second part of political economy is directly oriented toward non-Marxist disciplines. The counterpart to orthodox academia's coolness toward radical scholarship is seen in leftists' critiques of the orthodox social sciences. Many socialist scholars see themselves in a competition for intellectual superiority between paradigms. Thus we find articles that attack marginalist economics or chortle over the setbacks of general equilibrium theory. Orthodox development theory is shown to be wanting by radical theorists of underdevelopment; theoretical innovations in apolitical sociology are criticized from a Marxist perspective, and so on. These critiques typically debunk the claims of orthodox social science to scientific rigor and assert the superiority of radical approaches.

A third area of the new political economy consists of a large body of literature that analyzes the models and concepts of Marxist economic theory. This material expresses the goals of paradigm maintenance and extension. Two distinct idioms appear: one is exigetical, seeking to clarify Marx's own categories or analyses (such efforts invariably generate long debates); the second attempts to update the theory, to extend or modify Marxist economic analyses. Our earlier discussion of periodization notwithstanding, this is the area of most heated debate. This idiom also shades over into the previous one, since it is very common for individuals advancing new analyses to preface their works with quotations from Marx in order to show that their apparent innovations are really discoveries or extensions of what Marx himself intended. Polemics invariably fly as traditionalists seek to defend their paradigm from these distortions dressed in traditional garb. The battle for Marx's imprimatur has been going on for decades and shows no sign of abating.

In reviewing these debates, one is struck by the pluralism of theory among American left scholars. It is clear that one no longer has to follow *Capital* in a strict fashion to be published as or to be accepted as a leftist or Marxist scholar. The old guard has lost the battle to maintain as *the* Marxist paradigm the analysis of capitalism that appears in *Capital*. The postwar economic boom and the rise of monopoly, of welfare statism, of Keynesian economic management, and of trade unionism have convinced a sufficient proportion of the contemporary left that new models are necessary. The result is a heterodox and eclectic body of theory.

The left intellectual's identity as a Marxist is no longer based on adherence to one particular economic reading of the downfall of capitalism. Neo-Marxists and traditional Marxists mix in left journals and in the organizations of left scholars that sometimes accompany them. Rather than sharing an identity through a common analytic perspective, one sees a leftist identity forged through common moral-evaluatory critique, augmented by Marx's general theory of class struggle. This critique may or may not entail a commitment to the labor theory of value and certainly does not necessitate a belief in Marx's positions on the falling rate of profit or on colonialism-imperialism.

This observation brings us to the last and most common genre in the new political economy, the one that expresses the goal of moral critique. Certain topics that show the human suffering produced by capitalism are also areas for scientific analysis. Poverty, job alienation, racism, sexism, workplace injury, inadequate health care, and the economic travails of the Third World are all subjects that left theory addresses. This research is often dispassionate in tone, and it provides scientific description and causal analysis. However, although these topics have a legitimate place in the Marxist paradigm, much of their appeal derives from their humanistic importance. Left research in these areas is scholarly, but there is also a moral message, often left unsaid: "This suffering is unnecessary. It is caused by capitalism and could be avoided."

Chapter Two

THEORIES OF ECONOMIC SEGMENTATION
AND POVERTY

ONE OF THE MOST INTERESTING areas of the new political economy began as a relatively apolitical response to President Lyndon Johnson's War on Poverty. In the period from 1961 to 1968 federal expenditures for research and demonstration projects on poverty leapt to $400 million per annum. Much of this money flowed into academia in the form of research grants and predoctoral student support, stimulating social scientists of every theoretical and political persuasion to turn their attention to the problem of poverty.

Among these academics were graduate students and young faculty who had become politicized by the civil rights movement, the free speech movement, and other radicalizing influences of the sixties. Issues such as poverty drew these socially concerned young academics like magnets, offering them the opportunity to express their political commitments through their scholarly activities. Out of this fusion of government money and radicalized scholarship came many of the advances in radical research on poverty, economic segmentation, racism, and sexism.

The earliest work under government funding was narrowly focused on the explanation of poverty among racial minorities. But as the theory developed, its level of generality increased. From an applied model it expanded first into a critique of the orthodox academic theories of poverty and income determination and finally into a general theory of segmentation within the American economy. Because there has been such a shift in focus over time, we shall distinguish among several distinct schools of thought.

Neoclassical and human capital theory. The dominant or orthodox system of economic theory in American academia is called "neoclassical economics." Human capital theory is a topic within neoclassical economics that tries to explain wage levels and hence, indirectly, poverty. We will need to review human capital theory because radical analyses were often developed consciously as alternatives to or critiques of this orthodox position.

Dual labor market theory. This theory was proposed in the late 1960s and early 1970s by a group of nonradical economists at Harvard, most notably Michael Piore and Peter Doeringer. However, these faculty members worked with several politicized graduate students who were involved in the research from its earliest stages and who subsequently developed a radical variant of dual labor market (DLM) theory. That version is mainly the work of these individuals, most especially David Gordon, Richard Edwards, and Michael Reich.

Industrial segmentation theory. At about the same time that DLM theory appeared, an independent but related approach emerged, stressing the relationship between poverty and industrial sectors of the economy. Barry Bluestone seems to have initiated this perspective, and others have subsequently elaborated upon it. This model is also called dual labor market theory, but this use of the term obscures important differences, which we shall explore below. For this reason I have coined a separate term for it, emphasizing industrial segmentation rather than labor markets.

Both DLM theory and the industrial segmentation approach share a basic notion that the American economy should be viewed as separated into distinct parts, each of which has different wage levels and working conditions, a different racial and sexual composition of the work force, and a different relationship to poverty. By contrast, the neoclassical tradition draws upon a core image of a unitary economy in which various parts are linked through flows of capital and labor. In the neoclassical model, different parts of the economy do not go their own separate ways, because competition and flows of resources between sectors bring about equilibration or balancing between parts.

Here, then, is the central conceptual question that divides radical theory and its orthodox counterpart: Is the economy segmented or relatively uniform? One's answer to this question leads one to very different analyses of poverty and other forms of inequality. We shall begin with the apolitical orthodox position and then see how the radical positions developed in opposition to it.

Neoclassical and Human Capital Approaches to Poverty

Both orthodox and radical theory face the same kinds of questions: Why are the poor poor? Why are ethnic minorities overrepresented among the poor? What forces perpetuate poverty and what forces might eradicate it?

Neoclassical economists analyze poverty under the theory of wage differentials: the poor are poor because they earn low wages. Within the neoclassical framework, differences in individuals' wages are viewed as stemming from two factors: differences in the kinds and quality of skills that workers have, and differences in the wages paid by different industries for any given kind of skill (Leftwich 1955). What is significant for our purposes is that neoclassical economics drop the second of these two factors—unequal wages in different industries for similar work skills—shortly after mentioning it. Thus Richard Leftwich notes: "The former [factor] is more fundamental."

The second factor is downplayed because labor is considered so mobile that imbalances between industries are considered to be of short duration and to be self-correcting. If one industry pays better wages for a given level of skill than another industry, workers will migrate from one to the other until wage levels even out, according to neoclassical economists. Given this perspective, neoclassical economists concentrate on "the productivity characteristics of workers, as measured by their skills, training, education, and experience" as being theoretically and empirically crucial in explaining wage differences (Cain 1975: 40).

This focus led Gary Becker, Lester Thurow, and others to conceptualize an individual's education, skills, and the like in terms of a variable called "human capital." A wage is understood as a monetary return to the "investment" an individual has within him/herself in terms of human capital. As a consequence:

> Human Capital (the skills and knowledge of the individuals) is one of the key determinants of the distribution of income. Individuals with little education, training, and skills have low marginal productivities and earn low incomes. With very little human capital they earn poverty incomes. Blacks who have less capital than whites earn less. (Thurow 1969: 85)

From this definition there followed policy conclusions that dominated federal antipoverty efforts for several decades: "More investment in human capital should help increase incomes. What might be called the productivity approach to the elimination of poverty and low Negro income is thus aimed at improving the quantity and distribution of human capital" (Thurow 1969: 85). The orthodox position on poverty and income differentials is therefore quite simple: we are paid for the skills we have acquired; workers who are poor are poor because they lack education and job skills.

One should note that human capital theory explains the inequality of poverty in terms of a more basic *equality* in the mechanism that determines wages. Everyone is paid an *equal* amount of return per unit of human capital: if a physician earns ten times the income of a filing clerk, it is primarily because the physician has ten times the skill, knowledge, or education of the clerk. Human capital theory is therefore a potent justification of wage differentials—whatever its merits as a scientific theory—for it implies that income differences (and poverty) are rationally based: to each according to his/her skill. Like many economic theories, however, it leaves unanswered the question of why some people have less human capital and others more.

If human capital theory's explanation of poverty is simple, the logic underlying it is more complex. In particular, the neoclassical model of economic processes builds upon certain assumptions regarding the mobility of labor and the nature of labor markets. These assumptions are basic to the neoclassical position. If they are false, then the argument regarding wage differentials and poverty is flawed.

One axiom of the neoclassical perspective is that a single market exists for the sale of labor rather than separate markets for each kind of skill or occupation. In other words, neoclassical theory does not conceive of bakers competing for one set of jobs and brain surgeons competing for a different set of jobs in totally separate labor markets. Instead, the theory requires some kind of competitive relationship between bakers and brain surgeons for jobs (cf. Kerr 1954), though not necessarily a direct one. It would suffice, for example, if prospective bakers chose instead to learn to be brain surgeons because the monetary return on education was better in the latter field.

Orthodox economists are forced into the assumption that there is only one job market in which every individual potentially competes against every other for jobs because mobility of labor from one occupation to another is the only mechanism that ensures that a given level of skill (or human capital) will be rewarded equally in all occupations and industries. Only to the extent that workers move out of low-paying sectors and into higher-paying ones (for a given level of skill) will different occupations or industries be forced to pay equal wages for a given kind of labor. If bakers and brain surgeons operate in distinct markets with little or no mobility between them, there is no mechanism to ensure that a given amount of education or training in baking will be rewarded equally with respect to an equivalent amount of training in surgery. Instead, each profession would be characterized by its own particular monetary reward per unit of education and training, which would not have any necessary relationship to the reward in any other occupation. The notion of a universal yardstick—Human Capital—that ensures equal pay per unit of education and skill would disappear.

A second central assumption of neoclassical theory is the belief that surpluses or shortages of any kind of labor "will set forces in motion to eliminate the surplus or shortage," in Leftwich's words. Given long-standing shortages of labor in some occupations or industries and surpluses in others, wages would be determined by the availability of a particular kind of labor rather than by the productivity or human capital of that type of labor. Once again, if this assumption underlying neoclassical theory does not hold, then the posited link between wages and human capital will not logically follow.

I have described these theoretical underpinnings of neoclassical theory and its conclusion that poverty flows from insufficient education and training because dual labor market theory begins with an opposite set of assumptions and, consequently, comes to a very different conclusion regarding poverty. The neoclassical model, based on free mobility of labor and self-liquidating shortages and surpluses of labor, is viewed by DLM theorists as incapable of explaining an occupational structure that is fraught with barriers to mobility (e.g., unions, giant corporations, seniority and tenure systems, professional certification, controls over training programs and numbers trained, and so on). Instead, dual labor market theory is built around assumptions of limited mobility, unequal rewards for equal human capital, and ongoing surpluses and shortages of various types of labor.

The Dual Market: The Institutionalists

The intellectual dominance of neoclassical human capital theory in the 1960s showed itself in the government's willingness to accept the theory's policy implications. Hence, during the first four or five years of the War on Poverty, government programs concentrated almost exclusively on upgrading work skills among poor minorities (Bluestone et al. 1973). This apparent hegemony of the human capital approach was not of long standing, however. Prior to the sixties, labor economics had been characterized by an "institutionalist approach" that was highly critical of the free-competition and marginal-productivity assumptions of neoclassical economics. E. Wright Bakke, Clark Kerr, John Dunlop, and others were impressed by the existence of barriers to mobility in the labor market, most especially those created by craft unionization on the one hand and by "internal labor markets" (job ladders within firms) on the other (Kerr 1954; Bakke 1954; Dunlop 1966). The details of this approach do not concern us here. What is significant for our analysis is that the major rival to the human capital school during the 1960s came from the next generation of institutionalists, Michael Piore and Peter Doeringer, who were one-time pupils of Dunlop and were later faculty members at Harvard.

Piore and Doeringer extended Clark Kerr's notion that labor markets are "Balkanized"—broken into small separate units—and argued for a dichotomous model: the labor market should be conceived of as divided into two sectors. In the primary sector, jobs are characterized by high wages, good working conditions, chances of advancement, stability of employment, and equity and due process in conflict situations. In contrast, jobs in the secondary sector are typically low-paying with poor working conditions, are unlikely to provide opportunities for advancement, and are subject to close personalized supervision and frequently capricious discipline by management. Most important, secondary sector jobs are characterized by employment instability and high turnover rates (Piore 1975).

Doeringer and Piore derived their model from several studies of ghetto labor markets in American cities. What makes the model more than a simple descriptive device are Doeringer and Piore's additional observations that racial minorities are largely confined to secondary sector occupations and that the high unemployment rate of the ghetto should be understood as the result of chronic job instability associated with the secondary sector rather than a lack of job opportunities:

The hypothesis was designed to explain the problems of disadvantaged, particularly black workers, in urban areas, which had previously been attributed to unemployment. It implied that the basic problem was that they were somehow confined to jobs within the secondary sector, and the reported unemployment rates were essentially a symptom of the instability of the jobs and the high turnover among the labor force which held them, rather than a literal inability to find work. The relative stability of jobs and workers in the two sectors also appeared to be the critically explanatory variable in understanding the origins of the two sectors, and other characteristics may be viewed as derivatives of this one factor. (Piore 1975: 126)

Black unemployment rates (and, implicitly, poverty) are analyzed in terms of the confinement of black workers to jobs that are unstable *and* in terms of poor blacks' voluntary cycling in and out of such jobs, with periods of unemployment in between. Of these two sources of instability—the fluctuating demand for labor and the departure from jobs by choice—Piore and Doeringer clearly believe that voluntary worker instability is of greater importance. Thus they discuss economically stable but low-paying jobs for ghetto workers, such as hospital and hotel work, and point out that these jobs are also subject to the very high voluntary employee turnover rates typical of the secondary sector (Doeringer and Piore 1971: 166).

Given this division of the job market into a well-paying primary sector and a low-paying secondary sector characterized by chronically high turnover rates, why are disadvantaged workers unable to escape the secondary sector and obtain work in primary sector occupations? Doeringer and Piore answer in two ways. At the most general level, disadvantaged workers "are confined to the secondary market by residence, inadequate skills, poor work histories, and discrimination" (Doeringer and Piore 1971: 166).

In other research Piore analyzed these factors in more detail in a five-part model. First, Piore argues, primary work is distinguished from secondary work in terms of the behavioral requirements demanded of the work force, especially with regard to employment stability. Thus, he writes, "Insofar as secondary workers are barred from primary jobs by real qualifications, it is generally their inability to show up for work regularly and on time. Secondary employers are far more tolerant of lateness and absenteeism . . ." (Piore 1970: 91).

Second, says Piore, a process of "statistical discrimination" comes into play. An idea developed by several neoclassical economists, statistical discrimination describes a component of racial discrimination in hiring practices (McCall 1971; Phelps 1972; Arrow 1973): employers, having limited information, use easily obtaintable data such as race, demeanor, years of education, and the like as a basis for making hiring decisions. These traits *are* related to work performance, on the basis of employers' prior experiences, but only in a statistical or probabilistic sense. Job candidates who lack education or are black are rejected because statistically, a high proportion of individuals who lack education or are black have proven to be unstable workers in the past (Piore 1970: 91). This type of statistical discrimination, especially when allied with "discrimination pure and simple," acts to exclude many secondary market workers from the primary job market, whether or not their individual work histories show them to be stable and steady workers.

A third factor that maintains the separation between primary and secondary markets involves technology. Piore suggests that many jobs could be organized either along primary sector lines, which require a stable work force, or along secondary sector lines, which employ an unstable work force. However, the type of technology that one adopts for a stable work force is different from the type of technology one chooses with an unstable work force in mind. In other words, the choice of technological options depends upon the degree of labor discipline among one's work force. Once a business opts for one technology or the other, a considerable investment has been made, and, in essence, a particular type of worker behavior has been specified (Piore 1970: 92). The business is therefore locked into either the primary or the secondary labor market.

A fourth element in Piore's model involves a system of life style adaptation. Even persons with "good" behavioral traits, if they are trapped within secondary labor markets and live among people with a typical secondary market unstable life style, tend to develop the unstable traits over time (Piore 1970: 92). Thus, just as statistical discrimination keeps stable, dependable workers out of the primary labor markets, cultural adaptation traps them in the secondary labor market.

Finally, Piore notes a compatibility between the irregular work patterns of secondary market employment and the demands of public assistance and illicit activity within the ghetto: "The public assistance system discourages full-time work, and forces those on welfare into jobs which are either part-time or which pay income in cash which will not be reported to the social worker or can be quickly dropped or delayed when the social worker discovers them or seems in danger of doing so" (Piore 1970: 92). Similarly, illicit activities can more easily be integrated with irregular work than with a steady nine-to-five job.

As one can see from the description above, Piore and Doeringer developed the institutionalist concerns of Kerr and Dunlop into a "culture of poverty" explanation of labor markets. The poor are identified as those who work casually or intermittently in low-paying jobs. The central factor in explaining why disadvantaged workers cannot escape such jobs is the behavioral unsuitability of secondary workers for primary sector jobs, their chronic absenteeism and lateness. Despite the introduction of structural factors such as discrimination and technology, Doeringer and Piore's argument revolves around these individual behavioral traits. Structural factors interact with these traits, *but do not cause them*.

Piore has since extended this model, adding a description of the primary sector to his previous characterization of the secondary (i.e., disadvantaged) sector. His new model proposes three labor market divisions: an "upper tier" of the primary sector, consisting of nonroutinized technical, professional, and managerial jobs, which involve an internalized code of work ethics; a "lower tier" of the primary sector, composed of well-paid jobs involving routinized tasks performed under elaborate sets of work rules and administrative procedures; and the poorly paid secondary sector, where jobs have close personalized supervision and are essentially nonroutinized. Against these three divisions Piore juxtaposes three class subcultures: middle class, working class, and lower class. He argues that each subculture is "supportive" of work in a particular labor market segment. Thus the working class, which he models on Herbert Gans's *Urban Villagers* (1962), enjoys a stable, routinized life style centered on the extended family unit and long-time friends made during adolescence. Self-definition in the working class is based primarily on personal relationships, and work is seen as a means to an end (supporting family and friends). According to Piore, working-class persons view education as an instrument to find work. Thus working-class culture

appears supportive of work in the lower tier of the primary sector, which seems, like the basic life-style, to be stable and routinized.

The priority accorded to family life enables one to bear the lack of challenge on the job, whereas the challenge, were it to exist, might distract from family activities. (Piore 1975: 127)

In contrast, for the middle classes there is a blurring of family, work, and education. Work and education are considered rewarding in themselves, and friends are often drawn from work. Consequently,

The middle class subculture is well adapted to the support of upper-tier work patterns: the nuclear family and professional friendships facilitate geographical and social mobility and permit intellectually demanding and time consuming jobs. The view of education is supportive of extensive prework schooling far removed from the payoff, and of no immediate relevance. (Piore 1975: 127)

In the same way, the culture of lower-class communities is seen to fit the needs of the secondary labor force. Here Piore leans upon Elliot Liebow's characterization of streetcorner cliques in *Tally's Corner* (1967):

Lower class men have a highly personalized conception of themselves, divorced from and independent of a network of relationships with family and friends. Such relationships thus tend to be volatile, short-lived, and unstable, and their life appears to be an effort to escape routine through action and adventure. It is thus a pattern consistent with the erratic employment of the secondary labor market as well as with other characteristics such as the personal relationships between worker and supervisor. (Piore 1975: 128)

This instability, adventure-seeking, and general anomie of urban lower-class life style is viewed by Piore as a variant of working-class adolescent life style. The lack of steady jobs and family formation among lower-class individuals leads to their failure "to make a transition into a routine lifestyle pattern as adults . . ." (Piore 1975: 146). Blocked from the opportunity to create stabilizing adult job and family formations, lower-class culture retains the adolescent institutions and values of working-class teenagers—gangs, adventure, machismo, and so on. These adolescent features of lower-class culture are also reinforced by the process of immigration, according to Piore. Since most immigrants leave home during the transition from adolescence to adulthood, they have not yet created stable family groups. This influx of single migrants (or men who leave wives behind), combined with the lack of new jobs and the lack of a continuing supportive peer group, adds to the anomic adolescent life style of lower-class ghettos.

With the addition of this subcultural argument, Piore fulfills his goal of developing a systematic explanation of labor market segmentation. The *supply* of labor for each of his three segments—upper-tier primary sector, lower-tier primary sector, and secondary sector—is explained by his description of class subcultures. Each subculture, in reproducing itself successively, provides workers for each of the three labor markets.

With regard to the *demand* for the various types of labor and changes in that demand, Piore chooses to turn to an analysis of technology. Since his argument proceeds in several stages, we must first discuss routinized versus nonroutinized jobs arising from different types of technology. Then follows the issue of types of skills implied by certain technological processes. Finally, these two issues will be tied together to explain the three labor market segments.

Piore first observes that industries can adopt two different types of productive processes. One type involves a detailed division of labor: jobs become very repetitive and routinized and can easily be mechanized. This type of technology leads to jobs in the lower-tier primary labor market (e.g., an auto worker on the assembly line). An alternative type of production technology involves less mechanization, less capital equipment, and a less detailed division of labor. Each worker has a range of tasks. This second type of technology produces two kinds of jobs. At one extreme are nonroutine jobs requiring complex judgments and considerable knowledge. These are held by professionals or highly trained craftspeople. At the other extreme are jobs that are nonroutinized but are basically menial and involve general skills and the kinds of obvious judgments that anyone can make. Such nonroutinized menial jobs constitute the secondary labor market, according to Piore (1975: 141).

Now we turn to the issue of skills. Specific skills, as opposed to general ones, are adaptations to specific machines or particular work situations. They are usually acquired in an informal manner, as part of the on-the-job learning, by "osmosis." Piore contends that such skills develop in highly routinized machine technology jobs. Specific skills make an experienced worker considerably more efficient—and hence more valuable to management—than an inexperienced worker. There is an implicit assumption that these on-the-job specific skills are learned over some considerable time period. Hence stable, long-term employees will possess these machine-specific skills, whereas short-term, transient workers will not have acquired them. Management therefore tries to keep experienced workers and selects as new workers stable individuals who will remain on the job long enough to acquire these types of skills.

In contrast to specific skills, general skills are applicable to non-routinized work situations and are transferable from job to job. General skills come from two sources. Some are capacities that our society develops in all adults (literacy, the ability to carry or clean things, etc.); others require advanced education or lengthy craft training.

Combining the arguments on routinization with those about skill provides additional insight into the three labor market segments. Highly routinized and capital-intensive techniques imply that specific skills will be important. Employers will therefore seek persons with stable work habits and proven abilities with regard to the acquisition of on-the-job specific skills. In order to attract and hold such workers, they must pay good wages. This, then, is the lower tier of the primary sector: routinized specific-skill jobs, filled by persons from the working class.

Nonroutinized technologies imply general skills on the part of workers. If these general skills require lengthy formal education or theoretical training, they are associated with professional or craft jobs and pay well. This is the upper tier of the primary sector and, according to Piore, is staffed predominantly by middle-class people.

Nonroutinized work requiring the kind of general skills that all people have is often called menial work. Because these general skills are in plentiful supply and are brought to the job rather than learned there, employers need not pay high wages for them, and there is no special advantage to holding onto experienced workers. Hence, menial, nonroutinized work characterizes the low-paid secondary labor market. This market is disproportionately filled with lower-class workers with unstable work histories.

Piore has provided us with a creative and wide-ranging synthesis of economic and sociological materials in his explanation of labor market segmentation. By showing the links among technology, skills, and class subcultures, he offers a challenging theory of economic segmentation.

His theory is not immune from criticism, however. The two most questionable issues are whether the secondary sector is accurately portrayed in terms of unstable workers, and whether poorly paid secondary work is, as Piore says, "quite unskilled, involving menial work and obvious but non-routine judgments." These are questions amenable to empirical testing, and we shall return to them shortly. But first we shall look at two alternative approaches.

Radical DLM Theory

Doeringer and Piore's theory is not in any obvious way politically partisan. Insofar as it raises issues of statistical and simple discrimination, it has a certain critical element. Nevertheless, it projects a "blame the victim" quality in its focus on the behavioral instability of secondary workers as the central cause of their exclusion from primary sector jobs.

Surprisingly, radical theorists such as David Gordon, Richard Edwards, and Michael Reich have played a major part in the development of DLM theory and typically share the unstable worker explanation of dualism. However, they give their arguments an emphasis that avoids blaming the victim. For Edwards (1975: 19–20), the tendency of secondary workers to quit jobs, be late, and be absent from work is a *result* of dualism and not just a cause. Since the wage levels of the secondary sector are so low, and since there is no chance of advancement or increased wages if one stays in a given job, there is no monetary incentive for the worker to be stable and punctual. If one is fired for instability, one finds an equally unsatisfactory job elsewhere; if one is a long-term punctual, conscientious worker, one is not rewarded for these characteristics in the secondary sector. Thus, for the radical DLM theorists, low wages and poor conditions cause secondary sector workers to be unstable, which in turn causes labor market segmentation.

This perspective may have removed some of the "culture of poverty" causation and "blame the victim" elements from Piore's argument, but it does not obviate other weaknesses in his argument, as we shall see below.

Industrial Segmentation

An approach that avoids the culture of poverty and instead examines structural variables underlying economic dualism was developed independently of Doeringer and Piore's efforts and dates to 1968. Radicals such as Barry Bluestone, Howard Wachtel, and Randall Hodson have contributed to its formulation.

In October 1968, in the journal *Dissent*, Bluestone published an analysis of American poverty. He began with the assertion that the then current belief that poverty results from structural unemployment due to the inability of unskilled persons to fulfill the requirements of a technologically advanced society was erroneous. The cause of poverty, Bluestone argued, is neither a lack of jobs nor a lack of skills. Rather, it is the lack of adequately paying jobs: the problem of poverty is largely a problem of the working poor.

Focusing on nonparticipants in the labor force—the old, the handicapped, mothers with dependent children, and the unemployed—leads to an erroneous analysis of poverty in terms of inability to enter the work force. Here Bluestone agrees with Doeringer and Piore. However, rather than examining the intermittently working urban males of *Tally's Corner*, Bluestone concentrates on a revealing statistic: "*Nearly a third of all families living in poverty in 1964 were headed by a person who worked 50–52 weeks a year at a full-time job*" (Bluestone 1968a: 410). Full-time regular work, not casual labor interspersed with unemployment, is the experience of an important sector of the poor.

The crucial feature of such full-time work is the low pay. In 1963, 8.5 million people—nearly one-fifth of the total full-time employed work force—appeared on the job for the entire year and earned less than $3,000. Yet $3,000 was approximately the poverty income level for a family of four. It follows that approximately 20 percent of the work force could not support a family of four above the poverty line even by working full time all year. Of course, not all 8.5 million are family breadwinners. But presenting the figures in this way reveals that poverty may be understood as part of a larger phenomenon: namely, the existence of a large low-wage sector in the American economy (Bluestone 1968a: 411). Thus, the analysis that follows concentrates upon the working poor, but many of the findings speak to a much larger constituency—the 20 percent of the full-time work force in the low-wage sector of a dual U.S. economy.

Bluestone continues with a statistical breakdown of data on the working poor. Contrary to some opinions (e.g., Piore 1970: 93), full-time, full-year, low-wage workers are not predominantly rural agricultural workers. Thirty percent *do* work in agriculture, forestry, and fisheries, but the remaining 70 percent work in urban occupations such as manufacturing (15 percent), retail trade (15 percent), personal services (10 percent), construction (9 percent), and miscellaneous non-agricultural work (21 percent).

Demographic statistics on the poor reveal that approximately one-third of the working poor families are black. One should also note that among the poor in general the proportion of poor blacks who work full time is about the same as the proportion of poor whites who work full time. When one considers only male heads of poor households, a somewhat different picture emerges: some two-thirds of black male heads of households worked full time versus only about one-third of white male heads of households. Thus the image of the full-time working poor fits black poor even more closely than it does white poor (Bluestone 1968a: 412).

Focusing further on the working poor, Bluestone turns to the structural characteristics of low-wage industries in an attempt to understand the origins of this wage dualism. One of the most obvious potential explanations might be that low-wage industries are declining industries, ones for whom the product demand is disappearing and whose importance in the economy is declining. Not so, suggests Bluestone. Taking changes in employment patterns (i.e., the increasing or decreasing number of persons employed in an industry) as the measure of expansion/decline reveals that many low-wage industries are expanding. Among these are apparel, furniture and fixtures, and, most noticeably, the retail trade. On the other hand, some low-wage industries—lumber and wood products, textiles, leather goods, and footwear—do fit the declining employment image. It therefore appears that the expansion or contraction of employment in an industry is not a crucial factor in its wage level (Bluestone 1968b).

As a second possible factor contributing to wage dualism, Bluestone considers the productivity of low-wage industries, as measured by the value added per production worker per hour. In fact, a considerable gap in productivity shows up between the low-wage sector and the non-low wage sector: the mean productivity of the former is only about half the mean productivity of the latter. Yet, interestingly, the low-wage industries are not stagnating with regard to productivity change over time. Their productivity seems to be increasing as fast as that in other industries; they simply have a long way to catch up.

But why do these industries have relatively low productivity and low wages? Bluestone amasses evidence on several points. Low wage industries are also low-profit industries. They tend to be concentrated in much more competitive markets than the rest of American industry. They are likely to invest less capital per worker, and they tend to operate in product markets susceptible to foreign competition. They also generally produce goods for which there is a high elasticity of demand: if prices are raised, sales drop sharply.

What all these data add up to is a picture of low wages associated with a sectorial division in the American economy. On the one hand, oligopolistic, fairly profitable industries operate in markets where demand is relatively price inelastic. They are highly capital intensive and hence have high productivity, and their wages are relatively high. At the other extreme are less profitable industries that face competition internally and from abroad. Demand for their products is very elastic with regard to price. These industries tend to be more labor intensive, have lower productivity, and pay low wages.

In several subsequent publications Bluestone has extended and detailed this working-poor model, contrasting it with the human capital approach and drawing policy conclusions from the model (Bluestone 1968b; Bluestone 1970; Bluestone et al. 1973). For our purposes, two features of the later work are of special importance: an attempt to specify the barriers to mobility that act to keep the individual in one labor market, and an attempt to modify the two-sector model into a three-sector model of the economy, with an attendant explanation for the separation of the three segments.

Considering the issue of mobility, Bluestone discusses individual, industrial, and social barriers, emphasizing that the individual worker has little if any control over the latter two types of barriers. Parenthetically, the reader should note the importance for left theorists of reversing the "blame the victim" stance and the way in which structural factors beyond the individual's ability to choose or control are consistently stressed.

Individual Barriers to Mobility
Insufficient education
Insufficient training and skills
History of unreliable job performance
Disutility of geographical mobility
Disutility of occupational mobility

Industrial Barriers to Mobility
Hiring and on-the-job racial discrimination
Hiring and on-the-job sexual discrimination
Trade union barriers to entry
Use of educational level as a pure rationing device

Social Barriers to Mobility
High financial cost of geographic relocation
Personal risk attached to mobility
High levels of aggregate unemployment
Racism
Sexism
Lack of labor market information

(from Bluestone 1970: 23)

In discussing the relative importance of each type of barrier to mobility, Bluestone makes a point that is central to neo-Marxist analyses of poverty and explains to some degree why they tend to give less theoretical weight to the issue of labor mobility in general. Efforts to increase labor mobility will not in themselves result in the disappearance of poverty. Free mobility would only achieve a situation where race or sex would no longer be a barrier to job entry and where the good jobs would presumably go to those with greater education and skills. But the large low-wage sector would *not* be eliminated, and hence poverty would not be eradicated. Rather, poverty would only be racially and sexually integrated (Bluestone 1970: 23–24).

This position contrasts with the neoclassical approach of orthodox economics. In a truly homogeneous free competitive market with no barriers to labor mobility, workers would leave low-wage industries in droves for higher-wage ones. If low-wage industries did not offer better wages, they would collapse for lack of labor power. The radical response to this analysis is twofold. Even allowing for mobility, the low-wage economy can persist because of the excess of workers: the reserve army of the unemployed prevents labor shortages. Second, and most important, the low-wage sector does not pay low wages because it chooses to but because it cannot exist at the levels of the high-wage sector. This leads us to Bluestone's second development: a tripartite model that views the economy as having a core, a peripheral, and an irregular sector.

The core sector, as discussed before, is characterized by high productivity, high profitability, capital intensiveness, oligopolistic market power, and a high degree of unionization. Its advantages, which enable a higher general wage rate and separate it from the peripheral sector, include

(1) extensive assets which allow center firms to outspend smaller peripheral firms; (2) better geographic and product diversification which allows center firms to withstand losses in one area or on one product almost indefinitely; (3) vertical integration which allows center firms to underbid free agent and forward satellite retailers for large contracts; (4) the ability of center firms to become their own suppliers and distributors, thus insuring low-cost inputs and a distribution network; (5) favored access to finance when credit is scarce or restricted; and (6) political advantages: center firms can maintain a staff in Washington to advise on the locus of critical decision making, what information to prepare, and who to see it. Such factors are often decisive in gaining favorable laws and administrative rulings on such matters as tariffs, taxes, and subsidies, as well as successful contract bids. In addition, the extensive resources available to the core economy firm allow such firms to spend the great amounts on research and development necessary for continued high profits in a dynamic economy. (Bluestone 1970: 24)

By contrast, the peripheral sector, consisting of smaller, highly competitive firms with low productivity and low capital/labor ratios, lacks all the above advantages. These firms live a precarious existence, as evidenced by very high bankruptcy rates, and succeed only by paying most of their employees very low wages. This situation has continued to be the case historically, and most of these industries are specifically exempted from minimum wage legislation, which further encourages the tendency toward low wages.

The third sector of the economy, the "irregular economy," consists of jobs disconnected from regular enterprises. These involve

> (1) informal work patterns that are frequently invisible to outside observers; (2) an organized set of occupational roles specific to ghetto life; (3) work skills and competencies that are a product of ghetto life; and (4) the acquisition of work skills and competencies through nontraditional channels. Some of the work opportunities in the irregular economy are deviant by middle class moral and legal standards, but most are not; job activities may range from daily contract work for gardening to plumbing, electrical work, and automobile repair. These job experiences allow the worker to engage in pseudoentrepreneurial activity that is closed to him in the other two sectors of the economy. . . . The nonunion or nonlicensed craftsman, the home appliance "Mr. Fixit," the street or door-to-door hustler, all fall within the irregular ghetto economy. In addition, illegal activities—dope peddling, prostitution, gambling, etc.—are part of this economic sector. (Bluestone 1970: 26)

Since the working conditions of the irregular economy are often better than those of the periphery, especially in terms of pay, many people opt for the former. Although Bluestone does not discuss the specific barriers to mobility between the irregular and core sectors, one may suggest lack of state licensing, union membership (for plumbers, electricians, etc.), or formal credentials and criminal records (for the various illicit professions) as factors that inhibit mobility.

To summarize Bluestone's contributions, one should first note that he emphasizes the working poor. Second, he indicates a hierarchy of the barriers to mobility that prevent impoverished individuals from gaining access to other jobs. (A detailed examination of some of these factors will be given later.) Third, he describes a segmentation of the economy itself into sectors that differ significantly in their abilities to pay wages, irrespective of the skills of their work forces. It is in this last aspect that the theory moves most clearly into traditionally Marxist territory. By considering the economy in terms of sectors of capital with different abilities to accumulate capital and thus to reproduce themselves, Bluestone encompasses orthodox Marxism. Poverty becomes a special case, a consequence, in fact, of the uneven development of capitalist economies and especially of the interaction of oligopoly and competition in advanced capitalism. To understand the future of poverty, therefore, one must look at the interpenetration of oligopoly and competitive and state activity and their development over time.

Before pursuing the radical model further in its various twistings and windings, I wish to pause and take stock. I have presented the neoclassical approach to labor allocation and wage differentials and followed that with two varieties of economic segmentation theory. But, as presented, these positions lack a very important dimension that is quite evident in the original texts. I have tended to present each theory within its own analytical framework. However, much of the radical work was conceived in debate with—one might almost say in order to debate with—the neoclassical human capital approach. I have tended to downplay this aspect in order to simplify the presentation of the individual theories. But it now behooves us to return to the three models and follow the debate between them.

Neoclassical versus Dual Labor Market Theory

Several statements that follow from the human capital model are in principle open to empirical examination:

1. Workers can and do move from job to job to maximize their income.
2. Observed differences in income levels will occur only where there are differences in human capital.
3. The greater a worker's human capital, the higher his/her income will be.
4. Workers with equal human capital will receive equal wages.

The essence of the dual labor market (DLM) position is that there are separate labor markets with different individuals competing in each. Further, some mechanism acts to prevent free mobility between markets. Consequently:

1. Workers are unable to move from job to job (or market to market) to maximize their income.
2. Observed differences in income levels may occur where there are no differences in human capital (in separate labor markets).
3. Greater human capital will not necessarily result in increased income, since individuals lack mobility to find those jobs where they can utilize fully the value of their human capital.
4. Workers with equal human capital may be paid unequal incomes both within and between labor markets.

Let us review the evidence that speaks to these issues. One of the first and simplest tests of DLM statement (2), one that does not even involve a detailed definition of dual labor markets, can be made simply by looking at black versus white income, statistically controlling for education and other human capital variables. The evidence is so abundant and so overwhelming that neoclassical and human capital theorists do not even contest the facts: blacks and whites with equivalent education receive different wages. This discrepancy has been studied exhaustively both by orthodox economists and by radical social scientists. Their conclusions are based on a variety of strong data, including census figures, and show that for any given level of education, as measured by years of schooling, years of college, postcollege education, and so on, there are large disparities in income ("returns to education") between blacks and whites. Both Gary Becker, who founded the human capital approach, and economist Kenneth Arrow admit this apparent contradiction. As Arrow says: "Since in fact racial discrimination has survived for a long time, we must assume that the [neoclassical] model . . . must have some limitation" (1973: 10).

But, as in the case of any well-developed paradigm, neoclassical economists can generate an explanation of this anomaly within the assumptions of the paradigm. That is, they can explain the apparent breach of the rules in terms of some higher rule. Becker, in particular, has an elaborately developed explanation (Becker 1962): racist employers manifest their "taste" for discrimination by hiring whites rather than blacks. Given that this practice reduces competition between black and white labor and removes the possibility of access to cheaper black labor, racist employers end up paying more for labor than would be the case if they did not discriminate. This should cause racist employers to go out of business in the long run. Competing employers who do not discriminate would profit by hiring integrated labor at a lower cost and would eventually drive the racist employers out of business by underselling them.

Similarly, if the taste for discrimination was present among (white) employees, those employees would have to pay for the cost of segregation. In practice, they would either take lower wages in order to work in segregated shops or, what is equivalent, not move from a segregated to a nonsegregated plant without being paid extra income. As Glen Cain points out, employers would respond by hiring only racially homogenous work forces. However, competition in the long run should equalize pay rates among racially segregated companies (Cain 1975: 47).

The radical response to these neoclassical arguments emphasizes several points. First, the human capital theorists' notion that competition will bankrupt discriminatory practices over time evokes the question: How long does discrimination have to last before such a theory is proven wrong? Discriminatory income levels for equal human capital still persist (see Farley 1977 for a detailed analysis). Moreover, the improvements that have taken place seem to have occurred only after legislative action prohibiting discrimination rather than as a natural operation of the free market.

Second, the latter of Becker's two situations—the one in which white employees have a taste for discrimination and are willing to take lower wages to maintain a segregated workplace—leads to an equalization of black and white wage rates but a racial segregation of workplaces. This explanation is unconvincing. Available data show that white employee wage rates for equivalent occupations and education are consistently higher than those of blacks, even where segregation occurs. We are therefore left with Becker's alternative possibility, in which it is employers who discriminate and hence, according to neoclassical theory, who "pay" for this discriminatory preference by offering above-average wages to obtain an all-white work force. This situation should lead to lower profits and, ultimately, to bankruptcy, as discriminatory employers fail to compete with firms that do not have to pay higher wages.

If Becker is right, areas where black/white economic inequality is greatest should also be those where white employers are relatively worse off. In areas with less black/white inequality, white employers should be relatively better off. Radical scholars have tested Becker's theory empirically by comparing local labor markets in the U.S. and have found that it fails to fit available data. Michael Reich (1971) was the first to test the theory. When comparing urban areas known as Standard Metropolitan Statistical Areas (SMSAs), he found the opposite of Becker's scenario: the greater the inequality in income between blacks and whites, the better off were white employers. Also contrary to Becker's theory, higher black/white inequality was associated with higher inequality among whites, implying that working-class whites were worse off vis-à-vis upper-class whites where racial inequalities were greatest.

Reich's early test had certain weaknesses; most notably, he used relative family incomes as his measure, rather than individuals' incomes. His work was repeated and extended by Albert Szymanski (1976), who used individual earnings by state to calculate racial economic inequality. Szymanski controlled for several variables that could potentially skew the findings: degree of urbanism, percent of minorities in each state, region, and percent of the work force in manufacturing. He found that white median income was highest where blacks were least discriminated against and that inequality among whites was least where blacks were least discriminated against. Again the results contradicted those suggested by Becker.

Having found that most whites lose economically from racial inequality and that wealthy (employer) whites gain from economic racism, Szymanski sought a mechanism that would produce these results. He was able to demonstrate that working-class solidarity—the proportion of the work force that is unionized—was the explanation. In those areas where racial inequities were greatest, union membership was lowest, and white working peoples' incomes were also diminished vis-à-vis those of wealthier whites (cf. Roemer 1979).

Wayne Villemez (1978) critiqued both Reich and Szymanski's findings, objecting to their measures of inequality (gini coefficients; ratios of black/white median income; income share of the top 1 percent of whites), to the samples used (SMSAs, states), and to the view that racism operates in terms of relative incomes of blacks and whites. In my opinion, Szymanski's (1978) reanalysis and the elaborate tests in Reich's (1981) book defuse Villemez's dubious objections. Using a wide variety of measures of inequality and several specifications of the sample, they repeatedly find the same results: rich whites gain from minority/white economic inequality; poorer whites lose.[1]

Thus, neither of the necessary consequences of discrimination postulated by human capital and neoclassical theory occur empirically. White employee gain does not necessarily accompany white employer loss. Nor is white employee loss evident in Becker's special sense: namely, that whites earn the same as blacks in order to work in segregated workplaces.

But even if the neoclassical logic for explaining the necessary consequences of discrimination seems faulty, its assertions concerning black/white income differences still remain: that is, differences in income are to be understood in terms of differences in human capital. Despite the evidence cited above concerning inequalities in returns to education for blacks and whites, the human capital theorist can always rejoin that any apparent inequality in income in cases where blacks and whites have the same years of education can be attributed to differences in more complex human capital variables. For example, it might be argued that employers know that whites obtain better quality high school education than blacks and that a white high school diploma is therefore worth more pay than a black one. As various authors have pointed out, the human capital theorists can repeat *ad infinitum* that observed income differences are due to differences in human capital, even if those differences are not easily measurable.

At this point I think it is fair to comment on such infinite regress situations. Human capital theorists have been quick to raise the possibility of subtle differences in human capital as the cause of observed income differences between persons with superficially equivalent skills. They have *not*, to the best of my knowledge, tried to demon-

---

1 E. M. Beck (1980) tested Reich and Szymanski's findings and claimed that his study found neither that rich whites gained nor that poorer whites lost from racial inequality. However, Beck's study used a rather odd approach to the issue. He took aggregated data for the entire U.S. rather than labor markets, as the theory implies. He then used annual time-series data to ask: Did white income change as discrimination changed, net of general trends in white income? Despite Beck's belief that this is a superior test, I think it is a rather poor one. Few theorists would treat the U.S. as one labor market, given its great diversity. We know, for example, that time trends in racial inequality differ considerably from region to region, as demonstrated by Reich (1981: 46). A national analysis throws together the relative shifts in white/nonwhite income across regions, across the urban/rural distinction (irrespective of the industrial structure of local economies), and so on, whereas Reich and Szymanski's analyses control for these features.

strate the salience of such differences empirically. Most particularly, they have not shown how employers (who, after all, set the salaries) are aware of and exploit such subtle or secondary human capital information in hiring and setting pay levels. I suggest that the onus at some point must rest upon human capital theorists to measure factors like richness of family socialization and differential quality of formal education and to show how employers and personnel managers take them into account. Until the subjective importance of such factors in decision making is demonstrated, human capital theorists' appeal to a variety of subtle factors should be judged as special pleading, as an attempt to avoid genuine theoretical and empirical counter-evidence.

For our purposes, however, the only way of cutting through this Gordian knot, and hence coming to terms with the conflict between human capital and dual labor market explanations, is to escape the race issue entirely and examine income differentials with respect to labor markets, preferably considering a racially homogeneous sample or, at second best, statistically controlling for race. For if a DLM explanation holds even for white males of equal education, how can human capital theory explain the existence of income differentials? Clearly, appeals to factors such as differential quality of high school education or differential family socialization become much less believable. How is an employer supposed to make judgments, and upon what basis? Between blacks and whites an employer could, in principle, make a probabilistic judgment on such issues based on "common knowledge," but this approach is severely limited when the choice is between white male and white male. Thus, an examination of income differentials that controls for race in some manner will provide a much more straightforward contrast of the human capital and dual labor market theories. Several theorists have already attempted such comparisons. We shall begin with the simplest examples and move to the more complex.

A direct approach is to assert that in large sectors of the economy there is no relationship between human capital and income level. This proposition follows from a dual labor market analysis: if one cannot move into jobs where one's education counts and is rewarded, one has no choice but to work in unskilled jobs. Consequently, a dual labor market analysis would predict that a wide range of educational abilities will exist in the secondary market with no concomittant differentials in income.

Several researchers have attempted such analyses, using regression equations in which human capital variables act as predictors of income for some subset of the work force deemed to be in a secondary labor market. Paul Andrisani (1973) selected those industries whose median wages were in the bottom third of the wage distribution for all industries. These he then treated as a secondary sector. Regression analysis showed that for this sector of the economy human capital variables had little relationship to income. Similar results are reported by Paul Osterman (1975), Barry Bluestone et al. (1973), and Peter Doeringer et al. (1972). All indicate that education and other human capital variables are of comparatively low explanatory power in predicting variations in wage levels in considerable sections of the labor market (albeit with varying definitions of secondary sector for each author).

The significance of such findings in regard to the human capital approach are clear. If only one labor market exists in which employees are mobile, individuals with greater human capital should gravitate to the better paying jobs. Indeed, the only criteria for paying different wages to individuals should be varying amounts of human capital, since supply and demand considerations are supposed to average out in the long run (Cain 1975: 40). If dual labor market theorists have adequately proven that human capital variables explain little or none of the variation in income for a large sector of the labor force, the human capital approach itself, or, alternatively, the assumption of one homogeneous labor market, fails.

These findings have been critiqued by Glen Cain, a neoclassical theorist, on the basis of statistical bias. Cain argues that the above analyses, by taking some subset of the labor market (e.g., the poorest one-third), truncate the range of values of the dependent variable (income) and thus automatically lower the correlation between education and income: "indeed, it is not surprising to see [the correlation] approach zero" (Cain 1975: 82).

The apparent validity of Cain's argument does not hold on deeper inspection. It is true that by taking a restricted range of incomes the impact of education upon income may be artificially lowered. The correlation between education and income would be stronger if we included the whole range of educations and incomes, from brain surgeon to illiterate ditch digger, so to speak. But Cain errs in suggesting that truncation will lead to the total disappearance of any statistical effect. The severity of the truncation effect is a function of the narrowness of the sample chosen. A test of the human capital theory that considered only individuals with annual incomes from $10,000 to $10,100 would indeed be illegitimate. But taking the bottom third of all incomes is another matter. Truncation in the latter situation should slightly lower the power of human capital variables; it should not lead to a complete absence of correlation between human capital and income.

Human capital theory predicts not just a relationship between human capital and income for the aggregate entire economy. Nor does it simply state that income extremes should show human capital differences. In fact, the human capital approach predicts that income and human capital should be correlated at all points along the education-income curve. That several authors have demonstrated a lack of correlation between income and human capital for large swaths of the income curve (e.g., the bottom 33 percent) therefore suggests a major flaw in human capital theory. Furthermore, the findings that discredit human capital theory are consonant with a dual labor market approach. The latter, by assuming lack of mobility, predicts that individuals with widely varying degrees of human capital will be found working in identical jobs for identical pay.

An alternative approach to the human capital–dual labor market controversy is to examine the relative contribution of each to explaining income inequality. It should be noted at this point that the dual labor market perspective does *not* suggest that human capital is totally irrelevant for determining wages. On the contrary, education and skill levels play a part in separating markets. Rather, the various segmentation theories argue that income differentials cannot be explained solely in terms of human capital. Lack of mobility between markets or economic sectors will prevent persons from obtaining jobs where they can use their human capital to full advantage. Furthermore, the theories that stress low-wage industries point out that wage levels are more closely related to the ability of industries to pay than to the characteristics of individual employees.

Thus, one test of the industrial segmentation hypothesis involves comparing the relative explanatory power of individual characteristics (human capital) versus industry characteristics (concentration, capital intensity, etc.). One should note that from a Human Capital perspective there should be *no* interindustry wage-level variation where workers' human capital levels are equal, for workers would leave the low-paying industries for the higher-paying ones, thus forcing up wages in the former.

Howard Wachtel and Charles Betsey (1972) present an analysis of full-time, full-year workers that speaks to these issues, though it is unfortunately truncated to a certain degree in that managerial and professional occupations are excluded. Cain's objection could therefore be raised, but one should note that Wachtel and Betsey's analysis did include a wide range of occupations, from craftsmen, operatives, and service workers to laborers, and is not simply an analysis of the poor. (Only 14 percent of the sample were "working poor" by the Social Security Administration definition.)

Wachtel and Betsey first performed a regression analysis to discover the effects of personal characteristics (human capital variables, sex, and race) upon wages. They then calculated an adjusted wage variable that expressed the variation in wages *after* the effects of personal characteristics had been removed. A second regression then analyzed the adjusted wage variable in terms of structural variables (i.e., occupation-industry, region, union membership, city size) that pertain to a segmentation approach. The process was then reversed in order to test the impact of personal characteristic variables on wages after the structural effects had been removed.

In the analysis that began by assessing personal characteristic effects, the human capital variables appeared to be significant predictors, as did such non–human capital ascriptive factors as race, sex, and marital status. With regard to the structural variables, occupation-industry, region, city size, and union status all proved to be significant predictors, explaining almost as much variation in wages as the combined personal characteristics. Reversing the process, the first regression involving structural characteristics proved significant with a larger predictive power (R^2) than previously. Personal characteristics still proved significant, but at a lower level.

In summary, Wachtel and Betsey showed, using stringent methods, that even after the impact of human capital and potential discrimination variables (e.g., race, sex) had been controlled for statistically, there remained significant differentials between industries. Their evidence, I suggest, goes far to prove the existence of economic segments that pay different wages for equivalent skills.

Finally, there is a third type of analysis advanced by radical theorists. The particular advantage of these data is that race is eliminated directly: instead of statistically controlling for race and sex, one simply limits the analysis to white males, thus avoiding the complications arising from theories of racial statistical discrimination and differences in the assumed value of human capital. Since the analysis also deals with all levels of education and skill, Cain's truncation objection does not apply.

In an important article entitled "Labor Force Participation and Earnings in the Core, Peripheral, and State Sectors of Production," Randall Hodson (1977) examines 1973 data to establish the existence of labor market segmentation in the U.S. economy. One should note that the basis of his segmentation (core, periphery, and state sectors) is not quite the same as that employed by the theorists discussed above. For our purposes, however, the important point is that human capital theory predicts no wage differences (given equal human capital) whatever the criteria used to define different sectors. Hodson's mean income figures for white male workers in the labor force show that there are quite large differences in income for equivalent education and for equivalent job categories across the core, periphery, and state sectors (Hodson 1977: 41). Again, I suggest that these data provide strong support for the segmentation as against the human capital approach.

The evidence is not decisive, however. It might still be argued by human capital proponents, for example, that systematic on-the-job skill differences between core, state, and periphery workers could account for the differentials in pay. Although I find it implausible that such differences would exist across all levels of education, all occupations, and all three sectors in such a systematic way, one must admit that such possibilities have not been ruled out by Hodson's data. But I believe that the burden now lies upon human capital theorists to document such differentials—even among white males of equal education. In the meantime, Hodson's is about the strongest case that can be made against human capital, given present data sources.

At this point it may help to summarize the empirical attacks that have been made by DLM and industrial segmentation theorists against the one-labor-market human capital approach. The data we have described fall into three categories. First are the studies that show that for major sections of the income distribution there is little relationship between human capital variables and income levels. Such studies look at regression equations that use human capital variables as predictors of incomes for truncated sections of the income curve. Second are the studies like Wachtel and Betsey's that show that even after the variation in income due to human capital differences and race and sex has been removed, there remains a substantial amount of "unexplained" variance in income, significant amounts of which can be accounted for by structural variables (such as industry sector) that derive from DLM and segmentation theory. Finally, there is Hodson's study, which shows systematic intersectorial income differentials after sex, race, education, and occupation have been held constant. Taken together, these studies place a substantial dent in the case for the empirical validity of human capital theory. At the very least, they show the existence of important factors operating in addition to those of human capital in determining income.

Given this examination of human capital theory and the indirect support it gives for dual labor market theory, is it also possible to find more direct evidence for DLM theory? Here one has to look at a single aspect of DLM theory—namely, the notion of separation of labor markets—and its corollary, mobility or immobility of workers between markets. One reason that human capital theorists regard the U.S. as having one labor market is their assumption that workers would move out of low-paying sectors or jobs and transfer to better paying ones. Thus mobility acts as a mechanism to assure equal reward for equal skills across the entire economy. Conversely, DLM theorists have to assume real barriers to mobility or a consistent excess of labor in order to explain the persistence of low-wage sectors in a surrounding high-wage economy.

It is not clear from DLM theory exactly how much mobility could be tolerated and yet still provide the low-wage sector with workers. This issue is confounded by two factors: a reserve army of the unemployed, and intergenerational effects. Thus, for example, one could posit a fairly considerable level of movement of secondary market workers out of the secondary sector into higher-paying primary sector jobs, alongside high wage differentials between the sectors, so long as there was a fairly steady excess of available labor as an input into the secondary sector. Similarly, one could imagine quite a lot of intersector mobility within workers' lifespans if older, more experienced workers who shifted out of the secondary sector were regularly replaced by youths. Nevertheless, DLM theory cannot really encompass totally free mobility of workers, or the low-wage sector would cease to exist.

A few studies of labor mobility speak to this issue. Optimally, one would wish to follow a representative sample of workers over many years, noting job changes and the like at regular intervals. In practice, no one has data of this quality. At best, we have self-reported information on limited samples, which usually compare an individual's present job with his/her first job. There are obviously a number of methodological difficulties with such data, particularly in using first full-time job as a baseline. Nevertheless, the importance of the issue justifies a cautious examination of such data sources.

Samuel Rosenberg (1975) presents data on males aged 21–64 living in low-income areas of Brooklyn, Cleveland, Detroit, and Ohio. Thus one is comparing not primary sector workers in general with secondary sector workers in general but only those residing in poverty areas. Rosenberg's analyses demonstrate first that there is a significant correlation between first job (i.e., whether it was in the primary or secondary sector) and present job, as dual labor market theory would predict. Nevertheless, the data show that for all cities, over half of the men initially taking jobs in the secondary labor sector succeed at some point in moving to primary sector jobs—blacks as well as whites. Similarly, a study by Paul Andrisani (1973), which unfortunately contains a rather dubious definition of primary versus secondary sector, also reports mobility rates of approximately 50 percent between the sectors.

Finally, Howard Birnbaum (1975) reports data from a sample drawn from the 1966 National Longitundinal Survey of Men, 45–59 years old. Unfortunately, his categorization of sectors is based on skill levels rather than dual labor markets. Even given this limitation, Birnbaum's analysis shows a consistently higher degree of mobility from first job to present job than one might expect. Some 50 percent of the men in the lowest skill level advance to a higher category. About 33 percent of those in the next higher skill level become upwardly mobile, and about 25 percent of the high-skill group advance. Thus to the extent that one accepts Birnbaum's four categories as a surrogate for a dual labor market model, his study appears to suggest considerable mobility between sectors.

Where do these studies leave us? We have shown that, contrary to the predictions of the human capital approach, considerable variations in income exist for apparently equal qualifications, even among race-sex homogeneous groups. Thus the notions upon which neoclassical economics rests—that labor would migrate from low-wage to high-wage sectors and, therefore, that observed income differentials parallel human capital differentials—seem not to hold up in the light of empirical evidence. In addition, we have seen that the industry divisions that segmentation theorists emphasize are indeed empirically relevant in terms of explaining wage levels. However, the fairly high mobility rates of black and white males between the secondary and the primary sector indicate that the dual labor market is not adequately represented in terms of two *isolated* markets: there *is* intermarket mobility within an individual's working career for some 50 percent of male secondary workers.

These pieces of evidence point toward the value of a modified dual labor market or segmentation model. Segmentation is demonstrated by the existence of different wages for the same qualifications in different sectors. It also involves racism and sexism: women and ethnic minorities disproportionately find their first jobs in the secondary sector, and they appear to be less likely than white males to escape into the primary sector. Nevertheless, significant mobility does occur over time even for minorities and women.

I therefore suggest that radical theory must integrate supply and demand variables into the theory in a more explicit way than previously. Poorly paid workers are not easily able to move into better paying jobs. Labor supply in the U.S. consistently exceeds demand via a reserve army of unemployed and a steady influx of youth and immigrants into the secondary labor market. Racism, sexism, and education appear to influence both the likelihood of gaining a primary sector job as one's first job and the likelihood of transferring from the secondary to the primary sector at some point in one's working life. These observations lead to a "bottleneck" or "queue" version of dual labor market theory, which explains a significant degree of income inequality among working people and its interaction with race, age, and sex variables.

Having looked at the empirical evidence that bears upon the DLM–human capital controversy and concluded that a modified DLM or segmentation theory seems to account for the evidence more effectively, we may now go on to look at the several varieties of radical theory. To what extent is each supported by empirical observations, and to what extent do these theories provide conflicting or complementary views?

Dual Labor Markets and Industrial Segments

In earlier sections we described two variants of radical theory. In one sense they are ideal types in that some authors incorporate elements of both types in their work. But for analytic clarity it is worthwhile to separate them. One approach, most closely associated with Michael Piore and Peter Doeringer, stresses the instability of worker employment patterns in the secondary labor market as a cause of labor market dualism. It therefore stays within the bounds of human capital theory insofar as it stresses individual worker characteristics as causes of differential income or work status. (These individual characteristics are, however, sometimes seen as interacting with structural variables—racial discrimination, technology, etc.) The second approach, most clearly seen in the work of Barry Bluestone, emphasizes institutional factors, especially the market structure of industrial sectors, as the cause of dualism in wages. In some ways these two theories also represent competing stereotypes of the poor: Piore and Doeringer focus on young black males who work irregularly, whereas Bluestone does not confine himself to any one sex or race and emphasizes steady but low-paid work.

Clearly, both theories may have some validity. But it is important to examine their relative empirical importance and the degree to which the proposed mechanisms of dualism are supported by evidence. Piore (1970: 937) seems to believe that the image of full-time working poor is illusory; hence, indirectly he denies Bluestone's model. He suggests instead that the working poor are limited to the South. These are issues that we can examine empiricially by considering two questions. First, how extensive is the full-year, full-time, low-wage type of poverty, and is it limited to the South or rural areas? Second, is the high-turnover-rate, casual-labor phenomenon truly characteristic of black urban residents, as Piore suggests?

The first set of relevant data stems from a survey conducted by the Department of Labor of poverty areas in six U.S. cities in 1968–1969: Atlanta, Chicago, Detroit, Houston, Los Angeles, and New York City. Data were obtained on some 815,000 men and women. Among the variety of employment statistics collected, the figures most relevant to Piore's assertion concern full-time, year-round work:

> Most UES (i.e., poverty area) workers were employed year round and full time. A low of 58 percent of adult men in Detroit worked

50 to 52 weeks at full-time jobs compared to a high of 76 percent in New York City and Chicago survey areas. In the US, as a whole, more than 70 percent of adult men worked 50 to 52 weeks at full-time jobs. (Bureau of Labor Statistics 1969)

These data describe poverty areas in general, not just individuals below the poverty line. Nevertheless, in examining Piore's "culture of black poverty" position, to take the poverty area as a whole is probably the most appropriate test of his theory. As the data show, some 58–76 percent of adult males in these areas, which are urban and include cities not in the South, worked full time, full year. Thus Piore's suggestion that the working poor are southern and rural seems to be contradicted.

A further examination involving solely poverty-level workers is given by Bluestone:

Nearly a third of all families living in poverty in 1964 were headed by a person who worked 50–52 weeks a year at a full-time job. . . . The working poor are located in every state in the union, but the heaviest concentration of employed poor is found in the South. In 1964 over half of all working poor families and a third of all fully employed individuals lived in the southern states. While a good number live in the "pockets of poverty" of the Ozark Plateau, the Down East section of the eastern coastline, and the cutover region of the Upper Great Lakes, a still greater number are crowded into the industrial ghettos of the northern and West Coast states. (Bluestone 1968a: 413)

We see in this description the origins of Piore's belief that working poverty is a rural southern phenomenon, but we also see the important limitation of that stereotype: nearly 50 percent of working poor families live *outside* the South.

Third, an analysis of 1967 Survey of Economic Opportunity data by Sally Bould Van Til speaks to the issue of urban versus rural working poor. She shows that about 50 percent of adult urban poor males work full time, full year. Contrary to Piore, therefore, working poverty is not simply a rural phenomenon. However, a higher proportion of rural poor aged 25–50 work full time than urban poor: 65.6 percent for whites and 59.5 percent for blacks (Bould Van Til 1974).

Thus we see that Piore's notion of rural southern working poor is correct in one sense: working poverty is higher in these areas than others. But the overall impression that Piore seeks to give—that working poverty is minimal in urban northern settings and is almost exclusively a southern rural phenomenon—is quite inaccurate. Substantial proportions of the northern and urban poor work full time, year round.

Where does this information leave us? Piore's stereotype of black urban ghetto dwellers as intermittent workers who are incapable or unwilling to work at steady full-time jobs, who live in a culture of poverty that emphasizes such traits, must be modified. In urban poverty areas somewhere between about 60 percent to 75 percent of adult males work full time, year round. Large numbers of women are similarly involved in regular year-round work. In such a socio-cultural milieu, in which steady workers outnumber intermittent ones among adults, is Piore's culture of poverty thesis persuasive? I suggest not. Piore makes much of the notion that ghetto unemployment is not really unemployment but rather reflects the deliberate cycling of blacks in and out of ghetto jobs and that this pattern mirrors the larger black ghetto culture, which he sees as "adolescent" in its values.

I believe that we can see both the truth and the limitations of Piore's stereotype in his use of *Tally's Corner* and similar ethnographies. Census data show that length of time worked per annum is inversely correlated with age. I suspect that Piore's analysis is heavily influenced by the employment behavior of young, single black males, for all the data show that this age group (16–21) is much more like the Piore stereotype than the majority of blacks. Piore's is a valid depiction of ghetto *youth*, but as a description of the ghetto in general it camouflages the large involvement of ghetto residents in year-round work, it underplays unemployment by treating it as "voluntary" gaps between jobs, and it distorts black cultural values by identifying youth culture as *the* ghetto culture.

These critical assertions are further supported by an examination of job tenure and quit rates among the poor. These, too, show that the intermittent worker is but part of a larger phenomenon and that Piore's picture of black workers rapidly cycling in and out of jobs is overdrawn. Rosenberg, for example, looks at the number of times that a person reports that he/she was looking for work in a given year, which provides an index of labor turnover. His data on Detroit, Cleveland, San Francisco, and Brooklyn show that the mean annual turnover rates for secondary sector men vary from about .29 to .57, which means that a person is out of work on average .29 to .57 times a year. These figures are not particularly high compared with primary sector workers in the same geographic areas: the equivalent figures for primary sector workers are .22 to .50. In particular, the proportion of workers who frequently cycle in and out of work (Piore's stereotype) is quite small: between about 2 percent and 6 percent of secondary workers were searching for jobs more than twice in one year. Thus, Rosenberg concludes: "In general, secondary workers exhibit higher turnover than primary workers though the differences are not as high as would be expected given the importance turnover plays in the dual labor market hypothesis. . . . Very rapid turnover is concentrated in only a small subset of the population" (1975: 40).

Job tenure data confirm this view. Even among urban secondary workers, mean length of time on one's current job is substantial, ranging from 5.10 years to 9.41 years in the cities studied. Rosenberg notes:

> However, notice the long average job tenure of secondary workers. This suggests that many secondary workers hold one job for a long period of time while previous results [i.e., Piore's studies] show that other secondary workers exhibit the high turnover postulated by dual labor market theories. This raises the possibility that dealing with averages may be masking an important phenomenon in the secondary labor market. Only a small part of the secondary labor force may exhibit the instability characteristic associated with secondary work while other workers in these same occupations do not. (Rosenberg 1975: 74)

Rosenberg could equally have put it the other way around: the participant-observation data of Piore and others tend to allow a small but visible group of highly unstable secondary workers to overshadow the comparatively stable work habits of the majority of secondary workers. (It is also instructive in this regard to note that Rosenberg's data show that black secondary sector workers in general hold their jobs longer than white secondary workers.)

To summarize these various sources of data, I believe that the evidence shows that the majority of adults in poor areas appear to work for fairly long periods in full-time jobs. Although unemployment is high among such people, the image of secondary workers rapidly cycling in and out of jobs is quite misleading: it is true of only a small proportion of these individuals. Therefore, Piore's characterization of secondary sector black male workers is an atypical stereotype biased heavily toward young single males. The experience of the majority of ghetto working people is more accurately depicted by Bluestone's image of predominantly low-paid, full-time working adults surrounded by significant levels of unemployment, especially among youth.

If this assessment is a valid one, Piore's notion that it is the irregular work patterns of black secondary workers that keeps them stuck in the secondary sector ceases to be convincing. On the other hand, Bluestone's model, while vindicated for a sizable proportion of urban poverty area dwellers, both white and black, needs to be integrated into a wider setting that includes substantial numbers of nonworking poor before a comprehensive theory of urban poverty can be achieved.

Toward a Synthesis

If we aim for an integrated or comprehensive theory of poverty, we must account for several distinct types of poor among the population as a whole, rather than develop an explanation of one type and project it upon poverty in general. The poverty groups that predominate numerically are: the aged poor; the urban working poor; the urban unemployed; the disabled and sick poor; female-headed households; and the rural working poor. A comprehensive approach has to show the factors underlying poverty for each of these groups and the relationships between these poor populations. Howard Wachtel has made a partial attempt at such a synthesis, using a neo-Marxist approach. By combining his work with Rae Blumberg's on female-headed families, and by incorporating certain other data, I believe we can obtain a credible general theory of poverty in America.

Wachtel (1971; 1972) begins by conceptualizing three institutional determinants of poverty: labor markets, social class divisions, and the state. Poverty is understood as a result of the normal functioning of these institutions within a capitalist society, and most especially as a result of the interrelations of these three institutions.

Let us begin with the institution of social class, which has as its primary dimension in the Marxist scheme the ownership or control of the means of production. It is a banality, but an important one, to note that capitalists rarely appear among the poor. Earnings from stocks and bonds are not tied to the work abilities or skills of capital owners; illness and old age are not a direct threat to the bourgeois livelihood. In contrast, wage earners are heavily dependent upon their continued health and skills. Sickness, pregnancy, disability, old age, lack of mobility—in short, any factor that reduces the work ability of a wage earner—is likely to result in the disappearance of income and transition into poverty status.

While the Marxist class distinction explains some of the variance in income, the second institution—labor markets—gives us a further insight into stratification within the working population. The secondary labor market, according to Bluestone, consists of the full-time, full-year working poor, who account for nearly one-third of all poor families. They are also related to the other kinds of poverty populations in three ways. First, the secondary labor market provides a large proportion of the elderly poor. Low-wage non-union employers frequently lack pension systems, and low-income workers receive low social security retirement benefits. Hence, the blight of low-income secondary sector employment follows these workers even after retirement.

Second, the working poor are related to the unemployed poor. The two groups compete for jobs in the secondary sector, which tends to keep wages low. In addition, the working poor are concentrated in industries that are most likely to lay off employees during economic recessions and least likely to pay benefits during lay-offs. Secondary workers are often fired rather than laid off, in order to lessen employers' liability for unemployment. The working poor and the unemployed are close kin; they typically live in the same urban areas, and individuals move from one status to the other. Urban unemployed youths eventually become low-wage workers; elderly low-wage workers are laid off in favor of younger, fitter persons.

Third, the working poor are related to the large proportion of poor families who are poor because their breadwinner is sick or disabled. Moreover, such sickness and disability are often related to prior occupational status in the work force. As Wachtel points out, the secondary labor market usually fails to provide adequate health care, disability coverage, or insurance to its low-paid workers. Preventative action against illness is consequently lowest among such people. In addition, it is likely that occupational hazards and opportunities for ill health are more concentrated in the secondary sector jobs, where older machinery and poor working conditions often predominate.

Thus we see the combined impact of social class and labor markets upon the aged poor, the working poor, the unemployed poor, and the sick or disabled poor. Each group is in a dependent relationship with the secondary sector in the economy. If we now look to the state, we can see how its activity reinforces these processes. As Wachtel points out (1971: 9), one must conceive of state activity in broad and narrow senses in order to understand its relationship to poverty. In the wide sense, government subsidies to rich industrialists and to farmers, the maze of loopholes for the very rich, smaller tax breaks for home-owners and the middle classes, heavy dependence upon sales taxes, and the like—all act to distribute income in a lopsided manner. There is considerable debate whether the overall effect of taxation in America (as distinct from its intent) is progressive or regressive. But no one, to the best of my knowledge, would argue that the state could not in prin-ciple redistribute revenue more equitably. In this sense, then, the state contributes to keeping poverty in existence.

In the narrow sense, we find that state activity is an important factor in maintaining the situations that generate poverty for at least three groups: the urban working poor, the aged poor, and the rural working poor. The urban working poor are particularly affected by government legislation regulating industries and wages. Secondary sector indus-tries are sustained by a series of exemptions from a variety of federal legislation, most especially minimum wage laws, which allows this sector to remain an enclave of low wages and poor working conditions. It may be argued that the secondary sector would go bankrupt if it had to pay primary sector wages. However, many secondary sector indus-tries provide necessary services to the economy as a whole, and it is likely that mandatory minimum wage laws in secondary industries would simply result in higher prices for goods made in the secondary sector.

The aged poor are affected by government policy on inflation, taxa-tion, and health costs. Retirees living on fixed incomes cannot, unlike employed workers, recapture lost income via pay hikes. The most sig-nificant impact of government on the elderly comes through Social Security retirement benefits, and here Wachtel offers us a useful analy-sis. Turning to the supposedly antipoverty activities of government, Wachtel discusses the unintended consequences of government inter-vention in several areas. The Social Security program was intended to relieve the fear of poverty among the aged. Yet Social Security is based on a very regressive tax: lower earners pay higher proportions of their incomes; wages are taxed, but property income of any kind is not. Nor are Social Security payments uniform: low earners receive lower benefits than high earners. Supplemental earnings from working result in a reduction of Social Security payments, but one can enjoy unlimited amounts of unearned income from stocks, bonds, rental property, and private pensions without losing benefits. As a final irony, poor people (especially ethnic minorities) live shorter lives and hence are in aggregate less likely to live to receive full benefits. The sum total of these effects is that Social Security passes on into old age the inequalities derived from class and labor market position: poor working people become poor retired people. Old age amounts to a period of poverty for about one-third of the age group over 65, and the elderly constitute about one-fourth of the American poor.

Government action is also particularly important in understanding rural poverty, since agriculture is closely tied to a system of federal price supports and other activities. At least two factors combine to sustain rural poverty. On the one hand laws regulating the minimum wage, laws concerning union organizing, and laws overseeing unemployment and disability coverage often exempt agricultural workers. Thus agricultural laborers are in a position analogous to, and sometimes worse than, that of workers in the secondary sector. Second, the structure of agriculture resembles that of industry insofar as it can also be divided into an oligopolistic sector of large enterprises and a sector of numerous small farms. Furthermore, government activity consistently gives a competitive advantage to the large enterprises, which receive disproportionate shares of government price supports and subsidies. Similarly, government research activities, irrigation services, and the like favor large over small producers. The overall effect of such government action, allied to the market structure of agriculture, has acted to squeeze more and more small farms out of business and to favor farm owners over farm employees (Wachtel 1972).

Finally, government activity strongly affects the unemployed. Policy on taxation, credit, the money supply, and so on causes unemployment to shift considerably. To a large extent recent government economic management, using Keynesian methods, has consisted of playing off the degree of unemployment against other economic factors (e.g., inflation, taxation, balance of payments).

Thus we can draw out interrelationships between five of our six kinds of poverty—the aged, the urban working poor, the unemployed, the disabled and sick, and the rural working poor—and social class, labor markets, and the state. One additional and much neglected poverty population involves female-headed households. Many female-headed households suffer from poverty in a double sense: poverty is often a cause of female-headed family structure, and such family structure frequently results in poverty for its members.

Rae Lesser Blumberg has demonstrated the former aspect in the context of wider concerns involving women's status in various societies (Blumberg 1977). She confronts the well-known culture of poverty argument, particularly the notion of congenital weakness in black family structure, with a variety of empirical data. Contrary to George Murdock and Suzanne Wilson's (1972) finding of "a nearly exclusive association between mother-child households and societies that are Negro in race," Blumberg shows that such a family structure exists among many nonblack populations. Blumberg also demonstrates a strong association between decreasing income and increased incidence of mother-headed families. She explains this phenomenon in terms of a complex model involving the economic utility of marriage to both men and women and the ability of each partner to maintain him/herself economically and to obtain work. Since Aid to Dependent Children and other welfare programs provide support for a family only if no adult male is present, an economic disutility is created in many cases against stable marriage and in favor of female-headed families. The operation of such economic forces in conjunction with other non-economic factors leads to a dramatically increased incidence of female-headed households among poor people of all races in America.

Blumberg's analysis goes much of the way toward explaining the frequency of female-headed families in poor and high unemployment areas. But we can also look at this question in another way. Why are families headed by women likely to be poor? Most especially, why are families headed by women who work likely to be poor? Part of the answer may be understood in terms of the dual labor market theory. As noted earlier, women and minorities tend to be drastically overrepresented in the low-paying secondary labor market. But there is an additional factor of more general relevance.

We earlier stated that class structure is a key dimension in understanding poverty because wage laborers are likely to be thrown into poverty if for any reason they become unable to work. Although this situation is true for any individual worker, it is increasingly becoming the case for the family as a unit. In America more and more families find it necessary to have two persons working in order to support themselves at a level above poverty. For evidence, one can compare the mean annual income of American workers and the poverty level income for a nonrural family of four. The average full-time year-round income is now *below* the poverty line for a family of four. In other words, the average American worker can no longer support a family of four on his/her income alone. One would expect such economic pressures to result in smaller families and/or more and more two-worker families. Conversely, those families who for a variety of reasons cannot send out two workers (including female-headed families) will find it increasingly difficult to stay above the poverty line. In sum, wage shifts are causing the single-headed household to slide into poverty, and two-worker households are increasingly the norm.

To summarize this section, we note that three social institutions combine to perpetuate poverty in America. Class structure, labor market structure, and governmental activity combine to place certain sectors of the population—especially those in the secondary labor market—at a disadvantage in maintaining themselves above the poverty level. Poverty in old age is often a consequence of these same factors. Unemployment and disability are intimately related to labor market structure and government activity. Single-headed households are in many instances a product of the interaction of high unemployment, low wages for women, and government welfare policies, and single-headed households move toward poverty as industry adjusts wage levels to take into account the greater predominance of dual-worker families. In sum, poverty is produced and replicated by the normal functioning of our economy, state, and property ownership system.

Sociological Advances

By 1976, the major ideas of dual labor market and industrial segmentation theory had been well developed by the economists whose work I have analyzed above. However, as this body of research diffused through the social sciences, it triggered great interest among sociologists. Since 1976, a score of articles, many appearing in the most prestigious sociological journals, have applied DLM theory to several sociological problems. This development has provoked considerable debate. The sociological studies have on the one hand strengthened the empirical case for a segmentation perspective; on the other hand, they have also highlighted some of the weaknesses of segmentation theory. Here I shall briefly review and assess this more recent body of literature.

Just as radical economists cast DLM theory as a critical rebuttal of the orthodox human capital approach, so too early sociological segmentation theorists used their version of DLM to attack the area of American sociological orthodoxy known as status attainment research, which examines processes of mobility and social stratification. Status attainment theorists have examined the links between the social origins (family background) of Americans and their subsequent occupational destinations, as well as the various determinants of individuals' occupational success. If I may characterize a voluminous body of research in one oversimplified statement, the status attainment theorists concluded that parental socioeconomic status does not determine one's occupational success to a major extent and that educational achievement is the strongest predictor of an individual's occupational attainment and income.

The sociological DLM theorists criticized this approach as individualistic, in that it examines only characteristics of individuals as predictors of attainment while ignoring more structural factors, such as the organizational power of certain occupational groups to obtain higher incomes or prestige, the sorting of workers into industrial sectors that pay different wages for similar skills, the role of occupational segregation by race and sex, and so on (Bibb and Form 1977; Horan 1978; Beck et al. 1978; Lord and Falk 1980). To substantiate their argument, DLM sociologists took an approach modeled on the DLM–human capital critique. They constructed mathematical models in which both structural variables measuring segmentation and variables measuring individual characteristics (education, experience, age, sex, race) were used to predict income or status for representative samples of the population (Bibb and Form 1977; Beck et al. 1978; Tolbert et al. 1980; Horan et al. 1980; Beck et al. 1980; Lord and Falk 1980; Parcel and Mueller 1983). Their findings corroborated those of earlier segmentation studies: structural variables measuring various aspects of economic segmentation do indeed predict individual income, over and above the effects of individual or human capital differences. In addition, several studies demonstrated differences in the demographic composition of the labor force for different economic sectors and attempted to evaluate the economic costs for certain demographic groups of being disproportionately allocated to "poorer" economic segments (Beck et al. 1978, 1980; Daymont 1980; Kaufman and Daymont 1981; Parcel and Mueller 1983). Some studies also argued that the processes of income attainment differed by sector: that is, human capital variables were less important in certain economic sectors but more important in others. These results suggested that the status attainment approach, which treats occupational success as an essentially uniform process across the whole economy, was wrong.[2]

I will not dwell on these studies because, although they are generally superior in both method and data to the earlier economic research, they typically corroborate the prior findings on economic segmentation. Instead I shall focus on some debates within the sociological literature that point to weaknesses in this segmentation approach. Such debates appear at first glance to be of two types. On the one hand there have been arguments about perceived methodological and conceptual inadequacies, especially concerning the ways in which segments are defined and their effects assessed (e.g., Kaufman et al. 1981; Hodson and Kaufman 1981, 1982; Baron and Bielby 1980; Stolzenberg 1975.) On the other hand, there have been substantive disputes over the accuracy of certain empirical claims by segmentation researchers (e.g., Hauser 1980; Kalleberg et al. 1981), including the assertion that segments as defined by several sociologists fail to support some hypotheses of early DLM theory regarding the sex, ethnic, and educational make-up of primary and secondary labor markets. I shall argue below that much of the confusion and dispute over the segmentation literature can be attributed to the tendency of both critics and adherents to conflate different types of segmentation into one simple scheme and that some of the apparent empirical failings are due to the fact that hypotheses derived from one tradition (DLM theory) are misapplied to analyses derived from another (industrial segmentation) and vice versa.

---

2 Robert Hauser (1980) appears to deny this in a rejoinder to Beck et al. in the *American Sociological Review*. His insistence that the status attainment tradition, of which he is a principal figure, has always viewed income determination in a heterogeneous (e.g., sectorial) fashion is quite surprising. His subsequent attempt to prove statistically that economic sectors do *not* differ in income attainment processes is eloquent proof of his general perspective that income determination may usefully be studied at the level of the aggregate economy, that the same causal factors operate for all groups, classes, or sectors, and so on. See Beck, Horan, and Tolbert's (1980b) re-analyse and defense of their original view.

These observations can best be explained by describing one part of the debate.

Most prolific among the sociological segmentation theorists is the team of Charles Tolbert, E. M. Beck, and Patrick M. Horan. These scholars treat the good jobs/bad jobs distinction of dual labor market theory as an outcome of a more basic phenomenon: the division of industries into core and periphery sectors. Thus their work falls within what I have called the industrial segmentation approach. They sort various industries into core and periphery groups by using a technique known as factor analysis, which combines or collapses a large number of variables into fewer underlying dimensions. In this case, industries are characterized in terms of market power, size, profits, political contributions, unionization, average wages, size of white-collar work force, and so on. After these multiple characteristics have been distilled into one aggregate dimension, each industry is assigned, according to its score on the one dimension, to the core or the periphery sector.

In a series of articles Tolbert, Beck, and Horan successfully demonstrated that workers in core industries earn more than equally qualified workers in periphery industries and that a larger proportion of periphery workers live in poverty than core workers. They also showed various demographic differences between core and periphery work forces, different mobility within segments (Tolbert 1982), and so on. What criticisms can there be of such a seemingly productive approach?

One objection, voiced by Hodson and Kaufman (1981), Kaufman et al. (1981), and others is that the method used by Tolbert and his followers is circular, that they define economic sectors partly in terms of workers' wages and benefits and should not therefore use segmentation as an independent predictor of wage differences. (See Horan et al. 1981 for a rebuttal.) Another, perhaps more telling, objection is that Tolbert's procedure inappropriately collapses or superimposes characteristics to distinguish industries. The effect of each characteristic— firm size, market concentration, unionization, and the like—on workers' incomes may well differ significantly from that of the others. Thus it is inappropriate to mix them into one unitary core-periphery dimension (cf. Kalleberg and Sorensen 1979; Stolzenberg 1978; Parcel and Mueller 1983). Also, critics have argued that a model that cuts the economy into two pieces is unnecessarily crude and sells the segmentation approach short. Hence Kaufman et al. (1981) have developed an alternative model, treating forty industrial characteristics separately and ending up with sixteen distinct industrial clusters or segments.

Here we see a clear trend in the segmentation literature away from simple dualistic models toward more complex, multidimensional typologies of industries and more elaborate kinds of labor market segments. The efficacy of this new approach has still to be proven, but early results suggest that multiple dimensions do have greater explanatory power (cf. Parcel and Mueller 1983).

An additional point of contention in the sociological literature concerns the appropriate unit of analysis in segmentation studies. Researchers like Tolbert and his colleagues typically use data on individual incomes and the occupation and industry in which each individual works. This constraint on the availability of data leads most segmentation researchers to conceptualize segments as groups of industries. They justify this decision by arguing that industries are relatively homogeneous in terms of technology, product markets, and so on. However, James Baron and William Bielby (1980) make a point with which I strongly agree: industries are not the appropriate unit or level of analysis. A mom and pop store is very dissimilar in terms of wages, working conditions, product markets, and other characteristics from a chain store; it does not make sense to place the two enterprises in the same economic segment just because they are in the same retail industry. Bielby and Baron argue that firms are the correct unit of analysis, not industries. This approach receives empirical support from Stolzenberg (1978), who has demonstrated that wages in big firms differ from those in smaller firms, net of worker skills and similar factors. Thus it would be preferable to consider economic segments as composed of firms with similar characteristics rather than as groups of similar industries, as has typically been the case in the literature up to the present. Unfortunately, this criticism has not been taken to heart, for many more industry-level data sets are available, as opposed to firm-level sets. However, Bielby and Baron are working on a project using this more detailed enterprise basis for constructing segments.

Another important objection to the Tolbert approach is best exemplified by Lynne Zucker and Carolyn Rosenstein (1981), who compared several typologies of industries used by different economic segmentation researchers. They found that certain industries were assigned to the core in one typology but to the periphery in another. Over and above these annoying inconsistencies, Zucker and Rosenstein noted strikingly different results regarding the demographic characteristics of the labor force in core and periphery across various typologies. Furthermore, the work force characteristics implied by DLM theory did not always fit the core/periphery data as analyzed by these researchers. For example, worker unemployment was higher in the core than in the periphery, education was not markedly different in the periphery and core, and so on.

Zucker and Rosenstein somewhat overstated their case: the typologies did show the predicted earnings and poverty differences between sectors. They also misinterpreted some DLM theory. But in a larger sense the problems they identified point to a real difficulty that has been obscured: the industrial sectors defined by industrial segmentation theorists are not the same as the labor market segments envisioned by the earlier DLM theorists, even though industrial segmentation theorists have tended to treat them as if they were the same. For example, in contrast to the DLM image of a heavily female and minority secondary sector, the periphery, as defined in terms of industries, contained 12 percent minority workers compared to 9 percent in the core and 47 percent women compared to 37 percent in the core. Although these differences are in the predicted direction, they are by no means large enough to validate the original DLM model.

Obviously, there is a need for a more complex theory that can encompass several separate sources of segmentation, each of which affects wages and mobility, but each of which has its own independent effect. The two most important bases for defining segments are characteristics of firms (industrial segmentation) and characteristics of occupations (labor market or occupational segmentation). Ross Stolzenberg (1975, 1978) has demonstrated the significance and independence of these two types of segmentation. First, he proved that occupational segmentation exists and that a given amount of education, training, and experience will bring substantially different incomes depending on the occupational group to which a worker belongs. Second, he showed that industrial segmentation results in income differences after controlling for both human capital and occupational effects. Finally, he demonstrated that, while both industrial and occupational segmentation individually affect income, they also sometimes interact in complex ways. For example, some industries pay above normal wages for certain kinds of occupational labor but pay below average wages for other occupations.. Thus the two forms of segmentation have to be viewed as interlocking, sometimes working in opposite ways, sometimes reinforcing each other.

The recent emphasis on occupational segmentation does not pose a problem to theorists. Processes resulting in occupational segmentation have already been analyzed by numerous scholars, although an elegant synthesis is still lacking. Stolzenberg (1975) points out that the sheer time involved in training and gaining experience is one factor creating barriers between occupations. Eliot Friedson (1982) gives an excellent analysis of a tradition in sociology that studies "occupational shelters," especially the abilities of occupational groups to insulate themselves from market competition via professionalization, unionism, control over technique and training, and so on. Marcia Freedman (1976) has demonstrated the utility of this approach in examining income differences among occupations and in defining occupational segments. Randall Collins (1979) and Magali Sarfatti Larson (1977) have discussed the roles of credentialism and professionalism in creating occupational shelters.

The sociologists' introduction of occupational segmentation to complement the political economists' industrial segmentation perspective is therefore an important theoretical advance. Previously, DLM theory had an ill-informed sense of occupational segmentation (good jobs versus bad jobs). It was so tied into the characteristics of the persons filling the various occupational slots (e.g., Piore's notions of class and race subcultures, and the red herring of worker instability) that researchers neglected the impact that occupational barriers have beyond the particular social groups that happen to occupy the jobs in question at a given time. Certain occupations have retained a poor image and low wages despite a succession of different ethnic groups; other occupations, such as the law and medicine, still offer relatively high incomes even though more minority members and women have joined their ranks.

The more general point is that it is misleading to identify social groups as causes of economic segmentation and of poverty. Racism, sexism, and the overrepresentation of blacks and women in one sector of the labor market are of great empirical and theoretical relevance, but they are most probably not necessary for the existence of economic segmentation. One could envision racially and sexually integrated poverty and similarly integrated industrial and occupational labor markets. Nevertheless, poverty, income inequality, and segmentation would remain (Bluestone 1970).

Thus we need a two-part theory, one part dealing with the processes creating economic segmentation and the consequences of such segmentation, the other part explaining the mechanisms that allocate people or social groups to various segments and the interactions between segmentation processes and ethnic/sexual divisions. With the addition of occupational segmentation to industrial segmentation, we have the basic structure of the first part of the theory. The latter part is incomplete, but important progress has been made by David Gordon, Richard Edwards, and Michael Reich (1982) and by Edwards (1979), which will be discussed in the next chapter.

From Radical Critique to Mainstream Social Science

Despite occasional weaknesses in certain formulations, I find the segmentation approach to be greatly superior to economic formulations that argue that income attainment is a simple function of an individual's education and training and superior to the sociological equivalent in stratification theory. This is not to say that education and training are unimportant in understanding poverty and income determination; rather, they tell only half the story. Segmentation theory promises to fill in a large amount of evidence that has been missing and to take us one more step toward a comprehensive theory of economic stratification. It shows us that the economy is a highly structured entity in which some industries and some occupations are relatively sheltered from competitive market processes, whereas other segments behave more like open markets. The flow of people among segments is limited by processes as diverse as racism, sexism, credentialism, professional/ union control, and "queues," as well as by simple differences in the quality of labor. The result is a complex mosaic in which economic rewards to labor are a function of both the industrial/occupational/regional segment one works in and the skills and education one brings to the job (not to mention that some well-paying segments resist the entry of certain ethnic groups and women).

Returning to our sociology of knowledge, the example of economic segmentation theory nicely illustrates several themes discussed earlier.

The segmentation approach originated in part with a cohort of young radicalized economists. Seeking an intellectual outlet for their political commitments, they initially focused on explaining poverty and particularly the plight of ethnic minorities. Here we see what I called in Chapter One a "social problems orientation," the tendency of left scholarship to study and thereby highlight those areas in which capitalism is most destructive.

Beyond the details of particular segmentation analyses of poverty and inequality, one can identity two moral/critical themes or genres. One involves demonstrating how poverty is systematic in American society. Several authors attempted to show that poverty is not a historical hangover from the rural-urban shift or a dysfunction of capitalism soon to disappear, or a matter of racial or social groups who are left out of modern America. On the contrary, they emphasized the extent to which the poor are well integrated into the society, perform necessary roles, and yet are still poor. Thus the radical analyses explicated poverty's systematic causes and functions within the larger society.

A second theme concerned the task of shifting the locus of blame for poverty away from the poor themselves. Although one important exception, the nonradical Piore, did appear to indict minority and women workers of the secondary labor market for their poor work habits, this "blame the victim" stance was the antithesis of the radical approach. Edwards (1975: 19–20) hastened to explain that secondary workers' instability was a result of or rational response to other structural factors and not a cause of dualism. Readers were repeatedly reminded of the lack of control that the poor have over their own lives and of the institutional factors that generate or maintain poverty.

These two themes are examples of what I have described as radical scholarship's interest in systematizing blame. Systematizing is to be understood in two senses: showing the causal rather than the incidental nature of a phenomenon, and showing its locus in system-level macro-structural features rather than at the level of individual responsibility or action. Systematizing blame epitomizes the first of the three goals that I earlier suggested are characteristic of radical scholarship: the goal of developing a moral-evaluatory critique of capitalism. The two other goals of Marxist scholarship—paradigm maintenance and the analysis of contemporary affairs—are much less evident in economic segmentation literature. Why should this be so?

Unlike other topics, the economic segmentation perspective did not come into conflict with orthodox Marxism, because classical Marxism is almost silent on the issue of labor markets and income differentials within the working class. Perhaps this omission was owing to Marx's expectation that immiseration would reduce the whole proletariat to a single sorry state. In any event, segmentation theorists were able to construct their theory without challenging or even encountering an existing Marxist orthodoxy. Thus many of the potential problems of integrating theoretical innovations into a current paradigm never arose. For example, the textbook *The Capitalist System* presents the DLM approach alongside traditional Marxist economic writings, giving a clear impression that the two are complementary.

The paradigm maintenance problem of segmentation theory, if it had one at all, was that the theory was isolated intellectually from mainstream Marxist theory. Other than its efficacy as critique, what was specifically Marxist about economic segmentation? Two theoretical bridges to orthodox Marxism were subsequently constructed to remedy this problem. First, the shift in emphasis from labor market dualism to industrial segmentation partly integrated the new research with classical Marxism. The core/periphery and oligopoly/competitive distinctions of industrial segmentation theory fit nicely into an older Marxist tradition that stressed the uneven development of capitalism, the tendency toward industrial concentration and oligopoly, and the antagonistic coexistence of competitive and monopolistic sectors of capitalism. Half of segmentation theory could therefore be brought into the Marxist fold. Second, DLM theory has been integrated with Marxist theory by linking labor markets to historical changes in the labor process and to shifting forms of labor discipline, as in Edwards's (1979) work, which we shall discuss in the next chapter.

In sum, the goal of paradigm maintenance and paradigm extension was achieved relatively painlessly in this body of scholarship: the segmentation approach escaped several internal tensions that we earlier described as molding Marxist scholarship. With regard to external tensions, however, one can clearly see how the social dilemmas of these scholars have affected their work. The radical segmentation theorists were young academics intent on pursuing university careers. According to our model in Chapter One, this goal involved the tricky task of balancing political commitment and professional career. How could their intellectual work be political and critical and yet be considered legitimate and scholarly by non-Marxist professional colleagues? The attempts by radicals to satisfy the requirements of academia and hold on to their jobs can be viewed as structural constraints molding their scholarship in several ways.

The most obvious outcome is seen in the style of these scholars' work. Minimally rhetorical, eschewing the violent polemical style of Marxist-Leninism for a quieter academic style of presentation, the work also took a strongly empirical approach. If non-Marxist scholars stressed objectivity and data, then radicals legitimated their work by elaborate documentation and the use of unimpeachable data sources, such as government censuses and surveys.

Academic legitimation was also achieved in part by following the methodological dictates of the orthodox discipline. The economists have used historical statistics and case materials, regression and factor analyses. The sociologists have elaborated new realms of quantitative sophistication, adding log-linear models and cluster analyses to the methodological armamentarium.

The problem of where to publish has proved to be a thorny one. The earlier articles were often published in one form in left journals such as *Politics and Society, The Insurgent Sociologist*, and the *Review of Radical Political Economics*, and then in slightly different form in the prestige journals of the discipline or as monographs from scholarly presses.

How, then, is the political commitment maintained and expressed? At one level the critique is implicit. If one demonstrates that women and minorities, for example, are consistently underpaid because of their industrial/occupational segregation and not because of their lesser skills or education, one has established a critical point about capitalism *soto voce*. At another level, I believe that the political commitment has been expressed by a tendency to use segmentation analyses to prove the inadequacies of the established (nonradical) economic or sociological theories. Why should radical perspectives repeatedly test their models against human capital or sociological attainment ones? In part, radical scholars may feel a need to legitimate their choice of a Marxist approach to their nonradical colleagues by first showing the inadequacies of established formulations and by demonstrating their thorough understanding of that orthodoxy. However, beyond this, radical scholars have come to express their political commitment by attacking those theories of economics or sociology that justify the status quo or imply that present social arrangements are logical or functional. Thus the critique of capitalism has become displaced into a critique of theories that seem to legitimate capitalism, such as human capital theory.

In sum, the professional pressures on American radical academics have led them, not unwillingly, to embrace the mainstream canons of academic method and discourse while expressing their radicalism in terms of their choice of topics, the critical message embedded in their findings, and their overt criticisms of more established/establishment theoretical positions. This approach has been successful in many ways. A coherent body of left scholarship, much of it quite innovative, has been developed. Many of the early radical scholars have achieved tenure, albeit after hard struggles, owing to their evident scholarly productivity. But there has been a cost, which is seen most clearly in the contemporary sociological segmentation literature. Least important, but worthy of note, is that extraordinary energies are spent in methodological sophistication and in acrimonious debates over fine points of quantification. More important, the critical-evaluatory aspect has become so understated that in many cases it is no longer clear whether some segmentation authors are Marxists or simply nonpolitical scholars who have jumped on a new theoretical bandwagon for their own intellectual or career reasons. From one perspective, the evident success of segmentation theory can be read as the triumph of Marxist scholarship over its bourgeois opponent, a step toward the intellectual hegemony of critical scholarship. But from another point of view, the same success can be read as the absorption of the radical paradigm into the sociological mainstream, cleansed of its critical political origins.

Chapter Three

THEORIES OF THE LABOR PROCESS AND

THE FIRM

NON-MARXISTS CANNOT but be puzzled by the fact that, a century or more after Marx and Engels, radicals still return to the topic of the labor process under capitalism. Why should they, given that this is the one topic that received the full scrutiny of the masters themselves? Entire chapters of *Capital* are devoted to the subject; indeed, it is treated in virtually every one of Marx's major works. The reason that contemporary American radicals come back to the theme of technology, work, and social change can only be that each new generation of Marxists is dissatisfied with the conclusions derived by the previous generation from the classics. For a variety of political reasons that we shall probe, the moral-evaluatory stance toward technology has shifted at various points in the history of Marxism.

In Marx himself we find an attitude toward modern technology that, if not actually ambivalent, is certainly multifaceted. Matching the chapters of *Capital* devoted to the degradation of work caused by the development of industrial production are the passages in the *Communist Manifesto* and elsewhere lauding the progressive function of modern technology. These seemingly opposite views are related to Marx's conception of technological change as a major driving force behind social change. In the *Manifesto* and in the preface to *A Contribution to the Critique of Political Economy*, changes in the forces of production are regarded as pre-eminent factors in the impetus toward socialism (Tucker 1972: 4). It is this dual perspective, whereby Marx acknowledges both the exploitative role of technology in capitalist production

93

and its positive role of "bursting asunder" capitalism fetters and hastening revolution, that provides for contrasting positions within Marxist theory.

The Russian Revolution brought the positive Enlightenment view of technology to the fore among Marxists. The official Soviet view of modern industry was uncritically positive: remove the exploitative social relations of capitalism, and the Western factory system could be envied. Hence we find Lenin eulogizing Taylorism:

> Like all capitalist progress, [Taylorism] is a combination of the refined brutality of bourgeois exploitation and a number of the greatest scientific achievements in the field of analyzing mechanical motions during work, the elimination of superfluous and awkward motions, the elaboration of correct methods of work, the introduction of the best system of accounting and control, etc. The Soviet Republic must at all costs adopt all that is valuable in the achievements of science and technology in this field. (Quoted in Braverman 1974: 12)

Of course, one must determine what part of modern industrial technique is valuable and what part is intrinsically capitalist and alienating. The answer in the Soviet Union, evidently, was that the only capitalist part of modern industry was the capitalist himself; once expropriated by socialists, capitalist technology could be adopted lock, stock, and barrel. Reinhart Bendix (1956) describes in detail the zeal with which Soviet leaders and many workers approached Western technology, as evidenced by the slogan of "Communist Americanism," the formation of the "Time League," and so on. Kendall Bailes (1977; 1978: 50) sketches a similar picture in his studies of early Soviet engineering.

The blithe indifference with which Lenin and other Russian communists viewed such industrial phenomena as job hierarchies, the fine division of labor, labor discipline, and especially managerial authority was in harmony with most earlier nineteenth-century Marxist thought. Only anarchists and syndicalists had seriously challenged these aspects of work, and they had generally received short shrift from the Marxist left. As Engels remarked:

> If man, by dint of his knowledge and inventive genius, has subdued the forces of nature, the latter avenge themselves upon him

by subjecting him, insofar as he employs them, to a veritable des-
potism independent of all social organization. Wanting to abolish
authority in large-scale industry is tantamount to wanting to abolish industry itself, to destroy the power loom in order to return to
the spinning wheel. (In Tucker 1972: 662–665)

This uncritical stance toward industrial organization has remained
the party line in most Soviet-allied Communist parties up to the present.
In fact, rising criticism of the Soviet Union and the breakup of Soviet
hegemony over the intellectual left in various countries have been
partly responsible for the renewal of Marxist analyses of the labor process. This movement had various predecessors: in Soviet Russia the
workers' opposition criticized the wholesale adoption of factory hierarchies, and in Germany the Frankfurt School developed a critique of
Soviet practice and a reassessment of technology in general before
World War II. But in America and much of Europe it took the New
Left, the events of the sixties, and the defection of Communist parties
to Eurocommunism to reopen the debate on the labor process and
technology.

   In this chapter I shall examine this revival of interest in technology
and the labor process, particularly American research since the early
1970s. From this large and convoluted literature I have selected three
themes for consideration. The first concerns changes in the complexity
and quality of work following capitalist "rationalization" of the labor
process. The *leitmotif* of this research is the concept of deskilling, and
its most prominent theorist was Harry Braverman, although many have
follow this theme through the writings of Stephen Marglin, Katherine
Stone, David Noble, Richard Edwards, and others. The last theme
structure of work in the modern business enterprise is not the result of
technological imperatives but is instead the product of a centuries-old
attempt by capital to dominate and control its labor force. We shall
follow this theme through the writings of Stephan Marglin, Katherine
Stone, David Noble, Richard Edwards, and others. The last theme
questions the links between workplace behavior and workers' external
culture and community. Is the workplace best thought of as an autonomous realm with its own internal logic or as an arena that reflects the
culture and divisions of society outside the factory gates?

The Degradation and Deskilling of Work

Harry Braverman's *Labor and Monopoly Capital* (1974) was an instant success, a bestseller for its publisher and the subject of lavish praise from reviewers. Bob Rowthorn (1976: 59), writing in *New Left Review*, called it "one of the two most important works of Marxist political economy to have appeared in the last decade." Braverman's book inspired a score of works that have extended or applied his central thesis: that there is a pervasive tendency in contemporary capitalism for jobs to be reorganized at lower skill levels than previously. In short, capitalism degrades and deskills work (cf. *Monthly Review* 1976; Kraft 1977; Greenbaum 1976; Clark et al. 1978; Zimbalist 1979; Wallace and Kalleberg 1982).

Braverman draws his theoretical framework from Marx's *Capital*, especially Chapters 12–17 of volume one. A central point of Marx's (1967a) argument is that workers sell only their capacity to work (i.e., their labor power). Management must translate this capacity into work actually done in order to ensure profitability.

Braverman considers three implications of this capitalist logic for the organization of work. The first, suggested by Adam Smith (1937), is couched in the language of efficiency or productivity. Smith argued that one could increase productivity by dividing manufacture of an object into successive stages and by isolating each stage as a separate job filled by a worker trained for it. Braverman (1974) rejects this explanation of the detailed division of labor in modern industry, arguing that the efficiency gains described by Smith do not necessitate specialized workers. He is more sympathetic to an explanation of the division of labor that is based on the cost of labor. The principle attributed to Charles Babbage (1832) suggests that there is a capitalist imperative to substitute cheap labor for more expensive labor whenever possible. The easiest way to do this is to divide complex craft tasks into simple routinized steps that can be performed by cheap unskilled labor. Thus cost considerations dictate the deskilling of work and a fine division of labor.

Braverman accepts this position but also advances a further explanation of the industrial division of labor that focuses on control. Since management is responsible for making sure that workers' labor power is turned into labor actually done, management seeks to maximize its control over workers and to minimize its dependence upon them.

When workers monopolize knowledge of the production process, as in craft work, management is very dependent upon them. Consequently, over the last two centuries, management has attempted to enlarge its control over the production process by gaining knowledge of production and by reducing craft work, in which conception and execution are combined, to separate execution and conceptual jobs. With most work reorganized into narrow, low-skilled jobs with no conceptual content, the majority of workers become dependent on management, which has appropriated the intellectual skills once held by craft labor. Thus, according to Braverman, the Babbage principle and management's desire to turn employees into mere executors of work result in a steady degradation of labor. As jobs become narrow and meaningless, workers become more alienated.

Braverman makes certain modifications to this general picture. First, he stresses that the pace of deskilling varies across the economy. This uneven development expresses itself in the displacement of workers from automating or mechanizing industries and their relocation in other sectors of the economy. Second, he notes that the separation of conception from execution implies the creation of new, highly skilled intellectual jobs. However, Braverman minimizes the importance of this apparent counter-tendency to deskilling by stressing that these new technical jobs employ few workers (1974: 241–242). He also describes how these new experts themselves become deskilled over time.

Thus, while aware of potential counter-tendencies to deskilling, Braverman views them as minor eddies within the stronger current of work degradation: "In this manner short-term trends opening the way for the advancement of some workers . . . simply mask the secular trend toward the incessant lowering of the working class as a whole below its previous conditions of skill and labor" (1974: 129–130). In my opinion, this last point—that deskilling is a dominant tendency across the whole economy, resulting in a progressively more homogeneous unskilled proletariat—is the most contentious aspect of the theory of deskilling.

Braverman develops his arguments in the context of a historical analysis of labor and management over the last 150 years. Historically, as management transformed the labor process away from such semi-autonomous forms as subcontracting, putting out, and craft labor, it found itself drawn beyond its initial supervisory and sales functions toward a much more complex role embracing coordination, planning, measurement, and recordkeeping. In taking on responsibilities previously incorporated in skilled labor, management itself came to be a specialized professional function. Professional management increasingly appreciated the wider implications of enlarging the separation between conception and execution. That this was a conscious program became particularly clear with the development of Taylorism, or "scientific management," at the end of the nineteenth century. This theory stressed the importance of removing conceptual responsibilities from workers. It also emphasized management's need to gain a thorough understanding of the entire production process. Engineers were to design every detail of the work process according to scientific principles. There was "one best way" of performing any task, which could be determined by scientific methods. Workers were supposed to execute managerial orders without taking any initiative of their own. Braverman details Frederick Taylor's insights into this process and his application of it toward increasing the division of labor, speeding up work, setting piece rates, planning new work processes, implementing time and motion studies, and so on.

Braverman also examines mechanization and advanced machine technology, viewing the introduction of machinery as an extension of the logic of capitalist control over labor. Mechanization builds conceptual work into the machine, reduces the amount of skill needed from workers, and results in an ever narrower division of tasks.

An additional section of the book considers "the growing working-class occupations"—clerical, service, retail work—in order to demonstrate that his analysis applies not simply to "traditional" or declining sectors of the economy but also to presently expanding occupations. Through multiple case studies of various types of production, Braverman presents evidence that deskilling is ongoing and that ever finer divisions of labor are occurring.

An important factor to be considered with regard to this inexorable deskilling is its impact upon workers' feelings, wider consciousness, and culture. Consequently, it is aggravating to discover that in the introduction to his book Braverman specifically states that "no attempt will be made to deal with the modern working class on the level of consciousness. . . ." However, we can put aside this curious demurrer, for the book *does* give a very strong sense of the impact of deskilling on workers, though in an indirect way.

One way that Braverman indicts the process of deskilling—and no one can come away from the book without feeling that he/she has read an indictment—is through a historical description of working-class culture among American and British craftspeople in the eighteenth and nineteenth centuries. He depicts a literate, self-educated class, fascinated by science and technology to the point where craftspeople would gatecrash scientific meetings. Voluntary associations flourished among craftspeople for the study of arts and sciences; weavers were poets and botanists; and differential calculus was reputedly the subject of conversation in isolated villages.

Braverman provides no direct comparison of this lively craftwork culture with the modern deskilled proletariat. However, through description after description of deskilling, the reader senses the boredom and the deadening of mind and body that result from capitalist rationalization of the work process. In this regard Braverman is a master writer: he leaves it to the reader, through a process of personal experience or empathy, to fill in the subjective reaction to deskilling. Despite his demurrer, his own view comes through loud and clear:

> But beneath this apparent habituation, the hostility of workers to the degenerated forms of work which are forced upon them continues as a subterranean stream that makes its way to the surface when employment conditions permit, or when the capitalist drive for greater intensity of labor oversteps the bounds of physical and mental capacity. It renews itself in new generations, expresses itself in the unbounded cynicism and revulsion which large numbers of workers feel about their work, and comes to the fore repeatedly as a social issue demanding solution. (1974: 151)

It is interesting, in the light of our earlier discussions of the emphasis on scientific method in left intellectual work, to note that Braverman feels a need to downplay such lyrical expressions of subjective experience and to state that he will not attempt to analyze the consciousness of workers about deskilling because to do so would "derive the 'science before the science'" (1974: 26–27). Apparently he feels that it is more scientific to debate social scientists on the terrain of census figures than on the level of human feeling.

It is important to understand both the success of Braverman's work and the objections that have been leveled at it from some writers on the left, not simply because we need to assess the validity of his analyses, but also because the praise and criticism tell us a lot about the orientation of left scholars. In other words, a careful reading of the critical literature can inform our sociology of knowledge of left scholarship.

Why was the book so successful? Theoretical innovation is not the answer. As Paul Sweezy writes in the foreword to the book itself:

> What needed to be done was to apply Marx's theory to the new methods and occupations invented or created by Capital in its restless expansion. This is the task Harry Braverman has set himself. In terms of theory, as he would be the first to say, there is very little new in this book. (Braverman 1974: xi)

Here is the key. Braverman revived Marx's critique of the destruction of craft skill and argued that the work degradation that Marx described in the nineteenth-century transition from artisan production to modern industry has continued unabated in the twentieth century. He renewed a significant moral critique of capitalism, one that placed the majority of the work force in the role of victim. This approach proved enormously popular to the left in the seventies. A spate of studies soon appeared, each demonstrating for one occupation after another that deskilling was degrading the work of present-day Americans.

But, as I suggested in Chapter One, Marxist theory is a delicate balance of analytical concepts, critiques, and political positions. One can rarely introduce a new moral-evaluatory element without coming into tension with previous analytical frameworks or political positions (paradigm maintenance). Thus the very success of Braverman's critique created strains and conflicts within Marxist theory. In the next section we shall discuss two examples of such conflicts: in one, the acceptance of Braverman's deskilling thesis threw into question one version of DLM theory; in the other, his approach makes problematic the relative political quiescence of the working class.

Other Views on Skill

It should be apparent from the discussion above that Braverman believes that the majority of working people can exercise little or no skill in their jobs, especially in terms of conceptualization. Behind the apparently variegated occupations of late capitalism lies the polarized class model of Marx's *Capital*. However, other groups of left intellectuals take a rather different view of this matter. One such group includes David Gordon, Michael Reich, and Richard Edwards, whose work on poverty and dual labor markets was discussed in the previous chapter.

What concerns these scholars is not the notion of craft skill—that fund of knowledge, practices, and dexterity that a craftworker can carry from job to job. Rather, they propose a contrasting kind of skill: abilities developed specific to one machine or one job, abilities that increase and deepen with length of time on that particular job. Gordon (1971: 64–65) offers a variety of examples of such on-the-job skills. Routinized blue-collar workers, for instance, are more valuable to their firms if they can not only spot defective products but are also knowledgeable enough to identify the operation causing the defect. The value of routinized white-collar workers' knowledge becomes apparent when a form is lost and they can anticipate where to look for it. A secretary's value derives in part from knowing where certain people may be contacted on quick notice and so on.

Gordon asserts that, in spite of the fragmentation and deskilling of work (perhaps even because of it), workers' knowledge of the entire operation of the firm becomes very important for productivity. Obviously, he is contradicting Braverman's contention that detail workers are essentially kept ignorant of all but their own jobs. Instead, Gordon suggests that on-the-job-training imparts a significant degree of skill and that this skill matures with extended experience. Thus, in Gordon's model the craft deskilling that Braverman documents paradoxically leads to a *rise* in machine-specific skill. As a result, the homogeneity of labor that Braverman stresses—the notion that all labor is interchangeable because it is deskilled—is also reversed in Gordon's model. Workers with job-specific knowledge are regarded as superior, according to Gordon, and this consideration becomes so important to management that it will hire only those workers whom it expects to stay with the firm for long periods. This practice leads to a division of workers into stable workers versus short-term ones.

Personally, I find it difficult to shift from Braverman's detailed descriptions of the lack of content in modern jobs to Gordon's descriptions of on-the-job skills. One wonders whether a screw turner, to use one of Gordon's examples, typically bothers with diagnosing the origins of a defect. Equally, examples such as a form stamper called upon for a knowledge of the nuances of the firm's operation or a secretary's skill in knowing where the boss is seem a little forced. They certainly do not fit with the view of one manager, quoted by Braverman, who considered that "training a worker means mostly enabling him to carry out the directions of his work schedule. Once he can do this, his training is over, whatever his age" (Braverman 1974: 447). But perhaps this is giving Gordon's argument less than its due. There is clearly logical consistency in his notion that job tenure results in the acquisition of subtle on-the-job skills; that management recognizes this fact and hence aims for a stable and long-tenured work force; and finally that management therefore excludes "unstable" secondary sector workers.

The dispute over this alternative view can be resolved only by empirical examination of several points: How much time is required to train new employees for most contemporary jobs? Is the productivity of old-timers higher than that of relative newcomers or vice versa? If so, is it a matter of enhanced skills rather than, say, a more acquiescent stance by old-timers toward management pressure? And, finally, does management's penchant for stable, long-term employees derive from the felt need for on-the-job skill development, or are there other reasons not related to skill? Until these matters can be cleared up, we shall have two competing left theories of skill in the contemporary economy.

A position close to that of Gordon is offered by Ken Kusterer in a paper and in a book entitled *Workplace Know-How: The Important Working Knowledge of "Unskilled" Workers* (1978b). Like Gordon, Kusterer perceives an important residue of knowledge even after deskilling has taken place, but he does not believe that this knowledge gives a worker a wide-ranging appreciation of the entire production process. Rather, workers have a more modest "basic working knowledge of routine procedures, and supplementary working knowledge about the materials (or documents) handled, the machinery used, expected patterns of customer or client behavior, and the expected work-role behavior of others in the work organization (including management) with whom the worker must interact in the performance of his job" (Kusterer 1978a: 8).

For Kusterer, the significance of this working knowledge applies not to a theory of dual labor markets but to an understanding of alienation among workers. He sees these gray areas of skill and knowledge as the unalienated part of workers' experience, the areas in which their volition can make the job go better or not. Thus, by developing personal abilities, a worker can perform creatively, gaining pride and pleasure in doing the job right. This opportunity—at the margin, so to speak, of a deskilled job—explains why workers are not totally alienated and totally cynical about their labor. Work know-how forges one basis for commitment to work and a sense of pride and meaning in work (cf. Garson 1975).

A second feature of Kusterer's thesis is that working knowledge is also a basis for a work community in the factory or office. Thus alienation is also overcome via relationships with others in the workplace, mediated through shared working knowledge.

For Kusterer, Braverman is too caught up in nostalgia for the days of craftwork gone by. If work were as degraded as Braverman implies, there would be a total alienation on the part of workers. Instead, there is ambivalence. Work is perceived as alienating and oppressive. But there persists a positive orientation to work as a creative activity in terms of the personal discretion and power inherent in working knowledge and working skill. This dualism or ambivalence deriving from positive and negative work experiences, argues Kusterer, is present even in the meanest of low-paid jobs and explains the inconsistent attitudes that workers typically display toward their jobs.

Praise and Criticism of Braverman

The praise and criticism that Kusterer has for Braverman's work shows up in reviews by several other writers. Such responses are worth considering because they highlight what is considered good in a piece of contemporary Marxist work and what criteria come to the fore.

Rod Coombs picks out two "key respects" in which Braverman's book "represents a genuine and substantive advance." One of these is that Braverman combines "rigorous theoretical analysis with vehement and eloquent indictment of the effects of the capitalist labor process on the working class—a reintroduction of the critical and demystificatory element long absent from Marxist political economy" (Coombs 1978: 79). Coombs here gives a nice illustration of my earlier point that contemporary Marxist academics wish to develop a Marxism with scientific legitimacy ("rigorous theoretical analysis"), while simultaneously expressing their political identity through the practice of moral critique ("vehement . . . indictment").

Coombs also praises Braverman highly for locating the causal elements of change in the labor process rather than in the structure of economic distribution or in demand. This seemingly technical detail is in fact a good example of a reviewer undertaking paradigm maintenance by pointing out and praising a technically correct approach to Marxist analysis. To locate causal processes in the area of production rather than in distribution, exchange, or consumption has become *the* definition of Marxian analysis, as distinct from the Keynesian or Weberian traditions, according to some neo-Marxists.

In fact, concern for production has become something of an obsession in some left circles. Their view is based upon Marx's strong attack against economists who located the creation of profit in exchange. Marx insisted instead that profit (surplus value) was created in the production process. In a curious literal extension of Marx's point, any piece of research that locates causation in the realms of circulation, exchange, or consumption has come to be denounced as un-Marxist. (See, e.g., Gerstein's [1977] critique of Samir Amin.) We therefore see in Coombs's praise for Braverman an example of a critic policing the intellectual boundaries of the Marxist paradigm.

The most widespread criticism of Braverman, made by Michael Burawoy (1978a), Coombs, and David Stark (1978), is that he gives the working class no active role in his analysis of deskilling. These theorists argue that it is not enough to document that degradation occurs. We must know what the roles of class struggle and resistance are in the process. Once again we can detect a struggle over the definition of correct Marxist method. Braverman located the causes of deskilling in the logic of capitalist profit making ("capital logic"). Though a tradition of long standing in Marxism, this analysis comes into conflict with a more modern trend that eschews interpretations of historical developments in terms of the inexorable working out of capitalist logic (epithetically called "historicism"). Instead, it insists on seeing labor and capital as in constant struggle and on regarding automation, Taylorism, and the like as results of historical episodes of class struggle.

These reviewers criticisms of Braverman can be understood only in terms of a hidden battle over the definition of Marxist method (paradigm maintenance). Their call for more detail about the links between class struggle, capital accumulation, and technological change amounts to a demand for a historically sensitive Marxist scholarship that gives class struggle a central causal role. It is only this issue that leads neo-Marxists to disparage Braverman's book, for as a piece of moral-evaluatory work, of critical denunciation of capitalist work practices, it needs none of these theoretical elaborations. On the contrary, its moral critique is powerful: the degradation of work is systematically related to the needs of capitalism. Moreover, as critical theory, its great appeal is general. The analysis applies not simply to a subsection of the population, as critiques of poverty do; nor does it demand abstract identification with distant peoples, as critiques of imperialism do. Rather, it provides an indictment of domestic capitalism and identifies the victim as the entire American working class. This generality is the optimal goal of a Marxist analysis.

The critical reviews of Braverman's book demonstrate that such work is assessed on a dual basis: on the power and political correctness of its moral-evaluatory dimension, and on the power and analytic correctness of its theoretical analysis. A work may be judged successful on one dimension but lacking in the other. The consensus appears to be that, as a critique, Braverman's book excels, but that, as theoretical analysis, it needs to be expanded.

Yet a third level of criticism closes the circle. Braverman's theoretical analysis has been scanned for the "hidden" political implications of its conceptual approach. Thus Burawoy notes that the historicism of Braverman's analysis, his downplaying of the role of class struggle in the process of deskilling, leads to a pessimism or fatalism concerning the ability of class struggle to change such processes (Burawoy 1978a; cf. Coombs 1978: 94; Kusterer 1978a). Equally, Braverman's nostalgic use of the craftworker as a reference point from which to criticize capitalism is seen to lead to potential political difficulties with regard to the nature of the production process under socialism (Burawoy 1978a; Stark 1978: 41).

Braverman's book and the responses of the intellectual left to it give us several insights into the nature of left theory. We shall try to extend this discussion in a consideration of research on the development of the firm under contemporary capitalism. Both substantively and in terms of the sociology of knowledge, the work on the firm complements the previous research on the labor process.

Theories of the Firm

In his analysis of the labor process Braverman abstracted both from particular firms and from organizational structure in general. Prior to the publication of *Labor and Monopoly Capital*, several articles had appeared in radical journals that provided analyses similar to Braverman's but tended to give considerable weight to the organizational context of work—the effects of job ladders, seniority, and occupational segmentation—and to the historical particularities of specific industries. One issue underlying most of the radical studies of the capitalist enterprise is the role that technological necessity has played in creating the organizational structure of the modern firm. Is the hierarchical form of administration, with authority and decision making concentrated at the top and with a detailed division of tasks and responsibilities a technical necessity, the most efficient way to get the job done? Or does the present structure of capitalist firms reflect particular historical circumstances, such as the need to control alienated workers? Could production be organized differently, but efficiently, in a socialist society?

This question of whether the modern bureaucratic enterprise is a technologically superior or optimal form of organization has already generated several decades of debate among nonradical sociologists. Many sociologists have read Max Weber as a proponent of the view that bureaucratic hierarchy is objectively superior in terms of technological rationality to any other organizational form. In reaction, others have detailed the dysfunctional and irrational consequences of this form of organization. These sociologists did field research to document the control functions embodied in the structure of modern enterprises and showed many of the technical irrationalities (unintended consequences) that flowed from this system of governance (e.g., Gouldner 1954; Blau 1955; Merton 1968: 195–205). By contrast, radical scholars have taken to *historical reconstruction*. In documenting the origins of certain organizational features, they have demonstrated that many aspects of the modern firm originated from the need to control workers rather than from neutral considerations of technological efficiency. Radical histories of industries such as steel, cars, textiles, and farm machinery address this issue of technological necessity versus control.

This brings us to the second intellectual consideration informing these radical studies: namely, the place of consciousness and of actors in the historical development of the modern forces of production. As noted above, one of the most widespread criticisms of Braverman was that he tended to treat deskilling as if it were almost inevitable. One lost the sense of actors in his drama, at least insofar as workers were concerned. This objection led to charges of fatalism, that Braverman's perspective treated working-class reaction to capitalist rationalization so lightly as to dismiss its causal importance. By contrast, the radical theorists of the firm emphasize two warring factions in capitalist industry—labor and capitalists—and insist that the structure of the modern business enterprise embodies past struggles between them. Thus, as we shall see in the following case studies, the modern firm was created by management *and* labor, and many of its features represent compromises made between the two.

What Do Bosses Do?

The story begins with Stephen Marglin's (1974) account of the early days of capitalist manufacture in Britain, of how and why the factory system first came into existence. Marglin attempts to counter two related positions, each of which is invoked to justify capitalist forms of industrial stucture as "inevitable." The first position, a version of technological determinism, suggests that modern technology itself has certain "needs" that dictate the hierarchical division of labor that predominates in industry today. This position is held both by those who take literally Marx's aphorism that "the steam mill gives you the capitalist" and by those who, like Clark Kerr, believe that the objective requirements of industrialism push Soviet and capitalist societies onto converging paths.

In looking for data to counter this position, Marglin studied the *early* phase of British capitalism, a period of about 150 years. He discovered that capitalist and noncapitalist organizations of labor coexisted and that both used the same simple technology. Furthermore, the fine division of labor was well established *prior* to the introduction of water power, the steam mill, and other technological innovations. This evidence weakens the causal power of the technology argument considerably, for whatever led to the capitalist factory system involved some set of arrangements other than and historically prior to the needs of complex technological machinery.

The second position that Marglin seeks to refute is the "technological superiority" argument. Rather than harp on technology's needs for certain types of organizational structure, the technological superiority argument trades upon a "survival of the fittest" imagery. Its logic is that capitalist forms of organizational structure were adopted because they were the most efficient. In order to understand Marglin's refutation of this position we should first grasp his definition of technological efficiency: one technique is more efficient than another if it affords a larger output from the same amount of inputs. Given this definition, Marglin must convince us that whatever brought about the spread of capitalist industrial structure had little to do with technological superiority. Or, as he puts it:

> Rather than providing more output for the same inputs, these innovations in work organizations were introduced so that the capitalist got himself a larger share of the pie at the expense of the worker, and it is only the subsequent growth in the size of the pie that has obscured the class interest which was at the root of these innovations. (Marglin 1974: 34)

Adam Smith (1937: 7) gave the classical rationale for a fine division of labor some two hundred years ago. Three kinds of advantages flow from the division of labor, each of which contributes to higher productivity: there is an increase in dexterity due to specialization; time is saved by obviating the need to move from one task to another (i.e., specialization does away with "set-up time"); and there is an increase in invention of machines. Marglin argues against all three of these positions, but we shall focus on the most important, the increase in efficiency achieved by not moving from task to task.

Marglin concedes that separating tasks saves "the time that is commonly lost in passing from one species of work to another," but he argues that this reason "has little or nothing to do with the minute specialization that characterizes the capitalist division of labor." Peasants separate tasks to minimize set-up or transition time: they plough the whole field, then harrow all of it, then seed all of it, rather than complete the plough, harrow, and seed sequence for one row at a time. Similarly, guild craftsmen mark out cloth for many garments, then cut them all, then sew them all, and so on. According to Marglin, however, one can obtain the economies of reducing set-up time *without* specialization:

> A workman, with his wife and children, could have proceeded from task to task, first drawing out enough wire for hundreds and thousands of pins, then straightening it, cutting it, and so on with

each successive operation, thus realizing the advantages of dividing the overall production into separate tasks. (1974: 38)

The capitalist practice of minute division of tasks and of separate *personnel* for each task clearly goes beyond simply gaining the advantages of set-up savings. Why, then, did this type of labor appear as the first development peculiar to capitalist production, prior even to the factory system? The economic context prior to capitalism involved independent producers of craft goods. Each typically owned his/her own tools, and capital expenses were in any case small. One of Marglin's most crucial points is that the position of the nascent capitalist was marginal in such a system of self-sufficiency, since the actual contribution to production of any would-be capitalist was unimportant. About the only way one group could gain from the production of another was to try to play the middle-man role between producers and the market.

The first distinctly capitalist organization of production to emerge from this situation was the "putting-out system," where workers in textiles used their own simple machinery at home. A high division of labor characterized the putting-out system: a household carded wool, or spun thread, or wove; no household produced the entire product. The capitalist integrated these tasks, provided raw materials for each stage, and sold the final product. Marglin (1974: 38–39) asserts that the real contribution of the capitalist was negligible. Yet by separating the tasks into minute subdivisions and assigning workers to each one, the capitalist removed the individual producers from access to a market and made a handsome middle-man's profit. The fine division of labor guaranteed the capitalist a role in the whole affair and rendered the individual producers dependent upon him.

To give this argument the ring of truth, Marglin needs to persuade the reader of two things. First, if the capitalist was simply a middle-man, why did each producer not integrate his/her own work and eliminate the capitalist? Second, how aware were capitalists of their role, and how did they maintain their position? Marglin's explanation exhibits both strengths and weaknesses. With regard to the first question, Marglin invokes a logic of self-interest. Those workers capable of integrating others' work would become capitalist "putter-outers" themselves; organizing fellow workers into some kind of cooperative would dilute such a profit. If one had the resources, self-interest would drive one to become a capitalist putter-outer, not a cooperative.

This interpretation, in my opinion, is the weakest part of his argument. Fortunately, Marglin elsewhere offers a potentially stronger explanation of the relative dependence of the specialized workers in the putting-out system: debt. Putting-out involved partial prepayment of wages and advances of raw materials. Thus the putting-out households worked on someone else's raw materials to eradicate a debt. Their ability to cut out the middle-man was inhibited both by this debt and by the complexity of selling a partly processed product. In fact, despite this dependency, embezzlement and attempts to sell one's product to someone other than one's putter-outer were endemic, a situation that to some degree inspired the formation of the later factory system.

It is important to note that the role of the capitalist in the putting-out system was not secured by ownership of the means of production. In this early period machinery was simple, and it was owned by individual workers. Precisely because dependence of workers upon capitalists could not be attained via monopoly over the means of production, the specialization of labor and the debt system became indispensable methods of control. Marglin also shows the obverse of the argument. In those rare instances where the means of production were scarce, expensive, or otherwise amenable to monopolization by capitalists, there was no equivalent need for fine specialization of labor. He describes mining as a case in point: it was easy to monopolize ownership of mines, and the work system in mining was not specialized or finely divided in the manner typical of putting-out.

Marglin's interpretation of the origins and function of specialization and the division of labor gains additional plausibility from the evidence he provides of worker and capitalist perceptions of the process. As the following quotation from that period intimates, capitalists realized that the separation of functions contributed to maintaining workers' ignorance of the production process: "his manager Henry Hargreaves knows nothing about the mixing or costs of cotton so that he can never take his business away from him—all his overlookers' businesses are quite separate from each other and then no one knows what is going on but himself" (quoted in Marglin 1974: 40). Capitalists were aware of the value of a fine division of labor in keeping employees dependent upon them. Similarly, Marglin (1974: 40) shows that capitalists were aware of the dangers of being squeezed out by cooperative associations of workers. Thus the origins of the fine division of labor derived from the need to make workers dependent on the capitalist, and not from increased efficiency or other technological factors.

Marglin then extends his argument by looking at the origins of the factory system. To counter the widespread notion that factory production was made necessary by the needs of certain technological innovations (e.g., water power to drive factory machinery required centralization of workers in one shop), he proves that factories were widespread prior to the harnessing of water power. Moreover, the early factories used technology identical to that found in the putting-out cottages. What, then, inspired the creation of the factory system?

Fortunately, the historical record, including comments by participants, is fairly clear. The putting-out system did not allow capitalists enough control over worker output. The ruling logic of putting-out was to be found in the workers' relative preference for leisure versus cash and not in the capitalists' desire for increased production and profit. Cottage workers would work until they earned a satisfactory income; then they would stop. Raising wages to stimulate more production simply encouraged putting-out workers to maintain their previous income level by doing even less work. Marglin quotes early capitalists inveighing against what they perceived as the laziness and ill discipline of the cottage workers. They could not make extra profits until they could force an increase in production.

Initial attempts at a solution failed. Laws were passed to force putting-out workers to complete their tasks within set numbers of days. Successive laws tried to shorten the period and hence force higher production. More legal measures were enacted to repress the rampant embezzlement of goods. The factory system was born out of the capitalists' lack of control over cottage workers.

Marglin notes that factories could not successfully compete for labor in a free competitive market. Initially only the poorest members of society would look for employment there, because the work was longer and harder than the cottage regime. Thus factory organization, far from representing the survival of the technologically fittest, could succeed only by exercising extra-economic force. Marglin quotes from a nineteenth-century reviewer of Richard Arkwright's inventions, perhaps the most important technological developments of the period:

The main difficulty (faced by Arkwright) did not, to my apprehension, lie so much in the invention of a proper self-acting mechanism for drawing out and twisting cotton into a continuous thread, as in . . . training human beings to renounce their desultory habits of work, and to identify themselves with the unvarying regularity of the complex automation. To devise and administer a successful code of factory discipline, suited to the necessities of factory diligence, was the Herculean enterprise, the noble achievement of Arkwright. It required, in fact, a man of Napoleon nerve and ambition, to subdue the refractory tempers of workpeople accustomed to irregular paroxysms of diligence. . . . Such was Arkwright. (Quoted in Marglin 1974: 456)

Marglin provides a wealth of detail to show: (1) that the shift to the factory was not a process of free market competition between two modes of production; (2) that the productivity of the factory system (output per unit of input) was not superior to that of the cottage system; (3) that, as a system of least cost (by forcing more work for less pay), it *was* superior to putting-out; and (4) that contemporary capitalists and workers were aware that the issue was control over the work force rather than technology.

Politics played a crucial role in the timing of the emergence of the factory system. Marglin points out that the factory system (and certain machines that were invented but not adopted) was thwarted in earlier periods irrespective of "competition" or "superiority" because a politically weak capitalist class could not defeat legal limits imposed by a powerful guild coalition. Similarly, when putting-out workers later would not respond to capitalist interests, putting-out was restructured by legislative action.

Marglin never intended to dismiss or belittle the considerable technological breakthroughs that subsequently occurred in textile production. He simply wanted to highlight the sequence of events: struggle between quasi-independent producers led to a high division of labor in the putting-out system, which in turn succumbed to a factory system. *Then* systematic innovation became important, protected by the crucial patent system.

Generalizing from this scenario, Marglin argues that shifts in technology often signal previous shifts in the balance of class struggle (cf. Gordon et al. 1982: 115–116), that technologies facilitate the power of certain social groups over others, and that the adoption of new technologies often depends on the balance of legal or political power rather than on simple market competition. He sums up his findings by correcting one of Marx's most famous aphorisms in order to remove its technological determinist tone: "The steam mill didn't give us the capitalist, the capitalist gave us the steam mill. . . . It was not the handmill that gave us feudalism, but the feudal lord that gave us the water mill" (1974: 55, 57).

Steel, Cars, and Tractors

Marglin's work provides a good introduction to neo-Marxist perspectives on the firm, but as Marglin himself pointed out, it is only a first step. To demonstrate that two important features of the firm predate modern technology and reflect issues of capitalist domination is not the same as tackling the complexities of organization apparent in the modern giant corporation, with its job ladders, seniority systems, white- and blue-collar divisions, and sexual and racial stratifications. Most significantly, Marglin's interpretation of the importance of control vis-à-vis technology for the early capitalist era cannot be assumed to hold for the contemporary period. Fortunately, other left scholars have paralleled Marglin's historical approach in studies of later periods and so allow us to judge the validity of his conclusions for the modern period.

Katherine Stone's (1974) account of the steel industry is drawn from the work of David Brody (1960) and other historians. It begins with the 1880s, when steel was a highly skilled craft industry. During that period management had a relatively small role, since workers essentially subcontracted to produce a given quantity of steel and organized most of the specifics of production for themselves. Management's problem of making a profit was simplified by a novel wage system: workers were paid some fraction of the price for which the company sold the steel. Thus management was assured of a profit, and workers' salaries moved up and down according to the price per ton obtained for the steel they produced. Workers also arranged their own system of dividing the per-ton payment among the various skilled and unskilled jobs.

By 1920 these features of the steel industry had disappeared, replaced by a highly mechanized, deskilled system in which management made all the decisions. Job ladders, welfare systems, and the rigid divisions typical of the modern giant corporation characterized the new form of organization. U.S. Steel provides a useful case study of the major reorganizations that have produced the contemporary capitalist firm and the modern labor process.

Stone begins with the factors leading to the destruction of the craftworkers' per-ton payment system. In the late 1880s steel manufacturers were faced with the unusual combination of a rapidly rising demand for steel alongside falling prices. Owners realized that the kinds of changes needed in order to profit from the expansion—cheaper steel and faster production—could not be achieved so long as the power and prerogatives of the craftwork system continued.

The method by which U.S. Steel breached the old production system was remarkable only for its bloodiness; otherwise, it typified the pattern of lockouts and strikes at the turn of the century. The Homestead Mill strike began in 1892 as a lockout of the workers. The steel plant was surrounded by barbed wire and armed guards, strikebreakers were imported to run the factory, and, after a bloody and bitter confrontation, the steelworkers' union was defeated. By 1910 the steel industry was completely non-union. Once the power of the union was destroyed, U.S. Steel began a rapid and massive reorganization of its production and administrative practices. These changes and the conscious intent behind them form the analytic core of Stone's account.

Following the Homestead strike, U.S. Steel aggressively adopted mechanization both to replace the unskilled labor previously used to move steel from point to point around the factory and to obviate the need for skilled labor in several processes. The degree of mechanization was so great that the composition of the workforce changed drastically: skilled and unskilled positions disappeared, to be replaced by a large semiskilled category of machine feeders and machine minders.

Wages shifted, too. Although productivity leapt to three times its former level, the average wage rose by about one-fifth. The new semiskilled workers were paid better than the former unskilled laborers. However, many skilled workers lost their jobs or were transferred to semiskilled positions. Even those who retained skilled jobs suffered a rapid 70 percent drop in wages. The wage differential between skilled and unskilled work dropped to a fraction of its former level.

The overall impact of this process was to bring greater profits to U.S. Steel and to cheapen the costs of labor for the company. However, this reorganization had an unanticipated consequence of great import. As skilled and unskilled positions disappeared and wage differentials shrank, employees at U.S. Steel became increasingly homogeneous with respect to income and work experience, which in turn led to a more unified work force that could recognize its common interests.

Stone demonstrates that management was conscious of this development and that it experimented with a variety of organizational devices to stave off potential worker unrest. Again, the crucial point is that these changes were not inspired by technological or efficiency needs— the breakthrough in productivity had already been achieved—but represented conscious attempts to use organizational structure to dominate and divide employees.

Stone documents managerial intentions through numerous quotations from steel industry publications, such as *Iron Age*, in which industry spokesmen expressed their fears and their plans with extraordinary openness. For example, Frederick Taylor, the inventor of Taylorism and scientific management, was a manager in the steel industry and wrote several books extolling the methods he devised. The first managerial tactic developed to counter worker solidarity was the use of incentive systems such as piece rates. Taylor praised piece rates as mechanisms for dividing fast workers from slower ones, since the former would get paid more than the latter. As one manufacturer put it: "There are not likely to be union strikes where there is no union of interest" (quoted in Stone 1974: 72). Nevertheless, this strategy did not quell conflict. As has been documented by dozens of industrial sociologists, the piece-rate system leads to a cat-and-mouse game between labor and management. Management sets a rate; workers work harder and earn more. Management decides that it does not want to pay such high wages, despite the increased productivity, so it lowers the piece-rate payment. Workers respond by collusion and produce slower in order to put pressure on management to raise the piece rate again. At U.S. Steel, worker militancy grew, strikes broke out in 1910, and in each case worker demands centered on the reinstitution of a uniform hourly rate. These demands were not met by management. Instead there appears to have been a deadlock of sorts: the unrest continued alongside differential piece rates.

A second tactic designed to lessen labor unrest involved the construction of job ladders. Jobs were ranked hierarchically, wages were paid according to relative position in the hierarchy, and workers were allowed to progress up the ladder. Stone makes two points about this system, which has become widespread in large corporations. First, neither management nor the workers believed that the ranking of jobs and the pay differentials between jobs reflected true skill differences. Jobs at the top were not especially complex; nor did a worker need considerable experience at lower levels in order to be able to manage the higher tasks. On the contrary, Stone quotes the president of U.S. Steel to the effect that the top position on the job ladder could be taught to an agricultural laborer in six to eight weeks. Unskilled, inexperienced "blacklegs" were used successfully at all tiers of the job hierarchy during strikes.

Thus, job ladders and their differential pay rates did not reflect substantial skill differences or technological needs. Instead, they resulted from management's realization that a homogeneous work force bred discontent, whereas the possibility of upward mobility would pacify workers. The job ladder technique rapidly caught on as managerial magazines urged corporations to institute systems of promotion from within. Both management and workers soon discovered that workers oriented toward "collecting certificates" (promises of promotion) were pliable and obedient.

U.S. Steel's third strategy to prevent labor unrest and to stave off unionization centered on welfare measures, including stock subscriptions, health and injury benefits, housing loans, and pension schemes. The welfare period of U.S. Steel and other industrial giants elicited considerable comment at the time and has been scrutinized by such leftist historians as James Weinstein and Robert Weibe. Thus the details of the welfare schemes and the intentions of their originators are easily accessible. Although the record is full of rhapsodic statements of the firm's altruism, it also contains hardnosed managerial assessments that workers who participated in company schemes such as home ownership loans were less likely to listen to union agitators. Moreover, many of the incentives were limited in some way—for example, to those who showed a "proper interest" in the company's welfare or progress—and they excluded persons whom the firm deemed guilty of misconduct. As one worker put it, company benefits were "a scheme to keep out unionism and prevent the men from protesting against bad conditions" (Stone 1974: 76).

Stone also examines the impact of Taylorism in removing skill and knowledge from workers and re-establishing it in specialized management-controlled occupations. Since we have discussed this development at length in the context of Braverman's book, we shall note only one point here. In the same way that Braverman argued that deskilling created new skilled trades that lacked the autonomy of earlier crafts,

Stone shows how this new generation of quasi-craftworkers was kept dependent on the corporation. She quotes *Iron Age* and the president of one large steel firm, who advised that company-trained mechanics would be so specialized in the particular techniques of their firm that they would not be able to transfer these skills by moving to other corporations. We see here another purpose of minute specialization: the creation of workers who are almost totally dependent on one employer.

Technical colleges and trade schools were also established to train these new specialists. This program was financed by business management and opposed by unions as an overt method of taking the training and socialization of new skilled workers out of union purview.

Finally, Stone focuses on the impact of unionization after the late 1930s, finding that unionization did not threaten the job promotion hierarchy or the company's wage incentive schemes but rather acted to simplify them and make the criteria for pay and advancement more explicit. The union succeeded in reorienting the promotional system to stress seniority rather than good behavior, but it challenged neither the basic notion of the promotion ladder nor the accompanying fine division of labor.

Based on her historical research Stone concludes that the organizational features of the contemporary steel industry cannot be viewed as determined by technological imperatives and that job hierarchies did not reflect the complexity of tasks but were a device consciously adopted to counter the increasingly homogeneous nature of the work force and to undercut worker solidarity. She argues that the organization of work is best regarded as the outcome of decades of struggle between workers and employers.

Engineering and Capitalism

Stone's approach is complemented by the work of David Noble (1977, 1979), who shows the complex intertwining of technology and capitalism through a social history of engineering. He argues that engineers became "the agents of corporate capital":

> [Engineers] hardly proceeded according to the dictates of some logically consistent "technical reason" blindly advancing the frontiers of human enterprise, but rather informed their work with

the historical imperatives of corporate growth, stability and control: as their technology progressed, so too did the science-based industrial corporations which they served. (Noble 1977: xxiv)

The fusion of technological knowledge and managerial interests was attained through the professionalization of engineering. Corporate capitalists founded institutes and universities to provide engineering education and pressured educators when those schools failed to provide the right kind of engineers for industry. The patent system allowed corporations to monopolize engineering innovations and gave business an incentive to invest in engineering research. Out of these developments, according to Noble, came a profession oriented simultaneously toward technical issues and toward the wider issues of profitability and managing workers. The human factor was joined with technical factors as engineering absorbed insights from industrial psychology and personnel management. Engineers were confronted with the tasks of managing recalcitrant workers and maximizing productivity by manipulating the social relations of the workplace. In addition to showing the links between modern engineering and capitalist production in these terms, Noble also examines a particular technological invention—automated machine tools—"to determine precisely how extra-technical considerations, such as managerial control over the workforce, inform machine design and deployment" (1977: xxiv).

Machine tools (lathes, milling machines, etc.) are devices for cutting and forming metal into machine parts with specified shapes. Manual machine tools require an expert machinist who guides the cutting tool, adjusts the machine to allow for imperfections in materials, and is responsible for producing parts within a few thousandths of an inch of the specified size. The promise of automated machine tools is that, once they have been programmed with the shape to be cut, they can produce part after part without further human involvement.

Noble (1979) finds that social choices have been central to the development of these automated tools. For example, numerical control machines, a type of automatically controlled machine tools that requires complex computer programming, have become widespread in the industry in recent years. Once programmed, they can cut complex shapes to fine tolerances. However, a simpler, earlier technology, known as record-playback, was developed in the forties but was not adopted by industry. This earlier technique required a skilled machinist to make the first part manually while the machine recorded the movements of the lathe. Subsequently, the machine "played back" these movements, allowing part after part to be cut without the machinist's intervention. Noble argues that, technically, record-playback was as good an option as numerical control but that social factors led to the choice of the latter system over the former. These factors included management's desire to be independent of the skilled machinists needed to set up the record-playback machines. With numerical control, managers hoped to remove all decision making from the shop floor (Noble 1979: 36). Thus Noble concludes that issues of social control become fused with issues of technological rationality in the development of machines and industrial processes: technological rationality alone does not guide changes in the labor process in a capitalist society.

In this work by Noble, as in Stone's study of U.S. Steel, Francesca Maltese's (1973) inquiry into the automobile industry, Mario Barrera's (1976) analysis of International Harvester, and various subsequent papers, we see the creation of a distinct subparadigm: a neo-Marxist approach to the development of the modern firm and its structuring of the work process. The elements of the approach remain relatively constant—a historical analysis aimed at revealing the origins of particular organizational features and an explication of the intentions behind the historical developments. As the case studies proliferate, the evidence accumulates against a technological-determinist reading of organizational history and in favor of a conflict approach that views organizational structures as embodying strategies for controlling workers' behavior. With each additional study, the political conclusion that production could be oriented in some other way gains strength.

Richard Edwards on the Firm

Richard Edwards prefaces his work with a discussion of his broader theoretical purposes. As in the research just discussed, he wishes to counter two intellectual arguments: the notion that the structure of the contemporary firm is inevitable and corresponds to technological necessity or optimum efficiency, and the view that class struggle is unimportant for an understanding of the organizational structure of industrial enterprise. In contrast, he attempts to demonstrate that many important features of the modern business enterprise are the outcome of class struggles.

Edwards has a second purpose as well. If one accepts, as he does, the notion that deskilling and rationalization have led to a relatively homogeneous work force, one must ask why this development has not resulted in a corresponding rise in working-class solidarity and militancy. Since Edwards believes that a working-class consciousness is primarily formed by experiences in the workplace, he looks to changes there in order to explain the quiescence of workers in the present period. His answer hangs upon a periodization of the labor process. Prior to the 1930s, deskilling and homogenization did appear to be occurring, accompanied by a marked increase in working-class militancy. After the 1930s, however, something intervened to reverse this process of homogenization, polarization, and militancy.

Edwards constructs a general model in which class struggles are closely linked to the organizational structure of business enterprises, and especially to the strategies used by management to control workers. Furthermore, he regards control as a contradictory process: each control system embodies certain contradictions that, over time, undermine its own efficacy and therefore provide an impetus for management to adopt a new form of control. The new system of control also involves contradictions, which in turn lead to its demise, and so on.

To fill out this theoretical model, Edwards relies on two sets of materials. On the one hand, he uses articles by Stone, Marglin, Maltese, and others to build a composite picture of the empirical changes that have occurred in the manufacturing economy over the last two hundred years. He often returns to the original historical research upon which these case studies were based and thus draws from the work of an earlier generation of political and apolitical historians of business, including Robert Ozanne, Alfred Chandler, Caroline Ware, David Brody, James Weinstein, David Montgomery, and Robert Weibe, in order to detail the development of organizational structures of business and their surrounding context of labor history. The second tradition that Edwards uses is far less apparent in his work but can be seen in his footnotes and references. It consists of a body of "orthodox" sociology of formal organizations, especially works that view organizations in terms of power, control, and compliance (e.g., Alvin Gouldner, Michael Crozier, Amatai Etzioni, and so on). Edwards synthesizes these two sets of materials to develop a typology of control systems, which he organizes in a historical sequence to show the ebb and flow of control strategies, their origins in class struggles, and their institutionalization in particular organizational structures and practices.

The following diagram schematizes Edwards's model as a four-stage process. The general transition from simple control systems to structural control systems is the crucial one.

entrepreneurial→ hierarchical→ technical→ bureaucratic

Simple Control Systems   Structural Control Systems

Entrepreneurial control was characteristic of businesses in America prior to the 1880s. This was an era of small firms. With the exception of textiles and the railroads, even large corporations employed fewer than two hundred workers. The typical manufacturing enterprise was family owned or a partnership and produced goods sold in a competitive market within the local region. In such businesses the owner was typically also the manager: hence Edwards's label "entrepreneurial control." The firms were small enough that all questions were referred to the owner-manager for his personal decision. Little or no decision-making power was lodged in the position of the foreman, and the work process tended to be informal and largely self-regulated, governed by the boss's decisions and by craft tradition, rather than by written rules and regulations. The entrepreneur attempted to use leadership and personal charisma to motivate his workers. The firm's success depended on the entrepreneur's sales abilities and his good relationship with his workers. A sociologist would call this type of organization a patrimonial bureaucracy administering craft and/or small batch production.

The downfall of this form of business and of the entrepreneurial system of control resulted from the expansion of markets following the consolidation of the railroads in the period 1860–1890. As freight rates decreased, firms began to manufacture for the national market instead of local or regional ones, and the size of companies increased rapidly in response. According to Edwards, as companies grew too large and too dispersed for direct entrepreneurial supervision, a new kind of administration and control became necessary, so industrialists followed the example of large textile mills and railroads.

The new system, hierarchical control, involved the delegation of some of the boss's authority to a complex hierarchy of supervisory personnel. This type of organization, with nested pyramids of authority, organizational charts, separate divisions, and so on, was loosely modeled on the army and its chain of command. One important feature of this hierarchical system was that the power to hire and fire workers was delegated to the foremen, who exercised close personal supervision over the workers. The opening up of national markets also introduced an era of intense competition. Close supervision and harsh, often capricious discipline by foremen were used to obtain maximum output per worker.

The period from the 1890s to the 1920s represents a transitional phase in Edwards' schema, in which drastic changes took place in the organization of the American economy. Between 1892 and 1902 a wave of mergers resulted in the consolidation of a large sector of capital. Edwards discusses several causes: the previous period of ruinous competition, the growth of trusts, public financing of stocks due to changes in corporate law in the 1890s, an influx of British capital, and so on. In the arena of production this period was characterized by what Edwards calls a "crisis of control." In my opinion, two processes seem to have been taking place, although Edwards stresses the second one.

Historically, the first conflicts occurred in those economic sectors where the rise of giant corporations had been accomplished without a shift to hierarchical control, owing to the continuing power of craft unions. Stone's study of U.S. Steel is a case in point. These craftsmen continued to administer much of the process of production in a quasi-autonomous fashion via the contract system, thus obviating the need for an elaborate hierarchical control system. In these kinds of industries an early crisis of control occurred when management attempted to pre-empt these craft prerogatives by instituting hierarchical control. We discussed earlier the bitter clashes that resulted and the subsequent defeat of craft unions, followed by a rapid program of mechanization and deskilling as management sought to replace skilled with semi-skilled labor.

The second process, which lies at the heart of Edwards's characterization of the crisis of control within the firm, followed this destruction of craft unionism and the onset of hierarchical control. After 1901 the locus of union militancy moved away from craft unionism to industrywide CIO unions. Deskilling forged an increasingly homogeneous semiskilled work force, its common work experience reinforced by a high rate of interfirm mobility, which created a class of workers well aware of their common interests. This awareness showed itself in the increasing frequency of sympathy strikes. Class solidarity was further strengthened by the practice of soldiering—a collective decision to work slowly in an attempt to force an increase in piece rates.

Edwards characterizes the period 1890–1920 as one of escalating industrial conflict, especially over the issue of direct supervision by foremen. As the typical firm shifted from entrepreneurial to hierarchical control, considerable power was delegated to foremen and supervisors. This power, including the right to fire workers summarily, led to cronyism combined with arbitrary dismissal in a system of control that Alvin Gouldner (1954), in a different context, aptly labeled "punitive bureaucracy." Close supervision and arbitrary sanctions led to a rapid polarization of workers against supervisors and an increase in worker militancy. In the furious series of strikes that occurred from 1901 through 1919 worker demands were aimed as much against the autocratic control of supervisors as for wage increases. Senate subcommittees that probed worker dissatisfaction during this period provide us with extensive documentation of this aspect of the crisis of control.

Thus, for Edwards, the rise of the giant corporation produced a system of hierarchical control that in time generated its own contradiction in the form of a militant work force, whose solidarity was ensured by the punitive aspects of hierarchical control itself. At the same time, the giant corporations faced difficulties outside the realm of production. The enormous degree of corporate consolidation that took place between 1898 and 1902 produced industrial giants whose size went well beyond that needed for economies of scale. The fact that each giant enterprise controlled such a large proportion of the market raised for the first time the possibility of price collusion and oligopoly. In practice, however, the transformation of market power into oligopoly proved difficult in many industries, and corporate giants continued to compete for increased market shares.

The oligopolies also faced political problems. The rise of big business had produced an antagonistic coalition of small capitalists, farmers, intellectuals, and working-class organizations such as the Socialist party, the Wobblies, and the noncraft unions. These forces coalesced into a general antitrust movement that for several years threatened to hamper the activities of the newly consolidated industrial giants.

In summary, during the period of transition, from approximately 1890 to 1920, the giant corporations faced three problems: rising working-class militancy in the factories; the need to avoid ruinous competition from other industrial giants; and political coalitions aimed at dismembering the trusts. Edwards contends that the latter two problems were solved by America's entry into World War I. Public antagonism to big business evaporated in the face of the need to produce for a war economy. The problem of competition between corporate giants was alleviated by the insatiable demands of the war boom and most especially by the highly profitable price system developed by the businessmen drafted onto the War Industries Board. By the end of the war the shift in public attitudes and the development of oligopoly among the giants during the war years meant that monopoly capitalism was quite secure.

But the war did not solve the industrial relations problem. The punitive hierarchical control system continued to polarize workers and mold them into solidary groups. The AFL and CIO no-strike pledges during the war did not stop strikes, despite jailings and other government coercion. Rather, the policy allowed more radical forces, such as the IWW, to co-opt labor militancy. The end of the war signaled a rash of major strikes.

It took a long time for corporate management to find a strategy to cope with the polarization and militancy produced by hierarchical control. From 1919 to about 1925 individual corporations experimented (Edwards's term) with repression, welfare capitalism, Taylorism, company unions, industrial psychology, and so on. These methods were intended not to replace hierarchical control but to mitigate its consequences by dividing and "buying off" workers in a variety of ways. Taylorism, with its differential wage rates for "average" and "superior" workers, and welfare capitalism, with its housing, health, and pension benefits for "good" workers, each tried in its own way to reverse the homogenization of labor and to tie the interests of individual workers to the firm rather than to fellow workers. By and large, these schemes did not work. Hierarchical control continued to inspire solidarity among semiskilled workers. From 1919 to the late 1920s firms that offered welfare measures suffered strikes. Bitter managers berated workers' ingratitude, and many firms dismantled their welfare programs.

The solution to the contradictory outcome of hierarchical control involved a shift to alternative forms of controlling workers. Edwards identifies two variants of the new "structural" systems of control: technical control and bureaucratic control. Both exist in contemporary enterprises, often side by side, but Edwards sees them as distinct phenomena. He also postulates a historical trend toward an increasing emphasis on bureaucratic over technical control in modern corporations.

Technical control, in Edwards's formulation, relies on designing machinery to minimize the labor/labor power problem as well as to maximize efficiency. Machines that dictate the type, amount, and pace of work force each worker to produce more. Such machine pacing has been in use since the early nineteenth century in textiles, but it did not become widespread in American industry until the development of the "disassembly" line in meat packing in 1905 and the Ford assembly line in 1913. It is important to note that Edwards reserves the term "technical control" not for just any machine with a fixed speed but rather for a sequence of such machines, an entire production line, where each part of production is tied to a common rhythm or pace.

The importance of technical control is twofold. First, it removes the need for constant confrontation between supervisors and individual workers over the speed of their work, since work speed is set for all at the steady pace of the line. Second, the system isolates workers from one another. Where previously workers moved around the factory and had a wide number of contacts, the assembly line forces workers to remain stationary at one fabrication point. There is no simple means by which workers at one point in the process can interact with others involved in different tasks.

The implementation of assembly-line techniques in industries such as automobiles led to a rapid shift in the nature of supervision in those firms and a concurrent modification of industrial conflict. Foremen no longer needed to direct work tasks or to cajole workers into speeding up, since these functions were built into the machines. Consequently, the role of foremen changed. They lost their power to fire workers outright and instead shifted their efforts to surveillance of the quality of work and to trouble-shooting technical problems on the assembly line.

In examining the wider implications of technical control and its developments since World War I, Edwards makes several additional points. Citing Braverman, he mentions the extension of technical control into white-collar work and into many areas not traditionally mechanized. He also notes that technical control continued certain trends initiated by hierarchical control. For example, like hierarchical control, technical control continued to homogenize the work force by means of deskilled jobs and to offer mainly negative sanctions. Since there are usually no piece rates on an assembly line (all work is at one pace), the only effective control is the fear of dismissal. As a result, the introduction of technical control was accompanied by spectacularly high quit rates. Management responded by paying high wages (Ford's famous five dollars per day) and by seeking a constant surplus of potential workers. Auto manufacturers were among the first to encourage southern rural blacks to move north (Maltese 1973).

Edwards believes that technical control did solve some of the problems of hierarchical control. It depersonalized and disguised the exercise of power by building control into the machines themselves and removing it from foremen, thus relieving some of the conflict between supervisors and workers. Nevertheless, the stress of assembly-line work continued to show up in high quit rates and absenteeism that even high wages could not mitigate. Also, technical control tended to generalize conflict in a factory. Since an entire assembly-line plant operates on a common rhythm and in sequence, the whole process can be instantly disrupted by one area stopping work. Industries based on technical control were and are highly susceptible to short sit-down or lightening strikes, and small groups of trade unionists can effectively dominate a plant by flaunting this threat. Nonetheless, technical control spread throughout American industry, and it continues to be a major control type in the core sector.

Edwards also develops the concept of a second kind of structural control—bureaucratic control—which has become increasingly important in industry in recent years. Although bureaucratic control is often used concurrently with technical control, Edwards regards it as an analytically separate phenomenon, a more advanced or modern type of control than the technical type. He argues that through a gradual shift, bureaucratic control now predominates.

Bureaucratic control differs from technical control in several ways. The advantage of technical control was that it routinized the management responsibility of defining and directing work tasks. However, technical control did not have as much impact upon two additional facets of organizational power: the need to supervise and evaluate, and the attempt to elicit worker compliance via rewards and punishments.

The significance of bureaucratic control is that it brings all three functions of managerial control—pacing and direction of work tasks, supervision/evaluation, and reward/punishment—into one integrated and predictable system. Bureaucratic control involves the manipulation of work behavior by means of detailed, written instructions and specified procedures. With regard to work tasks, bureaucratic control necessitates the detailed specification of each worker's responsibilities through explicit job descriptions and workplace rules. The principle is to spell out clearly all that is expected of a worker. Supervision and evaluation are similarly rendered predictable by formulating standard measurement procedures for judging workers' performances. Normally such procedures call for regular reviews by supervisors. According to Edwards (1979: 139), these evaluations stress adherence to rules and attitudes toward work as much as quantitative output.

Finally, the most dramatic advance embodied in the notion of bureaucratic control concerns employee compliance via rewards and punishments. In place of the basically negative sanctions of earlier control systems, bureaucratic control constructs an elaborate program of positive rewards, such as variable pay rates for the same job ("step levels"), elaborate job ladders accessible through promotion, and other material benefits. Negative sanctions are still present, but under bureaucratic control they also become rationalized. They flow strictly from a known body of regulations and are subject to formal grievance and appeal procedures.

It is unfortunate that in his treatment of bureaucratic control Edwards departs from his earlier model. He provides little historical data on the origins of bureaucratic control, and we therefore gain little sense of the history of the struggle and the consciousness of the actors involved in its formation. As a result, it is poorly integrated into his historical model of the development of processes of control. Although Edwards shows fairly well how hierarchical control grew in response to contradictions within entrepreneurial control and that technical control similarly stands as a response to certain problems of hierarchical control, he does not really do the same for bureaucratic control. What we need, then, is historical documentation of how and when bureaucratic control measures were adopted to overcome the failures of technical control.

There are other problems with Edwards's scheme. In particular, I believe that his separation of technical and bureaucratic control is forced and that he underemphasizes the role of unions in generating some of the features of bureaucratic control. He tends to view the latter system as originating at IBM and Polaroid in the postwar period. Yet we know that the "internal labor market"—the term that has come to designate the bureaucratic control system of job hierarchies, career ladders, and promotion from within—emerged as the only really successful strategy among the early experiments with welfare capitalism in the period 1901–1920. Senior workers did become more pliable under the incentive scheme of the internal labor market, and, unlike most welfare capitalism measures, the internal labor market was not abandoned after the late 1920s.

The elaborate system of placing workers at various pay steps, even for doing the same job, also originated prior to World War II. However, unionized sectors fought off this innovation. Unions modified bureaucratic control in several ways, most notably by insisting on seniority bidding rights for promotion systems, by fighting for rule-governed grievance procedures, and so forth.

Edwards's ideal type of bureaucratic control is modeled on certain non-unionized firms like IBM and Polaroid, which, in the absence of union opposition, were able to adapt earlier forms of bureaucratic control and elaborate them. Therefore, his model is somewhat strained, in that he wishes to associate technical control with the unionized mass-production industries and bureaucratic control with the high technology firms, and treat them as separate systems. However, they share important features. The auto industry does not depend on machine pacing alone; it also controls its work force through high pay and an elaborate promotion system, much as IBM does.

I am also skeptical of Edwards's insistence that bureaucratic control is applied to high-skill, craft, and professional jobs. In many ways, the elaborate evaluation systems of bureaucratic control, which emphasize rules orientation, dependability, thoroughness, and so on, are aimed at relatively low-level white-collar work and certain blue-collar tasks. Bureaucratic control provides an alternative system of evaluation for work where output is not easily measured (or machine paced) or where quality of output outweighs quantity. In such situations management is forced to focus on attitude and rules orientation because it has no more direct way of assessing worker performance. Such evaluation systems flourish in the white-collar worlds of banking, insurance, sales, and collections and affect workers from the lowly file clerk up to bottom management. They are by no means restricted to the highly skilled, as Edwards suggests.

These caveats apart, Edwards's book offers a powerful analysis of the evolution of systems of industrial control in the context of labor-management struggles. But he does not stop there. He goes on to integrate his theory of control mechanisms with that of labor market segmentation. At the most general level, Edwards (1979: 163) views the historical process of deskilling as having led to a relatively homogenized working class by the early 1900s. As a result, working-class militancy was high and socialist movements were relatively strong. However, subsequent changes in workplace organization, and especially the development of different forms of workplace control, have once again fragmented the work force, creating distinct labor markets and incorporating pre-existing racial and sexual divisions. The lines of fragmentation correspond to both the industrial control types and labor market segments.

Edwards (1979: 169–174) identifies three labor market segments: the secondary labor market, characterized by casual employment, low wages, and no income returns to on-the-job experience; a subordinate primary sector, involving repetitive, routinized, machine-paced work that is typically unionized, resulting in good wages, internal labor markets, and substantial returns to experience; and an independent primary sector containing white-collar workers as well as craftworkers and professionals. These segments correspond to the various control types. In fact, for Edwards, the control types bring about labor market segmentation.

Simple control involves direct surveillance and close supervision. It also implies a high degree of worker alienation and turnover. According to Edwards (1979: 179), the present-day secondary labor market corresponds to those relatively backward sectors of the economy that still operate on a simple control model: small manufacturers, service jobs, retail sales, temporary and typing-pool office work.

Historically, the mass production industries began by trying to take advantage of the secondary labor market. Thus in the early days technical control was accompanied by high worker turnover and low job security. However, unionization forced a compromise that resulted in the separation of the subordinate primary sector from the secondary labor market. Wages rose and turnover declined as the internal labor market developed its elaborate job ladders and high security. Nowadays, technical control coincides with the subordinate primary sector. Here one finds assembly-line work, other large-scale manufacturing, and machine-paced clerical work.

Edwards views bureaucratic control as the opposite of simple control. Instead of relying on punitive discipline and the reserve army of the unemployed, firms try to select and keep workers who evince a high sense of occupational or professional commitment and who will require relatively little supervision. This practice implies credentialism, a stable work force, and higher wages. Motivation is also generated by prospects for internal promotion. Bureaucratic control gives rise to the independent primary sector, encompassing craftwork, nonproduction staff jobs, and jobs in high technology firms like IBM and Polaroid.

Edwards has therefore provided a synthesis of the historical studies of the labor process and the studies of economic segmentation reviewed in Chapter Two. He strengthens the argument developed by Braverman, Marglin, and Stone that the history of the labor process and the firm cannot be understood in terms of functional prerequisites of technology or as a succession of more efficient techniques of production and administration. Rather, it is the outcome of the struggles between labor and management, of techniques of domination and control over the work force.

The Grand Synthesis

In their most recent work, David Gordon, Richard Edwards, and Michael Reich (1982) attempt a grand synthesis of theories of capital accumulation, labor markets, and the theory of the firm, drawing on the work of Edwards discussed above. They introduce the notion of "long swings": long-term periods of economic boom and decline that mark phases in capital accumulation. They have identified four long swings: from the 1790s to the mid-1840s; mid-1840s to late 1890s; late 1890s to World War II; and World War II to the present. They also develop the concept of "social structures of accumulation"—institutional arrangements between labor and capital that encourage capital accumulation. Included among the social structures of accumulation are labor markets and specific labor processes, as well as other economic institutions. The core of their book is a historical specification of the institutional arrangements and political struggles that constituted the various social structures of accumulation and caused the upswings and downswings of long waves.

Gordon et al. identify three periods that correspond to the long swings since the 1840s. First came a period of proletarianization. Initially, American capitalists faced a shortage of proletarian labor. After various experiments, mass immigration proved to be the basis of a new structure of accumulation, which set off a new boom in the mid-1840s. By the 1870s, however, problems had arisen with this structure of accumulation. Wages had begun to increase, but productivity remained stagnant, largely because craft labor resisted changes in the work process. Profits were therefore squeezed, and a long economic downturn began. This crisis was resolved by the introduction and spread of mechanization and by the defeat of craft unionism. By the late 1890s a new boom was under way as productivity and profits increased. But the destruction of craftwork led to a homogenization of the proletariat; semiskilled labor became the norm. The homogeneous nature of the work force encouraged trade unionism and working-class solidarity. These developments caused a decline in profits that led to an economic downswing (1918–1939). This crisis was solved in turn by the introduction of new institutional arrangements. Corporate acceptance of seniority systems, job ladders, and grievance procedures co-opted unionized labor in the core industries. Labor markets became segmented as unionized blue-collar work diverged from secondary labor markets on the one hand and professional labor on the other. This segmentation temporarily solved the problems of homogenization.

The underlying model is a dialectical one of crisis, boom, and decline. The cycle begins when social structures arise which are particularly propitious for capital accumulation. The resulting boom in investment and production sets off a new long swing of economic activity. After several decades, institutional problems, typically due to labor resistance, impede profitability. The long swing enters a decline phase. As stagnation continues, capitalists begin to experiment with new institutional arrangements, especially new ways of dealing with labor. Labor typically struggles against these innovations, but certain ones are eventually consolidated by capitalists. These conditions recreate an environment for profit making, and a new long swing of economic activity begins.

Work and Culture

The research by Gordon et al. represents the culmination of one theme in the radical study of the firm. We now turn to a quite different approach within the labor process literature, one that looks at group experiences outside of work for clues to unrest and/or acquiescence inside the workplace. Such research asks whether individuals' racial, class, or ethnic backgrounds have an impact on political consciousness as manifested at work. This is an important but neglected issue. Marxism has yet to address adequately the social origins of radicalism: Is a socialist consciousness generated by experiences at the point of production, or through participation in a radical community and nonwork culture?

Al Gedicks (1976) studied working-class activism in Western coal-mining towns during the nineteenth century. Since the mines in this period were the focus of intense struggles, they provided a good test case. Many of the workers in these mines were recent immigrants from rural Finland, and Gedicks questioned whether the miners' origins predicted their radicalism. He discovered that the mines with the greatest unrest had a high concentration of workers from districts in Finland where agricultural wage labor predominated. Finns from rural areas where peasants were self-employed smallholders were much less likely to be activists. Implicitly, the experience of wage labor in agrarian Finland built a socialist consciousness in a way that peasant production did not, and this consciousness was brought to America and into the new workplace.

Stanley Aronowitz (1974) discusses an analogous situation in the contemporary auto industry. In the 1960s the General Motors plant at Lordstown suffered from severe absenteeism and lateness problems. Workers were alienated and hostile toward management. Aronowitz argued that this was an age-specific phenomenon. Young workers, caught up in the relatively rebellious youth culture of the sixties, were much more alienated than their elders, who still maintained a culture that emphasized pride in one's work.

The overall implication of these studies is that Marxist scholarship needs to look at class formation as a cultural process outside of the workplace (cf. Bowles and Gintis 1976) and that specific variations in community, ethnicity, age, and race may prove essential in understanding variations in worker militancy and consciousness. This research agenda has not been widely adopted in the past, in part owing to a contrasting theoretical position, best exemplified by Burawoy (1978b).

Burawoy, using an Althusserian approach, views the realm of production as relatively autonomous: that is, it has a distinctive structure and dynamics. He does not consider workplace behavior to mirror external cultural concerns. On the contrary, he argues that the workplace socializes individuals regardless of their background or predispositions. After reviewing the Marxist theory of exploitation, Burawoy asks why workers typically accept work discipline and why they work as hard as they do. Based on his ethnographic research in a factory machine shop, he offers three answers. First, exploitation is obscured in capitalist production: there is no separation in time between work done for one's own wage and work done for the capitalist's profit. Unlike the feudal agrarian system, where the peasants worked several days on their own fields and then, at a different time and at a different place, tilled the lord's fields, under capitalism there is no visible or temporal demarcation of work done for oneself and work done for the capitalist. Hence exploitation is not self-evident. Second, Marx's assertion that workers and capitalists are engaged in a zero-sum struggle, that each can gain only at the other's expense, is not apparent in the workplace. In the context of expanding productivity, which presents an ever larger pie to be divided, the interests of capitalists and workers in the factory are parallel rather than contradictory. Subjectively, the personal interests of the individual worker are coordinated with those of the capitalist through productivity raises, piece rates, and greater fringe benefits.

A third facet of work life that encourages worker acquiescence involves the games workers play on the job. Burawoy seems to include in this category a variety of behaviors, the common feature of which is the exercise of personal autonomy. Whether a worker deliberately slows down his/her work pace, as in "soldiering"; whether he or she works extra rapidly in the morning in order to be able to slack off in the afternoon; or whether the worker takes pride in setting up some job in a particularly efficient manner—he or she is playing a game. Burawoy believes that the experience of such games, the manipulation of organizational structure for one's personal ends, gives rise to a subjective consciousness that allows the worker to accept the rules of the larger game (that he/she is a daily wage laborer) instead of rebelling. Thus games, in addition to productivity raises, help to co-opt workers into conforming to the capitalist industrial order. Burawoy also raises the issue of the proliferation of work rules and of grievance procedures in the modern factory. The worker is a pseudo-citizen under the rule of an impersonal factory law, which also tends to legitimate capitalist industry and increase workers' acceptance of the status quo.

Together, these features of capitalist production act to socialize workers within the workplace. For Burawoy, the immediacy of these experiences, combined with the pressures of supervision, erase any externally developed attitudes that a worker might bring to the factory. Everyone should be affected by these factors, irrespective of outside background. He tries to test this assertion statistically by analyzing workers' production levels using regression analyses with race, age, marital status, and education as predictors. For his argument to hold, external factors such as race and marital status should not lead to different production levels.

By and large, such analyses support Burawoy's hypothesis, although external factors do play a small but statistically significant role in explaining variations in production levels (1979: 147–148). These results lead him to reassert his thesis regarding the relative autonomy of the workplace and his opposition to analyses stressing the cultural factors behind worker resistance. He is nevertheless careful to qualify his position: his findings refer to worker response in *normal* capitalist production, not to extraordinary situations, such as during strikes or revolutionary upheavals.

Conclusion: Criticisms and Praise

In the sections above I have outlined several major lines of research literature. To simplify the presentation, I generally avoided interjecting my evaluation of the works under discussion. Here I shall consider the merits and faults of the labor process literature and locate it in my sociology of knowledge.

The deskilling thesis offers a powerful critique of the organization of work in contemporary America. Braverman's examples and the case studies undertaken by his followers fully convince me that the restructuring of work over the decades has led to routinization, a narrowing of tasks, and the loss of the conceptual part of work in many occupations. However, Braverman goes on to assert that deskilling is the foremost trend occurring across the whole economy and is resulting in a homogeneous unskilled proletariat.

My reading of the available empirical evidence leads me to disagree with this last point. Deskilling, though an important tendency, is balanced by a series of countervailing trends that destroy low-skill jobs and create higher-skilled ones. The most straightforward illustration of this observation is to be found in U.S. Census data. The proportion of higher-skilled labor (professional, technical, and crafts) has nearly doubled during this century, from 14.8 percent of the American labor force in 1900 to 28.8 percent in 1980. Other scholars interested in aggregate skill levels have also been unable to find evidence of overall deskilling (see Attewell 1982).

What trends balance the deskilling tendency, and why did Braverman miss them? First is the explosive growth of professional and technical labor during the twentieth century. Braverman mentions that as conceptual and manual work became separated, highly conceptual occupations came into existence. However, he downplays this point by suggesting that few workers are employed in such jobs (1974: 241–242) and that they do not belong to the working class. Yet 28 percent of the work force is too large a number to be dismissed so easily.

The second trend that Braverman neglects is the destruction of already deskilled jobs by automation. Braverman seems to suggest that the major effect of automation is to replace high-skill, craftlike jobs. This is not the typical case. Machines can easily replace standardized sequences of movements and simple perceptual tasks, but it is much harder to automate complex work that combines conceptual and execution tasks. Thus automation most easily replaces jobs that are already routinized and deskilled.

The proportion of high-skill jobs in the economy increases as automation destroys low-skill positions; at the same time, the professional/technical occupations expand. This current runs in the opposite direction from that observed by Braverman. Both currents exist; the relative strength of each is a matter for empirical study. I have reviewed the evidence as well as the theoretical issues in another paper (Attewell 1982). For most of the twentieth century, upgrading tendencies seem to have balanced deskilling ones. There has been no net deskilling in the industrial economy.

Beyond these issues, there is a problem with the way Braverman reads capital logic. The profit motive leads capitalists in an unceasing search for ways to increase productivity—that is, to reduce the costs of production per unit of output. But it is incorrect to suggest that replacing skilled labor with cheap detailed labor is the only or even the major way of achieving this. At certain places and times it does pay to deskill, but there are other ways of decreasing unit costs. As Marx described, the introduction of machinery dramatically reduces unit costs, gaining the innovative employer a "technological rent"—an extra margin of profit over his/her less mechanized competitors. Often it pays a capitalist to buy complex machines that require skilled support workers; the subsequent productivity increases are sufficiently large to pay for the higher-cost labor and still make a handsome profit. For example, in the contemporary micro-electronics industry, the introduction of automated bonding machines has eliminated low-paid jobs in Asian countries, and the bonding process has been repatriated to the United States. Bonding machines run by skilled technicians outcompete low-skill manual assembly in the Third World. Thus profit making does not dictate either a deskilling solution or an up-skilling solution. Capital is disinterested in skill; it chooses whichever strategem promises the greater profit (cf. Friedman 1977: 78–82).

In sum, the aggregate skill level of the American work force as a whole reflects a complex interaction of several processes: the relative growth rates of high-skill versus low-skill industrial sectors and occupations; the decisions of capitalists to raise productivity by increasing the division of labor or by introducing capital-intensive but highly efficient production processes; the changes in the import/export mix of the American economy, which affect what is produced here and what abroad; and so on. One cannot extract from this interplay (or from capital logic) one simple "master trend," as Braverman does.

To be sure, this criticism does not vitiate Braverman's critique of the many jobs that are deskilled or the numerous meaningless, deadening tasks performed by American workers. But his interpretation applies to only one part of the work force. Deskilling is not the fate of the work force as a whole. The proletariat is far from being the homogenous, unskilled mass that Braverman portrays.

Turning to the historical studies of Marglin, Stone, Noble, and the rest, I believe that these authors have succeeded in their initial task of demonstrating that the work process and institutional arrangements of the modern firm did not come about through the neutral workings of technological rationality or through market competition rewards to the most productive work process. They provide ample documentation that the history of capitalist enterprise in America is one of labor-management struggles, that technological change is an important weapon in these struggles, and that those who design new technologies are well aware of the need to address "the labor problem." In their enterprises these researchers have been greatly aided by the work of left-wing labor historians, including David Montgomery (1979), Herbert Gutman (1976), and Jeremy Brecher (1972).

I remain unsure, however, concerning their second conclusion: that by showing the capitalist context of the contemporary labor process and enterprise structure, they have demonstrated that industrial organization need not be this way. In account after account, following their evidence of the power struggles and interests that led to technological change, these authors also report the impressive increases in productivity that resulted. Marx's observation therefore still holds true: capitalism constantly extends the power of the forces of production and the productivity of social labor. An old dilemma remains: How can a society maintain such a high level of productivity without retaining the kind of labor process that capitalism has created? To use Michael Burawoy's felicitous phrase: How would "socialist machines" differ from capitalist ones? The present left literature on the labor process does not deal adequately with this issue, and so long as it fails to answer it, its critique of technology and the firm remains incomplete, always vulnerable to the retort: "How would you do it differently?"

I am an admirer of Richard Edwards's *Contested Terrain*. Although his discussion of control types is not news for industrial sociology, his book leaps well beyond that discipline by locating these types in historical contexts and proposing a dynamic movement from one type to the next. Previously, industrial sociologists had given wonderfully rich case studies of control systems within firms and impressive comparative analyses of control types (Etzioni 1961; Collins 1976). But this work remained in an ahistorical limbo until Edwards's book came along. I have discussed the weaknesses in some of the details of Edwards's work, but on the whole, I think his book has opened a new and fruitful approach to organizational theory.

The work of Gordon and his colleagues is also very important for locating changes in the structure of the firm in a historical context and for integrating the sequence of control types into the larger movement of proletarianization, homogenization, and segmentation. By syn-

thesizing the literature on the firm with that on labor market segmentation and long waves, they have created a powerful framework for integrating the various topics of radical political economy. I suspect that
their work will benefit from the careful scrutiny of economic historians. Their assertion that the period 1870–1920 witnessed the homogenization of labor remains contentious, and I have yet to be fully
convinced that the working population was more segmented in 1980
than in 1900. Their use of a dual core/periphery segmentation perspective also strikes me as unnecessarily crude. A more finely nuanced
analysis that identifies more than two industrial and occupational segments would, I believe, lead to a better understanding of the historical
processes they describe. However, these are minor reservations about a
richly textured and impressive analysis. I have no doubt that the book
will be very influential.

The analyses concerning the role of outside culture in workplace
behavior are still too few to afford any conclusions. Burawoy has
made a strong case for the "relative autonomy" of the workplace, but
other studies suggest the opposite, and much more research is needed.
Burawoy's work, in addition to its substantive contribution, points up
an important feature of many of the labor process studies: those aspects of the analysis of work that lead to the most successful moral-
evaluatory critiques of capitalism unfortunately tend to plunge the
theorist into pessimism concerning the potential for social change via
revolution. The same could not be said of Marx, of course. He argued
that the degradation of work will lead to the overthrow of capitalism
via the immiseration of the proletariat, the universalization of wage labor, and labor's increasing solidarity. But almost all of the factors once
thought to presage the fall of capitalism have been questioned by the
contemporary theorists of work. The notion of immiseration, for example fell out of favor as blue-collar wages rose in the post–World
War II expansion, and it has been replaced by a view that stresses the
conservative implications of working-class consumerism, repressive
desublimation, and the like (Marcuse 1964).

Braverman's analysis of deskilling, though trenchant as a critique,
shows little or no promise for social change. As a result, some reviewers assailed it for political pessimism. Though their point is well
taken, their own alternatives seem weak. The fragmentation of tasks
and the loss of the conceptual aspect of work would seem to leave little
room for finding material bases of political awareness in the workplace.

We do find some authors echoing the classical belief that, despite the degradation of work, capitalist industry also demands some kind of overall perception of the work process, which lays a material basis for future worker control of production. Gordon et al.'s formulation of this point was treated earlier. Coombs, having castigated Braverman for implying "that the domination of labor by capital within the labor-process is virtually complete," gives his own version of the classical position:

Simultaneously, these same relations of production create a working class which, as the degree of labor productivity increases, becomes a progressively more coherent and powerful collective laborer, *measured in terms of its objective ability to shoulder the task of organizing the administration of the entirety of society under the new social relations.* (1978: 94)

If one asks how this objective ability to organize the entirety of society is possible, in view of Braverman's interpretation of the fragmentation of conceptual and manual work, Coombs offers this answer:

The increased potential of the production process, its increasing complexity which renders it more susceptible to disruption by working-class action, and the progressive proletarianization of some of those who possess the technical knowledge to control it—all of these things objectively increase the collective power of the working class, despite the political obstacles to the implementation of that power. (1978: 94)

Thus the argument comes down to the possibility that those employees with sufficient technical knowledge to run the system are potentially allies of, if not part of, the proletariat.

If the degradation of work thesis tends to lead to pessimistic outcomes in terms of the political potential of workers, the few positions critical of Braverman's thesis leave even less room for revolt. We earlier discussed Kusterer's (1978a) argument that Braverman overstates deskilling and that residual areas of work skill and autonomy in work still exist in even the most routinized jobs. However, the political consequences of this island of autonomy in the sea of alienation are basically conservative. It is this small taste of pleasure that keeps workers relatively content with their lot, says Kusterer. Burawoy's position is similar, as we have seen.

My point in raising these perspectives on the labor process by

Coombs, Kusterer, and Burawoy is to reiterate an earlier argument concerning Marxist theorizing. In general, there is always the potential for tensions to occur between the moral-evaluatory aspects of any critique and its consequences for the larger body of Marxist theorizing. For the theory of the work process, such tensions appear endemic: the new formulations that seem to be most successful in terms of a moral-evaluatory critique of capitalism come into conflict with the wider theoretical framework of the theory of revolution. Success in the former tends to undermine traditional analyses in the latter and results in a politically pessimistic position. This pessimism is partially balanced by studies that point out the historical particularity of capitalist forms of work organization, in contrast to technological determinist perspectives, for they stress that work does not have to be this way. But in winning their theoretical point against technological determinism, the historical accounts of the labor process also undermine the theory of revolution. They all seem to breed a pessimism regarding the working class's defeat and its present cooperation in the most modern forms of work organization and managerial control. Nevertheless, each author feels compelled to include an analysis that (often via mental gymnastics) finds some way to reach a hopeful political conclusion.

Despite the tension between its moral-evaluatory dimension and its need to maintain the traditional paradigm regarding working-class revolution, contemporary labor process research does represent a return to the intellectual well-springs of Marxism. After decades of ambivalence regarding the American working class, of theories emphasizing its consumerism and one-dimensionality, of left-wing identification with the Third World, minorities, and women as surrogate proletariats, left scholars have resumed their interest in the situation of the American worker. The emphasis is on alienation rather than exploitation—because of capitalism's destruction of work as creative activity, because of the splitting of conception from execution, and because of workers' loss of control over their job processes. (An exploitation analysis would focus on workers' loss of their product, their economic loss.)

The literature we have reviewed epitomizes the intertwining of Marxism as moral critique and as analysis. With the one exception noted above, there is relatively little tension between the two: the deskilling critique is so much a part of the traditional Marxist paradigm that there is no need to bend the paradigm to allow for the critique.

Similarly, little or no strain is apparent between the goal of explaining current events and that of paradigm maintenance. Braverman's success derives from his ability to reapply Marx to contemporary occupations and the demise of skill in the twentieth century.

In style and orientation, the labor process literature illustrates our earlier comments about the close relationship between left scholarship and its nonradical twin. The radical work is scholarly and employs the entire methodological arsenal of the social sciences, including historical studies, ethnographic case studies, and statistics. The left work has not yet had the same impact on the wider disciplines of economics and sociology as the segmentation research described in the previous chapter, but there can be no doubt that radical analysis of the labor process is growing steadily more impressive as the years pass.

Chapter Four

CRISIS THEORY

CRISIS THEORY HAS ALWAYS occupied center stage in Marxist political economy, and little wonder, for economic crises have surely provided some of the more dramatic moments in capitalist history. For over two centuries the capitalist economies have suffered repeated paroxysms, causing commerce to slow to a crawl, throwing millions out of work, and often leaving governments teetering on the brink. On each such occasion since the 1850s, Marxists have been there, listening intently, waiting for the patient's last breath. Time after time the patient has recovered, sending Marxist economists back to their treatises, puzzling over the resilience of capitalism, yet still sure that the end must come.

Out of these reflections there have emerged several analyses of the crisis tendencies of the capitalist economies. In this chapter we shall review the major variants of crisis theory from Marx to the present period. I preface the analysis by defining the concept of crisis and linking it to notions of economic breakdown, social upheaval, and revolution. Then I outline several types of crisis theory, seeking to explain the logic of each position while deliberately avoiding discussions of where the theory came from, why and by whom it was created. In a third section I give a history of crisis theory (or theories), thus providing a context for the positions presented in the previous section. In the fourth and final section I draw some lessons from the history and from theory itself in terms of the sociology of knowledge framework developed in Chapter One.

What Are Crises?

For Marxists, the cycle of production—selling goods, reinvesting profits in new machines and a larger work force, and producing more goods—is not just an economic process: it is also a social one. Investment involves employing more workers on more machines and is therefore a reproduction and expansion of social relationships and social roles. The constant cycle of production is also a cycle of socialization—of workers coming to factories, of the daily recreation of the forms of activity and consciousness that keep capitalism going.

Approached from this vantage point, the significance of economic crises in the Marxist framework becomes clearer (Wright 1975: 6). If capital accumulation falters, so does the reproduction of capitalist socialization. Unemployment rises, and consequently worker consciousness is no longer generated in the daily interaction with capital that occurs in the workplace. The downturns of the capitalist economy are therefore not simply recessions, depressions, or slumps. They are crises of *social reproduction*, moments when capitalism stops reproducing itself.

However, it is a long distance, both theoretically and in reality, from an economic crisis to a political revolution, and although this link is implied in Marxist writings, it is not spelled out. All the theorists reviewed below believe that crises are a necessary and chronic feature of capitalist economies. At this point, however, agreement ends as to the mechanism linking recessions to political change. Without suggesting that the economy itself need get worse and worse over time, some writers imply that each downturn exacerbates the polarization of classes and provides further impetus for the socialist cause. Others, most notably Marx and Engels (1972: 41) in their earlier writings, anticipate a series of ever more extensive and destructive economic crises whose political ramifications become successively more severe. The most extreme position, known as breakdown theory, sees economic downturns intensifying over time until the capitalist economy grinds to a total halt, which precipitates or at least allows for a proletarian revolution (cf. Sweezy 1942: 190–209).

In short, the all-important question of whether the end of capitalism occurs via the indirect effect of successive economic downturns on wider socio-political forces or via a cataclysmic economic breakdown is left unanswered, a question mark at the center of Marxist theory. Instead we are given ambiguous formulations, such as this one from Marx and Engels:

In the face of this general prosperity, in which the productive forces are developing as exuberantly as is possible within the framework of bourgeois relations, it is not possible to talk of a real revolution. Such a revolution is possible only in periods in which these two factors—namely, modern productive forces and bourgeois forms of production—come into contradiction with one another. . . . A new revolution is possible only as a result of a new crisis. It is as inevitable as is the latter. (Quoted in Mandel 1971: 68–69)

Granting the indeterminacy of this position, we shall now turn to the crises themselves. Here observation and theory are much more complete, and we can present a simplified typology of the various causes that have been proposed for economic crises.

A Typology of Crisis Theories

There is no "official" crisis theory within Marxism, only an assortment of theories. The reason for this pluralism is that the object is not to describe what crises are but to determine the causes of crises and how these causes produce economic contractions. This leaves considerable room for debate, since what one theorist views as a cause of crises, another theorist considers a symptom or effect of some more basic causal factor. Marxism also has its pluralists and its monists: some theorists believe that several distinct causal mechanisms produce crises, whereas others hold that there is one and only one cause.

We shall draw five ideal types of crisis theory: disproportionality theory; underconsumption theory; theories based upon the rising organic composition of capital; theories based on rising wages; and the theory of the fiscal crisis of the state.[1] Disproportionality theory and underconsumption theory are sometimes subsumed under the term "realization crises." Profit is viewed as embodied in commodities, but it

---

1 The reader should note that these theories are often referred to in the literature as disproportionality *crises*, underconsumption *crises*, and so on. These are misnomers; the point is not that there are different kinds of crises but that theories differ on the causes of crises.

cannot be "realized" until those commodities are sold. Thus, a glut of commodities may result in a crisis if capitalists cannot realize profits embodied in (unsold) goods. Theories based upon the rising organic composition of capital and upon rising wages can be similarly subsumed under the label "falling rate of profit crises," since both are claimed to produce a falling rate of profit (Sweezy 1942: 153).

Disproportionality Theory

Given that capitalism is an unplanned economy, business people are left to decide themselves what volume of goods to produce such that all may be profitably sold. An incorrect decision in one factory does not simply affect the one manufacturer immediately concerned. Capitalists are linked in buyer-seller chains. Entrepreneur A sells products and then buys new raw materials from industrialist B, who will then buy goods from C in order to start a new production run, and so on. If A finds that s/he has overproduced, such that his/her product cannot be sold at a profit, s/he will probably cut back future production, thus causing B to cut back, and so on. As workers in these businesses are laid off, they curtail their purchases of goods, causing goods in other areas of the economy to go unsold and resulting in further layoffs. A system-wide crisis may result if these cutbacks are severe enough or if the industries concerned are major ones in the economy. Thus the "anarchy of production"—the fact that decisions on how much to produce are made without knowledge of the overall requirements of the system—may cause a crisis through disproportionate production of goods among the various units of industry.

A more systematic version of disproportionality theory concentrates on the relationship between two particular sectors of the economy: "Department One," which manufactures producer or capital goods (machinery and intermediary products), and "Department Two," which produces finished consumer goods ("wage goods"). For an economy to avoid crises of disproportionality, there must be some kind of balance between the amount of goods produced by Department One and the need for such goods in Department Two. Likewise, the outputs of Department Two must match the need for those goods in Department One.

The tenuousness of this balance is exacerbated by the fact that capitalism is a system of expanding commodity production; therefore

Departments One and Two are growing. To avoid crisis, the rate of investment in Department One, which determines its growth, must be in balance with the investment in and rate of growth of Department Two. Only under these conditions will the inputs and outputs of the two departments match in the future. The problem, then, is to balance both present and future production of the two sectors.

Disproportionality theory notes that a balance between these two sectors of the economy is possible theoretically. It does not argue for a systematic or chronic imbalance between enterprises or industrial sectors. But given the dispersal of investment decisions among hundreds of thousands of industrialists, it is likely that random imbalances will occur frequently. Though some will be completely trivial, others will trigger a series of cutbacks that can spiral into major economic recessions in an interrelated economy. Disproportionality theory therefore views the capitalist economy as a house of cards. The anarchy of production and investment decisions will generate shocks, guaranteeing that at some point the structure will fail.

Underconsumption Theory

Certain superficial similarities can be seen between underconsumption theory and disproportionality theory. However, the two are conceptually distinct. Underconsumption theory posits a *systematic long-term imbalance* between supply and demand in the economy, one that is not related to specific goods or to the anarchy of decision making. It deals with the balance of aggregate supply and aggregate demand in the economy, suggesting that the former consistently outstrips the latter.

Michael Bleaney (1976), in his definitive history of underconsumptionist thought, distinguishes two versions of the theory. One, dating back to Sismondi and Robertus, emphasizes that capitalism produces and reproduces a mass of relatively poor proletarians and a few rich capitalists. Because of this relative poverty, the workers' ability to buy mass-produced consumption goods consistently falls behind the available supply, thus causing a tendency toward overproduction, realization problems, and stagnation.

A second variant, most notably represented by Malthus, concentrates on the money held by capitalists. Since capitalists cannot hope to consume all of their income by buying goods, there is a danger of capitalist oversaving, which results in underconsumption of the goods currently available and hence a realization crisis. Capitalists cannot free themselves from this bind by investing their savings, thought Malthus, because such investment simply expands the productive power of industry and widens further the gap between supply and effective demand.

Finally, a third version of underconsumption theory hypothesizes a chronic imbalance in demand between Department One and Department Two.

Marxists who adhere to underconsumption theories quote the passage in *Capital* where Marx appears to endorse the Sismondian view:

> The last cause of all real crises always remains the poverty and restricted consumption of the masses as compared to the tendency of capitalist production to develop the productive forces in such a way that only the absolute power of consumption of the entire society would be their limit. (Marx 1967c: 484)

Capitalism is crisis-prone because individual capitalists tend to reinvest profits into industry, hence increasing productive capacity, while they simultaneously try to cut the costs of production by lowering or holding down their workers' wages. Aggregated across an entire economy, these practices lead to a chronic tendency to produce beyond the effective demand. Such a tendency can manifest itself in one of two ways: either production will continue, resulting in periodic gluts of commodities and crises of realization, or gluts may be anticipated and production cut back, resulting in long bouts of stagnation in which factories operate at some small proportion of their potential capacity. This is the core of underconsumptionist theory.

Marxist theoreticians often argue that underconsumption results from insufficient or restricted markets for goods. It follows that if a capitalist nation could find new markets, the crises of overproduction/underconsumption might be avoided, at least temporarily. (Here we see a link to one variety of imperialism theory.)

The second version of underconsumptionism (attributed to Malthus) may also be viewed as a market problem. Here the focus is upon the capitalists and oversaving. The issue for capitalists becomes where to invest the saved capital. Since existing markets are viewed as already overproductive, given the inadequate demand, one would not want to invest in them and exacerbate the situation. But if one could find new investment markets, then the capital underconsumption problem might be solved. (Here is the link to an alternative variety of imperialism theory.)

We shall be dealing with the specific theorists associated with these underconsumptionist positions in the next historical section. However, we should note at this point that Marx himself occasionally appeared to deny the relevance of underconsumptionism to crises:

> It is pure tautology to say that crises are caused by the scarcity of solvent consumers, or of a paying consumption . . . but if one were to attempt to clothe this tautology with a semblance of a pro-founder justification by saying that the working class receive too small a portion of their own product, and the evil would be reme-died by giving them a larger share of it, or raising their wages, we should reply that crises are precisely always preceded by a period in which wages rise generally and the working class actually gets a larger share of the annual product intended for consumption. From the point of view of the advocates of "simple" (!) common sense, such a period should rather remove a crisis. (Quoted in Bleaney 1976: 108)

Here Marx seems to contradict his earlier remarks that it is a restric-tion in workers' consumption vis-à-vis the supply of goods that pre-cipitates a crisis. If worker demand is going up just before the crisis strikes, we must look beyond underconsumption for an explanation of the onset of the crisis.

Rising Organic Composition Theory

In non-Marxist terminology organic composition is analogous to the capital intensiveness of economic production. Rising organic composi-tion is therefore analogous to a shift from labor-intensive to capital-intensive techniques—for example, mechanization.[2] Over time, the in-crease in the organic composition is said to lead to a fall in the rate of profit of business, hence triggering an economic contraction. The ris-

---

2 This explanation is simplified, since the issue does not hang on an increase in the number or size of machines as objects but depends upon the capital that is used in the production process, especially the ratio between that capital expended on machines, raw materials, etc. ("fixed capital") and that capital expended on wages ("variable capital"). In both cases the capital is conceived of in value terms, not in price terms.

ing organic composition argument involves two steps: first one must demonstrate that systematic forces exist that cause a rise in organic composition over time. One then needs to prove that this rise necessitates a fall in the rate of profit. Much of this argument is usually presented algebraically. To avoid the mathematics, I shall have to simplify the argument a little.

A capitalist introduces new machinery because s/he hopes to increase productivity, to produce items at a lower unit cost than previously. By mechanizing, a capitalist may produce certain goods much faster and more cheaply than competitors who are still using an older, less efficient technology that is more labor intensive. So long as the market price for the goods is fixed by the old, less productive technique, the innovative capitalist will make extra profits and be able to undercut competitors. This profit is a sufficient incentive to stimulate capitalists to introduce new and better machines whenever possible.

Once the new, more capital-intensive technique is generally adopted, the price of the goods involved will fall to reflect the new realities of productivity, putting the innovative manufacturer back where s/he started. However, the industry is now more capital intensive (less labor intensive) than before. The cycle repeats itself: a manufacturer considers introducing even more machinery in order to cut costs of production again. Generalized across the economy, there is a continual tendency for the average organic composition of capital to rise.

The next step concerns the impact of this steadily increasing organic composition upon capitalists' rate of profit. Those who support the theory argue that as the organic composition of capital increases, there is a tendency for the general rate of profit to fall.[3] This tendency can be offset temporarily in several ways. The exploitation of workers may be increased by cutting wages or by making employees work harder or lengthening hours. It may also be offset by opening up industries that are labor rather than capital intensive. Since the falling rate of profit takes place at the system-wide level, the effects of industries that have

---

3 It is impossible to explain how a rising organic composition leads to a falling rate of profit without explaining the whole labor theory of value—an effort that would take us too far from our path. Interested readers should refer to Mandel (1968), Wright (1975), Yaffe (1973), and Cogoy (1973) for successively more complex explanations of the falling rate of profit. Lebowitz (1976 and 1982) contends that their arguments are faulty and that the falling rate is not a necessary outcome; Hodgson (1974) and Van Parijs (1980) agree.

a high organic composition may be neutralized by others with a low composition. Cheapening other costs of production, such as raw materials and machinery, may also help to keep up the rate of profit. However, adherents of the theory believe that these counter-tendencies are only temporary.

How is rising organic composition (which leads to what Marx called "the law of the falling tendency of the rate of profit") related to economic crises? Proponents of the theory argue both cyclical and secular versions. In the cyclical version, a fall in the general rate of profit will send weak enterprises into bankruptcy; other enterprises will be unwilling or unable to invest, and hence demand for capital goods will decline. As realization problems emerge and workers are laid off, the economy enters the recession side of a business cycle. In this cyclical version, the recession restores the general rate of profit, in part by lowering the organic composition and in part by lowering wages.[4] The economy takes off again, only to repeat the whole cycle of boom and bust.

In the secular version of the theory, successive crises due to the falling rate of profit become worse and worse, since the organic composition of capital keeps rising over a series of business cycles. Thus the profit rate steadily declines, bringing the economy to the verge of collapse owing to insufficient investment and consequent overproduction.

One should note that the falling rate of profit crisis finally appears in a form similar to that described by underconsumption theory: there are gluts of unsold goods, workers are laid off, and so on. But underconsumption is viewed as a *consequence* of capitalists' cutbacks due to the falling rate of profit, rather than as a causal factor in its own right.

Marx presented the falling rate of profit theory in volume three of *Capital* (1967c). It has since been modified and elaborated by others.[5] Nevertheless, the theory has been attacked by Marxists at almost every point. Critics have suggested that there is no necessary increase in the organic composition and that, empirically, no such rise is evident; that

---

4 Stock prices fall in recessions. Such a statement in fact means that the value of corporate assets falls, including the value of their fixed capital. So, although the number of machines does not decrease, their value vis-à-vis variable capital is lessened, which is equivalent to a lowering of the organic composition. The new return on the devalued capital is better, and the rate of profit rises. Capital is also devalued more directly in recessions: companies go bankrupt, machines and goods are sold off cheaply, and so on.

5 See the references in note 3 above.

a rising organic composition, even if it does occur, does not logically necessitate a falling rate of profit and that empirical study shows no decline in the rate; that the so-called counter-tendencies are not just temporary but are as permanent as the tendency of the falling rate itself, thus effectively annulling it; and that contemporary alterations in the structure of capitalist enterprise, especially the growth in the service/bureaucracy sector, the growth in monopoly, and the involvement of the state, all render the law inoperative.

In sum, this type of crisis theory is at one and the same time the most widely accepted and the most widely criticized. We shall discuss some of these debates later, after completing our review of the theories themselves.

Rising Wage Theory

Rising wage theory (also known as neo-Ricardian and profit-squeeze), like rising organic composition, posits a mechanism that drives down the rate of profit, thus precipitating an economic crisis. However, its adherents argue that rising wages are the source of the profit squeeze. Cyclical and secular (long-term) variants of the theory are associated with different authors.

The logic of this position is simple. The cyclical version hypothesizes that as an economic cycle progresses, more and more investment occurs and increasing numbers of workers are hired. At some point, this expansion brings about a shortage of labor in general, as the army of the unemployed is depleted, and especially certain kinds of skilled labor. This shortage enables workers to bargain their wages higher, and wages rise significantly toward the end of the boom, just before the contraction begins (as Marx noted in an earlier quotation). These wage increases cut into profits and make further expansion very expensive. As the rate of profit begins to fall, investors cut back and stop expanding production. Demand declines across the whole economy, precipitating a crisis.

The secular version of this theory was developed with Britain in mind. It suggests that British capitalists are caught between international competition on the one hand and a powerful unionized work force on the other. Unions have succeeded in increasing wages beyond productivity gains, and intense international competition prevents capitalists from passing on these additional costs by raising prices. The lack of profitability leads to a slowdown in new investment, which brings about a long stagnation crisis.

It is a matter of dispute whether Marx accepted this type of wage-based profit squeeze. Those who support the theory quote one passage to legitimate their position (Marx 1967a: 620), but their opponents counter with another quotation:

> The tendency of the falling rate of profit is accompanied by a rising tendency of the rate of surplus value, that is, the rate of exploitation. Nothing is more absurd, for this reason, than to explain, a fall in the rate of profit by a rise in the rate of wages, although there may be exceptional cases when this may apply. (Quoted in Sherman 1976b: 28)

The Fiscal Crisis of the State

Another theory argues that in contemporary capitalist societies certain economically induced crises manifest themselves as fiscal crises of the state. Economic crises are displaced, so to speak, into the political realm. The core of this theory (O'Connor 1973) is that governments attempt to solve the problems of the capitalist economy by supporting unemployed and retired workers, by subsidizing businesses through government purchases and tax breaks, and by following Keynesian models of spending during economic downturns. However, someone has to pay for this spending, and business has sufficient political power to hold down its taxation burden. The result is a government caught between increasing demands for services and a static tax base. City, state, and federal governments are pushed toward bankruptcy or large-scale borrowing ("deficit financing") as they attempt to maintain services without sufficient tax income. The details of this process will be discussed in a later section.

The five varieties of crisis theory discussed above are ideal types. Individual theorists often differ on details, and some incorporate elements of more than one type. We shall now go on to consider the historical origins of the theories in the light of our sociology of knowledge interests. The theories will be linked to individuals, and we shall try to answer the difficult questions of why certain theories appeared when they did and how their appeal or lack of appeal can be explained. This exploration will lead us to a discussion of contemporary American Marxists and their relationship to these theories.

On the History of Crisis Theory

Marx and Engels

Economic crises were such dramatic features of mid-nineteenth-century life that they could hardly have escaped the notice of polymaths like Marx and Engels. Indeed, one finds discussions of economic crises throughout their early works: in the *1844 Manuscripts* and in *The Condition of the Working Class in England*, *The Poverty of Philosophy*, *The Communist Manifesto*, and *The German Ideology* (Mandel 1971: 69).[6] However, their major conceptual work on crises did not begin until shortly after the failure of the European uprisings of 1848. The timing was not coincidental: the revolutions of 1848 closely followed a major economic recession in 1847, and it was this event that cemented the intimate relationship between revolution and economic crises in the minds of Marx and Engels. In 1850 the collaborators began publishing retrospective studies of the economy from 1836 to 1850, plunging for the first time into the minutiae of credit, trade, and production data in an attempt to trace the development of an economic cycle.

It is difficult to juxtapose this image of Marx and Engels laboring over stacks of data, trying to unlock the logic of cycles and their periodicity, with the subsequent comments of twentieth-century Hegelianized Marxists. Trent Schroyer (1972: 106–125), writing on *Marx' Theory of the Crisis*, assures us that Marx was building a "genetic-historical phenomenology," to which the notion of empirical prediction was alien. The reality is more prosaic: between 1850 and 1857 Marx and Engels followed the movements of credit, prices, and the like, testing their initial understanding by means of a series of (largely unsuccessful) predictions. As Ernest Mandel tells us, the two forecasters incorrectly predicted slumps in 1852, 1853, and 1855. Finally, in 1857 they hit the mark, and Engels proclaimed "a magnificent crash" (Man-

---

6 My description of the origins of Marx and Engels' crisis theory is drawn from chapter 5 in Mandel (1971).

del 1971: 69–77). Subsequent detailed empirical analyses of the 1857–1858 crash enabled them to predict the periodicity of cycles in terms of the renewal of fixed capital and to assemble their general analysis of the business cycle. At the culmination of these studies in 1857, Marx wrote: "The present commercial crisis has induced me to devote myself now to close study of the fundamental features of the economy, and also to preparing something about this present crisis" (quoted in Mandel 1971: 79). The *Grundrisse* was begun in that year, followed in 1858–1859 by *A Contribution to the Critique of Political Economy* and thereafter by *Capital*.

Although the origins of Marxist crisis theory lie in the period 1850–1862, its transmission to the wider intellectual community proved to be a slow and tortuous process. Indeed, the twists and turns of subsequent crisis theory can be understood in part by realizing that Marx's clearest exposition on the subject, *Theories of Surplus Value* (especially Part 2), was not published until 1905–1910. Volume three of *Capital*, with its discussion of the law of the falling tendency of the rate of profit, first appeared in 1894, long after Volume two (1886) and its ambiguous references to underconsumptionism. The intellectual world received Marx's crisis theory in dribs and drabs, and, as we shall see, a good forty years passed before his overall conception was understood.

Russia (1860–1900)

Surprisingly, the first innovative uses (or misuses) of Marx's technical political-economic writings occurred in semifeudal Russia. The irony was not lost on Marx that his work was more enthusiastically received there than in many "advanced" nations. But the political situation in Russia was very volatile, and Marx and Engels were drawn into the intellectual and political debates of early Russian socialism.

Of particular relevance to crisis theory are the works of two economic writers of the "legal populist" movement, Vorontsov and Nikolayon.[7] (The latter translated the first volume of *Capital* into Russian.) Both theorists settled on the issue of whether capitalism could survive and grow in the context of Russia. Using underconsumptionist logic

---

7 In characterizing the economic theories of the Russian legal populists and their legal Marxist debators, I have drawn primarily from Luxemburg (1951), Jacoby (1975), Bleaney (1976), and Sweezy (1942).

and analyses based on Sismondi, Robertus, and Marx, they sought to show that capitalism could not exist for long in Russia because of an absence of markets. According to Rosa Luxemburg (1951: 279–281), this argument was derived from the first volume of Marx's *Capital*, especially the notion that workers cannot afford to buy all the available commodities because they are paid only a fraction of the value of the commodities they produce. This situation would result in a permanent excess of consumer goods.

This was the core of the Russian legal populists' analysis. They concluded that capitalism in Russia would suffer from a chronic underconsumption crisis. The bourgeoisie had no need of these mundane goods. Nor could the surplus goods be absorbed by the Russian peasantry, who had suffered disastrous income losses as capitalist industrial products replaced the peasant goods formerly sold to city dwellers. Furthermore, Marx had predicted the immiseration of the proletariat and the tendency toward mechanization and displacement of workers, both of which implied that the home market would shrink rather than expand. Finally, since Russia came late into the imperialist race for colonies, it lacked the external markets to which surplus products could be exported. Thus their reading of *Capital* in terms of the particular situation of Russia showed the legal populists that capitalism could not survive and spread in Russia. The paucity of internal and external markets would impede the expansion of those capitalist concerns already operating and inhibit entrepreneurs from opening new businesses.

The populist analyses were important as the first "foreign" attempts to adapt Marxist political economy to the analysis of a new phenomenon (namely, the appearance of capitalist production in Russia). They also led to an early association between Marxism and the underconsumptionist version of crisis theory.

The critics of the legal populist position came from another section of the Russian intelligentsia, the "legal Marxists," whose leading figures were Struve, Bulgakov, and Tugan-Baranowski. Though much of their attack on legal populism involved an empirical demonstration that capitalism had already taken a firm hold in Russia,[8] they too resorted to political economy to forge an argument.

The most influential of these figures at the time was Michael Tugan-

---

8 See Lenin's *The Development of Capitalism in Russia* (1967), a work in the legal Marxist tradition, intended to demonstrate that capitalism had taken a firm hold in Russia.

Baranowski, whose works appeared in Russian from 1894 on and were later published in German as *Studies on the Theory and History of Commercial Crises in England* (1901) and *Theoretical Foundations of Marxism* (1905). In debating the populists over whether capitalism could survive and prosper in Russia, Tugan-Baranowski was one of the first Russians to articulate the entirety of Marx's crisis theory. From the second volume of *Capital*, Tugan-Baranowski drew upon Marx's reproduction schemata. These consist of two equations, one for Department One (the capital goods sector) and another for Department Two (the wage goods sector), that describe the inputs (variable and constant capital, plus surplus value) of two industrial sectors and their outputs (the value of goods produced). The inputs of one equation become the outputs of the other and must therefore match. The reproduction schemata represent a significant intellectual advance because they enable one to consider the apportionment of value (investment) in the two sectors, the subsequent division of that value into wages and machinery, and the output. One can model one or more cycles of capitalist production and see how products produced by one department become inputs in the other and how the surplus produced during each cycle is reinvested.

Armed with this simplified model of capitalist production, Tugan-Baranowski contested the populists' underconsumptionist/limited markets view. For them, the problem appeared to be that capitalists would not spend all their money on goods and that the proletarians lacked the means to purchase the entirety of goods produced. The reproduction schema enables one to see this position as a misconceptualization of the problem. The excess goods produced over and above the consumption needs of the proletariat are bought by the capitalists, but not for their own consumption. Capitalists invest their surplus, which in real terms means that they purchase capital goods and consumer goods, which they then advance to their workers for subsistence in the next round of production. (The fact that they advance wages to the workers who then buy the consumer goods themselves does not alter the logic.) So in fact, as long as capitalists plow back the surplus into investments by expanding their factories and work forces, unsold goods and underconsumption are not inevitable. Investment expands the "impoverished" home market by setting new people and machines to work.[9]

---

9 This critique of underconsumptionism and of the apparent market problem stands today (cf. Bleaney 1976: 117–118). It can be readily demonstrated using the reproduction schema (with numerical examples if necessary) that the surplus product can be

Thus Tugan-Baranowski, applying Marx's theory, explained why capitalism had survived in Russia and was expanding. He did not stop there but examined other forms of crisis mechanisms through the heuristic device of the schemata. He also showed that the rising organic composition/falling rate of profit argument was erroneous (though he used numerical examples that in retrospect are seen to be unacceptable; cf. Dobb 1937: 101).

Having critiqued both underconsumptionism and the falling rate of profit, Tugan-Baranowski had all but disproven the necessity of crises under capitalism. As Rosa Luxemburg put it:

> There can be no doubt that the "legalist" Russian Marxists achieved a victory over their opponents, the "populists," but that victory was too thorough. In the heat of battle, all three—Struve, Bulgakov, and Tugan-Baranowski—overstated their case. The question was whether capitalism in general, and Russian capitalism in particular, is capable of development; these Marxists, however, proved this capacity to the extent of even offering theoretical proof that capitalism could go on forever. (1951: 325)

Luxemburg's remarks are a little misleading, for these arguments did not lead the legal Marxists into repudiating crises as such but only two mechanisms of crisis. In their place, Tugan-Baranowski developed a theory—again around the reproduction schema—of the inevitability of disproportionality crises. Since we reviewed the logic of this theory earlier, we need only recall that, although the schema indicate that the inputs and outputs of Departments One and Two can balance, the realities of capitalist decision making suggest that they often will not. Hence the imbalances trigger crises, as overproduced goods remain unsold.

This disproportionality theory developed by the legal Marxists was to be adopted by Lenin and the Bolsheviks, and it influenced Austrian and German theorists as well. A version of underconsumption theory also reappeared in Bolshevik writings (Jacoby 1975: 11–16). Nevertheless, for a substantial period disproportionality was *the* major theory of crisis for eastern European Marxists.

---

reinvested indefinitely. The only problem with this demonstration, if indeed it is a problem, is that one has to accept that capitalists will want to keep reinvesting a substantial share of their profits and will have some reason for expanding production indefinitely. It is around this point that debate followed.

Germany and Austria (1890–1914)

The death of Marx in 1883 and of Engels in 1895 left the socialist movement without its leading intellectuals and with a mass of manuscripts as its major guide to the future. The initial response was to use the writings of Marx and Engels as revolutionary gospels. Engels had earlier complained about the treatment of "writings and letters of Marx . . . exactly as if they were texts from the classics or from the New Testament" (quoted in Jacoby 1975: 8). But that was exactly what happened.

Several new developments demanded theoretical attention. The first, especially after 1870, centered on the spectacular electoral successes of socialist parties, especially in Germany. The second encompassed the rapid changes in the structure of capitalist industry, including the spread of monopolies and cartels, a general increase in the size of enterprises, and, most important, shifts in credit and corporate law leading to the proliferation of joint-stock companies and massive financial conglomerates. The third area of change involved the continued expansion of the European powers into the Third World, as Germany, France, and other nations vied with Britain and one another to create empires. It should be added that none of these phenomena was new in a qualitative sense; all had been present in some degree before 1890. But their greater prominence cried out for new analysis.

By and large, orthodox theorists responded to these events by letting reality drift gently away from theory or by turning to Engels's comments upon these phenomena. Until 1895 he acted as Marx's rearguard, adding analyses concerning new developments, especially in the introductions and afterwards that he wrote to various editions of Marx's works. Engels had noted the significance of electoral socialism and the need to revise tactics away from the uprisings of 1789 and 1848 to conform to the realities of mass left parties and modern standing armies (Colletti 1974: 45–48). He had also attempted to understand the twin issues of monopoly and imperialism, posing a question that came to the fore again in the 1960s. Did the rise of European industry in competition with the then dominant British economy indicate a reversion to competitive capitalism or an extension of the concentration and centralization of capital (Colletti 1974: 57–58; cf. Mandel 1970)?

Nevertheless, despite Engels's insights into the 1890s, based on his and Marx's earlier work, the era demanded new evaluation. As Lucio

Colletti documents, the long depression of 1873–1895 pushed laissez-faire capitalism to the wall. Protectionism replaced free trade, and an ambivalence regarding colonialism gave way to rampant imperialism (Colletti 1974: 58–72). These were the events that late-nineteenth-century Marxist theoreticians were forced to explain.

It took a new generation to respond to these events, and even then it needed the barbs of non-Marxists and the most eminent Marxist revisionist of them all, Eduard Bernstein, to set the debates rolling. In 1896 and 1897 Bernstein wrote his celebrated (now infamous) articles in the German Socialist party journal *Die Zeit*, in which he contrasted Marx's predictions with the reality of the post-1895 economic boom. A theoretical challenge to Marxist theory appeared in Eugen von Böhm-Bawerk's *Karl Marx and the Close of His System* (1896), and from 1894 on, Tugan-Baranowski published his refutations of much of Marxist crisis theory. Together these works shook every inch of Marxist political-economic terrain. Paradoxically, they thereby stimulated the first wave of post-Marxian political economy. By far the most influential and fundamental of these critiques was Bernstein's, so let us examine his work first.[10]

Though a revisionist in theory, Bernstein intended not to change the practice of German social democracy but to rid it of its revolutionary "metaphysic"—Marx's theory of class polarization, crisis, and revolution—which Bernstein saw as having little relationship to the reality of post-1870 Germany. Using census and other empirical materials, he disputed Marx's model and belief that the classes would become increasingly polarized in wealth; that the petty bourgeoisie was being forced into the proletariat; and that capital would be ever more centralized (joint-stock companies diluted ownership, Bernstein thought). Finally, and most importantly, Bernstein attacked the orthodox view that the internal contradictions of capitalist economy would eventually bring about its collapse.

Bernstein's critique of the notion of economic breakdown is subtle. The impassioned reactions of subsequent commentators have obscured its status as a logically tenable (though perhaps mistaken) extension of Marxist logic. Bernstein argued that the tendencies that Marx saw leading to crisis (the falling rate of profit, the tendency of production to

---

10 Data for my description of this period of German Marxism are derived from Colletti (1974: 45–110), Jacoby (1975), and Sweezy (1942: 190–207), among others.

exceed demand, crises of disproportionality) did indeed exist. However, structural changes in capitalism countered or negated these crisis tendencies. Monopolies avoided disproportionality via planning; working-class unionism raised wages and hence, along with credit, ameliorated underconsumptionism; monopoly pricing thwarted the falling rate of profit, and so on. All these elements can be seen as extensions of Marxist arguments: a changed capitalism could (and had) bypassed breakdown tendencies. Capitalism would not collapse.[11]

Contemporary reactions to Bernstein's attack on the theory of breakdown varied. Colletti argues that figures as important as Labriola and Lenin did not at first object. Kautsky, the leading intellectual of the German Communist Party, conceded Bernstein's point that a revision of Marxist economic theory was needed (Colletti 1974: 60). But he denied Bernstein's critique of breakdown, stating in effect that no one believed in breakdown anyway, only in the necessity of crises (Sweezy 1942: 194).

The most strident attacks on Bernstein came from figures to the left of the Party like Luxemburg and Parvus, for whom Bernstein's theoretical revisionism was the ultimate legitimation for the Party's already reformist tactics. Breakdown theory, Luxemburg argued, implied the necessity of socialism. To abandon it implied a turning away from revolutionary goals:

> If one admits with Bernstein that capitalist development does not move in the direction of its own ruin, then socialism ceases to be objectively necessary. . . . Bernstein began his revision of the Social Democracy by abandoning the theory of capitalist collapse. The latter, however, is the corner-stone of scientific socialism. (Luxemburg, quoted in Jacoby 1975: 22)

Luxemburg (1966) made her name in the Party through this attack on Bernstein in the pamphlet *Social Reform or Revolution?* However, such strong reactions to Bernstein pushed social democracy into a

---

11 It is very odd to find that usually circumspect commentators like Paul Sweezy lose all sense of proportion when describing Bernstein's work. It was, if we are to believe Sweezy, a "devious" attempt to "eradicate Marxism, root and branch, from the socialist movement" (Sweezy 1942: 193). This reaction is all the stranger, given that Sweezy himself argued later that monopolies reverse the falling rate of profit, resulting in a rising surplus (Baran and Sweezy 1966)—a formulation strongly reminiscent of Bernstein's.

quandary. It had not previously adopted a mechanistic breakdown theory of the purely economic demise of capitalism. But under the assault of the Party left it either had to accept the new dogmatism of breakdown to demonstrate its antirevisionism or, like Kautsky, attempt to evade the issue.

Shortly after Bernstein's articles appeared, Böhm-Bawerk's review of *Capital* was published. Following on the heels of an earlier attack on volume one of *Capital*, this work confronted Marxist value theory with the apparent contradictions between volumes one and three of *Capital*. It also attacked the labor theory of value from the new marginal utility perspective. Böhm-Bawerk's critique further intensified the direct pressure upon orthodox Marxists to respond. Whereas in an earlier period a passive and uncritical loyalty to Marx and Engels had led to a rift between theory and practice and a theoretical eclecticism, the pressure of outside critics forced the younger generation of intellectuals to defend the Marxist position actively. In the process, the orthodox writers strengthened some of Marx's arguments, hence unwittingly providing for an expansion of Marxist economic thought.

A third major stimulus to the reawakening of crisis theory came with the publication of Tugan-Baranowski's analyses in 1901. Tugan-Baranowski attempted to disprove the tendency of the falling rate of profit and the tendency toward underconsumptionism and substituted his own theory of disproportionality crises. Such an attack was too much even for the German revisionists. Bernstein himself had accepted the falling rate of profit and underconsumptionism; he merely documented counteracting tendencies. Tugan-Baranowski, on the other hand, denied even the logic of the original tendencies.

Every major theorist in German social democracy leaped to the attack. Kautsky, propelled leftward, spoke of the inevitability of "crises, wars, and catastrophes," of the intensifying severity of crises, and of chronic depression. Even revisionists like C. Schmidt defended underconsumptionism. Last, but by no means least, Rosa Luxemburg was moved to write a refutation of the entire Russian school of populist and legal Marxist political economy in order to rescue her theory of underconsumptionism. Thus, once again, the impetus to develop political economic arguments came from exterior attacks rather than internal dynamics.

By the turn of the century the crisis controversy had become almost sterile. It seems that revisionists had forced the ambiguities of the original Marxist conception of crisis and revolution to come under scrutiny. Bernstein, for example, had argued that cyclical economic contractions indeed occurred but that they were mitigated over time and in any event could not be considered crises in any real sense since capitalism recovered from them without apparent long-term effects. In response, the orthodoxy was forced to reassert the necessity of the fall of capitalism. Formulations that tended to emphasize long-term secular decay (and sometimes actual economic collapse) came to the fore, but theories emphasizing the purely cyclical aspects of crises remained in place.

Thus the response to outside attack changed crisis theory only insofar as it added an emphasis on long-term underconsumptionism as a guarantor of the inevitability of the demise of capitalism. The only requirement for wearing the mantle of orthodoxy was an acceptance of the inevitability of crises and revolution. Economic breakdown became an option that one could take or leave.

Orthodox Marxism experienced a second wave of revisionism in response to a more practical issue: the causes of imperialism. We are not concerned at this point with the substantive analyses of imperialism (these will be dealt with in the next chapter). Rather, imperialism theory was intimately linked with political economy, and especially with theories of economic crisis. It is this overlap that requires some attention.

I earlier suggested that the emergence of imperialism and monopoly capital aroused the interest of Marxist theoreticians. The two phenomena appeared to change the status quo so profoundly that individuals like Lenin interpreted them as a distinctly new stage of capitalism. But how were they integrated into Marxist political economy and crisis theory?

A major problem for Marxist intellectuals was to incorporate the rise of imperialism and of monopolies and cartels into the body of Marxist theory as *necessary* historical developments. Marx had already made the theory of the necessary concentration and growth of capital, of the transition from competitive capitalism to monopoly capitalism, a major theme in his political economic writings. On the other hand, Marx had indeed written of colonialism in numerous contexts, but as to its necessity, his position was less than clear. He showed that Britain's Indian markets were obviously crucial to certain manufacturers and merchants who reaped enormous profits from the colony. Yet he also noted that the costs of administering India as a colony sometimes exceeded profits. From discussions such as this, one can adduce the importance of imperialism for certain capitalists, but not its necessity for capitalism as a whole. Similarly, Marx believed that imperialism helped to offset the tendency of the falling rate of profit by supplying cheap raw materials, but he never stated that this advantage made imperialism necessary. Thus the generation of theorists after Marx was faced with the task of proving the historical necessity of imperialism.

An early attempt by Rudolf Hilferding partially succeeded. In *Das Finanzkapital* (1910) Hilferding linked the growth of monopolistic cartels, joint-stock companies, and large industrial empires controlled by banking firms to the rise of imperialism. Under competitive capitalism, he argued, Britain took a laissez-faire attitude. The state was anti-monopoly, and, indeed, a strong anticolonial feeling existed. But after 1875, as monopolization developed and as foreign monopolies began to compete with British ones, Britain shifted from a free trade policy to a protectionist and imperialist one. Monopolies did not want to increase production at home, since that could be achieved only by cutting prices and hence profits. Unable to invest in other sectors owing to already entrenched monopolies, they looked to foreign colonies for new markets and for new investment opportunities. Along with this shift from competition to monopoly and from free trade to protectionism, Hilferding sketched the rise of militarism and jingoistic patriotism. (See Sweezy's account of Hilferding; 1942: 287–328, 375–378.) Although Hilferding's book was lauded at the time, it had relatively little impact on crisis theory. Hilferding himself did not subscribe to breakdown theory and tended to discuss disproportionality crises, which he saw as partially solvable.

The first strong link between crisis theory and imperialism theory was forged by Rosa Luxemburg in *The Accumulation of Capital: A Contribution to the Economic Clarification of Imperialism* (1912–1913). Luxemburg (1951) seems to have had two goals. On the one hand, she argued that crisis theory had misconstrued the issue of capitalist reproduction. An understanding of the reproduction of capitalism requires a long-term (secular) analysis of the development of the capitalist economy, not a preoccupation with periodic cycles and crises:

> The attempt to solve the problem of reproduction in terms of crises is fundamentally a device of vulgar economics, just like the attempt to solve the problem of value in terms of fluctuations in

demand and supply. Nevertheless, we shall see in the course of our observations that as soon as economic theory gets an inkling of the problem of reproduction, it reveals a persistent tendency suddenly to transform the problem of reproduction into the problem of crises, thus barring its own way to the solution of the question. (Luxemburg 1951: 36)

Thus the necessity of collapse was to be found not in business cycles but in the long-term limits to the accumulation of capital (Luxemburg 1951: 325). To prove her point, Luxemburg turned to the version of crisis theory that is secular rather than cyclical: underconsumptionism.

A second issue was of great importance to Luxemburg both theoretically and politically. In attempting to analyze the reproduction of capitalism, the Russian legal Marxists like Tugan-Baranowski had adopted Marx's reproduction schema from volume two of *Capital*. Approximately half of *The Accumulation of Capital* is devoted to Luxemburg's contention that these schemata are abstractions that ignore important real-life phenomena, that the use of these schemata to understand capitalist reproduction is therefore flawed and leads to unwarranted conclusions. For example, reproduction theory fails to take into account the existence of classes other than the bourgeoisie and proletariat or the strength of foreign trade and imperialism. Neither of these features figure in Marx's reproduction model. Thus, although she differed from Bernstein in almost every political respect, Luxemburg derived her theoretical revision of Marx from a similar logic: some aspects of *Capital* (in her case the reproduction schema) simply did not fit reality. As she wrote in a response to critics of her book:

> There is no doubt that the explanation for the economic roots of imperialism must be deduced from the laws of capital accumulation, since, according to common empirical knowledge, imperialism as a whole is nothing but a specific method of accumulation. But how is that possible, if one does not question Marx's assumptions in the second volume of Capital which are constructed for a society in which capitalist production is the only form, where the entire population consists solely of capitalists and wage laborers?
>
> However one defines the inner economic mechanisms of imperialism, one thing is obvious and common knowledge: the expansion of the rule of capital from the old capitalist countries to the new areas, and the economic and political competition of those

countries for the new parts of the world. But Marx assumes as we have seen in the second volume of Capital, that the whole world is one capitalist nation, that all other forms of economy and society have already disappeared. How can one explain imperialism in a society where there is no longer any space for it? (Luxemburg and Bukharin 1972: 61)

The substance of Luxemburg's critique is well-known. Marx's schema implied, as Tugan-Baranowski pointed out, that capitalism can reproduce ad infinitum, with the exception of occasional disproportionality crises. Luxemburg (1951: 348) countered that, left to itself, a capitalist economy would collapse from underconsumptionism. However, realization of newly produced surplus value can be achieved through commerce with noncapitalist producers. Hence it is necessary for capitalism's reproduction that more and more noncapitalist areas—for example, colonies—be drawn into the capitalist orbit. Imperialism becomes necessary for capitalism, which will fail when external markets disappear.

The issue of imperialism became even more prominent with the onset of World War I. The war destroyed the international unity of the socialist parties; the majority of leftists supported their own nations rather than internationalism. Before, during, and after the war the theoretical debates over Luxemburg's thesis continued. In 1913 Otto Bauer attacked Luxemburg's understanding of reproduction and argued from the schema that capitalism could survive within an isolated country, given a balance between capital accumulation and population growth (i.e., growth of the working population could prevent what would otherwise be underconsumption crises). It followed from Bauer's logic that the primary function of imperialism was to provide more workers and thereby sustain higher capitalist growth rates than could otherwise be supported by the home population:

Accumulation is at first limited by the growth of the working population. Imperialism increases the number of workers who are forced to sell their labour power to capital. It accomplished this by destroying the old modes of production in colonial areas and thereby forcing millions either to emigrate to capitalist areas or to serve European or American capital in their native land, where the capital has been invested. Since with a given organic composition of capital the amount of accumulation is determined by the growth in the available working population, imperialism is in fact a means to enlarge the limits of accumulation. (Bauer, quoted in Luxemburg and Bukharin 1972: 141)

It is of no benefit for us to consider the validity of Luxemburg's and Bauer's arguments. Both have come under severe criticism from within the Marxist camp. But it is important to note that both Luxemburg and Bauer view imperialism as a mechanism by which otherwise inevitable crises of capitalism are avoided. For Luxemburg, imperialism solves the realization crisis; for Bauer, it slows an accumulation crisis by providing more workers. This interpretation of imperialism as a defense for capitalism, as a means of neutralizing breakdown or crisis tendencies, is an important and recurrent one in Marxism. It subsumes the theory of imperialism under the theory of accumulation crises.

However, this view is not without its detractors. In *Imperialism and the World Economy* (1915) and in a critique of Luxemburg, *Imperialism and the Accumulation of Capital* (1924), Nikolai Bukharin, a leading Bolshevik theorist, advanced a different analysis. Following Hilferding, Bukharin argues that imperialism represents the policy of monopolistic national capitalism as it comes into competition with other equivalent national capitalisms. But, unlike Luxemburg, he does not emphasize the necessity of imperialism. While granting that colonies certainly help as markets for excess goods during an overproduction or underconsumption crisis, he regards this outcome as essentially epiphenomenal (Bukharin 1972: 243). This is not to say that the process lacks empirical interest; in fact, he dedicates several sections of *Imperialism and the World Economy* to the dumping of goods on foreign markets by monopoly corporations. But the significance of imperialism, for Bukharin, stems from a different logic of the accumulation process: namely, the urge to maximize profit. Foreign markets are especially lucrative because the relatively inefficient techniques for producing goods in underdeveloped lands mean that the prices of goods are higher there than in the West. Hence products created in efficient mass-production processes can win super-profits from the high "native" price system. Furthermore, the greater degree of exploitation of labor in foreign countries allows for a greater general rate of profit. Capitalist exports of goods or capital to the Third World can therefore take advantage of these higher profits.

In recent years, such observations have generated theories of imperialism as "unequal exchange." We shall deal with these in the next chapter. It is important to note here that Bukharin and his followers demonstrated the systematicity and necessity of imperialism *without* linking it to the theories of crisis. Instead, they tie it to normal accumulation practices, such as the pursuit of profit.

A theorist who agreed with Bukharin that imperialism does not flow from the necessity to counteract or stave off crises was Karl Kautsky. In every other sense the two men were enemies. Bukharin spent pages of his first book lambasting Kautsky's theory of imperialism and viewed him as a traitor to the communist movement because Kautsky supported Germany in World War I. Kautsky saw imperialism as a tactic of capitalism, an aspect of its darker side, analogous to the viciousness of child labor in early capitalist industry. Kautsky regarded imperialism as unnecessary and argued that working-class political action could prevent imperialism, as it had prevented exploitation of child labor, through legislation. Thus he foresaw a future of "ultra-imperialism"— by which he meant post-imperialism—an era of peace between industrial powers and an end to colonialism.

This roll-call of theories cannot be concluded without mentioning Lenin's pamphlet of 1916, *Imperialism, The Highest Stage of Capitalism* (Lenin 1969). While repeating much of the substance of the Hilferding-Bukharin argument, Lenin nevertheless returns to the notion that imperialism is necessary in order for capitalism to avoid crises and/or breakdown. In this restricted sense his view resembles that of Luxemburg and Bauer. The argument, in barest outline, is that monopoly has led to the accumulation of "an enormous superabundance of capital" in the advanced countries. In a cheesy metaphor, Lenin describes such countries as "overripe." This overabundance of capital cannot be reinvested in the advanced countries because of the low consumption capacity of their "half-starved and poverty-stricken masses." Since they cannot find a "field for profitable investment" at home, capitalists adopt an imperialist stance. For Lenin, imperialism meant above all the export of capital (rather than goods) and its investment in underdeveloped nations. The crux of Lenin's argument is that imperialism enables capitalists to invest otherwise useless capital in new areas. Imperialism thus solves a contradiction of mature capitalism: the contradiction between expanding capital seeking investment and the restricted market for goods.

At this point we can halt our description of political economy prior to 1918 and summarize certain themes. We have argued that one can distinguish two waves, though they blur in some cases. The first wave of political economy emerged in response to revisionist attempts to mitigate a perceived lack of fit between Marxist theory and the reality of late-nineteenth-century events, especially with regard to economic stability and class structure. When Bernstein and Tugan-Baranowski suggested that crises or breakdowns were not inevitable under capitalism, orthodox Marxists attempted to reassert the *logical* necessity of crises and their intensification over time. In the process of refutation, some antirevisionists transformed the theory of cyclical crises and political revolutions into even more dramatic notions of the inevitability of secular (long-term) tendencies for the capitalist economies to collapse. (Luxemburg used the phrase "grind to a halt.")

A second wave of theorizing followed upon the need to explain the rise of financial conglomerates and monopolies in the industrial nations, the race for colonies, and the intensification of imperialist rivalries. These phenomena resulted in a series of modifications of Marxist political economy. Numerous theories treated imperialism as a mechanism by which the various forms of accumulation problems could be averted or ameliorated (e.g., Luxemburg and Bauer). Others linked imperialism to the normal functioning of the accumulation process and the search for maximum profit (e.g., Hilferding and Bukharin). Lenin seemed to span both camps with his notions of overripe capitalism and of imperialism as a response to the contradictions of this phase of capitalism. But all of these intellectuals saw the need to develop or recast Marxist political economy in order to account systematically for the new phenomena of imperialism and imperialist rivalry.

The Interwar Era (1918–1939)

Although the most innovative phase of Marxist political economy had already peaked, important developments in crisis theory itself and in its relationship to imperialism occurred in the postwar years.[12] Luxemburg's formulation of realization crises and of their link to imperialism provoked further debates as critical views of her position were published by Bukharin and Lenin. Bukharin's 1924 review of her and oth-

---

12 This period is described by Marramao (1975), Jacoby (1975), and Sweezy (1942).

ers' work, entitled *Imperialism and the Accumulation of Capital*, is probably the most definitive statement of the orthodox position on breakdown theory and its relation to imperialism (Bukharin 1972).

Breakdown theorists like Luxemburg believed that they had proven the limits of capitalism and the necessity of its downfall by demonstrating that capitalism could not sustain internal growth. They viewed the Third World as a mitigating factor that would suppress those crisis tendencies which would otherwise cause the collapse of European capitalism. The structure of argument was the same whether the role of the Third World was as a consumer market (Luxemburg), a labor market (Bauer), or a source of investment opportunities (Lenin).

Bukharin points out that, although this view appears to be an optimistic one, since it points to the necessary collapse of capitalism, it is in fact the opposite. The Third World contained untold millions of individuals who had yet to be fully integrated into capitalism. If the existence of Third World markets, labor, and investments truly negated the effects of capitalist contradictions in the advanced nations, then capitalism would not collapse for centuries. In 1924 only a tiny proportion of the world's population could be called capitalists or wage laborers, and it would take forever to absorb the massive noncapitalist labor reserve. Hence, breakdown theories that looked to the Third World to balance capitalist contradictions in Europe were actually condemning European revolutionaries to a *very* long wait. This criticism of the logic of Luxemburg's position is still relevant. The notion that Third World markets and imperialism negate contradictions in the capitalist accumulation process remains alive in Marxist thinking, often without confronting Bukharin's conclusion.

Luxemburg's works also provoked her opponents to refute her crisis theory and her objections to Marx's reproduction schema. Although Luxemburg denied the applicability of these schemata for analyzing capitalist reproduction tendencies, her critics did not refrain from using them. In fact, in the interwar period use of the schemata to deduce the ultimate breakdown became ever more popular. We have already mentioned Otto Bauer's critique of Luxemburg in 1913 and his population growth theory. Bauer reformulated it in 1936, again using the reproduction schema, as a crisis theory of "the discrepancy between the development of Department One, and the demand for means of production in Department Two" (Mandel 1975: 35).

Another critic of Luxemburg who developed Bauer's models of the reproduction schema was Henryk Grossman, an early and influential figure in the so-called Frankfurt school (Marramao 1975). Grossman's 1929 work, *The Law of Accumulation and Collapse of the Capitalist System*, is the apotheosis of that variant of crisis theory which emphasizes cumulative contradictions leading over time to a total economic breakdown. Using Bauer's version of the reproduction schema, Grossman followed the model for thirty-five years, at which point the share of surplus value available for consumption by capitalists dwindles to zero. Capitalism consequently collapses for lack of surplus value.

Grossman's theory has been criticized on a number of theoretical, methodological, and political grounds. Several commentators appear to agree that Grossman's collapse occurs only because he makes untenable assumptions concerning the parameters of the model: the rate of surplus value and the rate of accumulation are held as constants over the thirty-five-year period (Pannekoek 1977: 67; Sweezy 1942: 210; Mandel 1975: 31–37). Beyond these technical issues, Grossman's theory has also been attacked for implying that capitalism simply falls apart economically without the intervention of human agency—a kind of fatalism remarkable even among Marxists (Pannekoek 1977: 68–69). However, contemporary supporters of Grossman deny this interpretation (Marramao 1975: 63).

For us, Grossman's work is significant for two reasons. First, as the ultimate mechanical breakdown theory, it ended the era (1895–1939) of shifts and counter-shifts in Marxist theories of crisis and illustrates the move away from cyclical theories of crisis (and revolution) to hypotheses of long-term dislocations ending in economic breakdown. Each of these two alternatives tends to exclude the other, or at least it minimizes the importance of the other. As Mandel says in his discussion of Grossman, a theory of reproduction that shows all going well until a final collapse in year thirty-five has little explanatory power regarding the five-, seven-, and ten-year cycles observed in capitalism (Mandel 1975: 31–32). Similarly, the logic of cyclical crises does not lend itself to predictions of a final, cataclysmic breakdown occurring in year thirty-five or its equivalent. Thus we see two very different notions of crisis theory emerging from Marxism.

Grossman's work is also important in a historical sense, in that it has been disseminated by his student Paul Mattick to some of the present generation of crisis theorists, including David Yaffe and Mario Cogoy. It therefore retains its position in intellectual debates.

The interwar theorists discussed above continued debates that had originated before the war. However, two events of the interwar era provided another stimulus for Marxian political economy. First, the success of the Bolshevik revolution in Russia opened a new horizon for Marxist political economy. Overnight the political economy of socialism turned from a hypothetical abstraction into an empirical fact. Thus, as the Soviet Union began to reorganize its economy (while fighting off invasions, blockades, and civil war), Marxist theoreticians hoped to witness their political-economic theories established in fact.

Theoretically, this excitement took the form of a revival of interest in economic planning, for in place of the anarchy of capitalist production, the Soviet Union aimed to institute a consciously planned economy. In terms of crisis theory, this development corresponded to the issue of disproportionality. As mentioned earlier, Russian legal Marxists and Bolsheviks had emphasized this aspect of crisis theory in contrast to the many German theoreticians who tended to concentrate on the falling rate of profit, realization crises, and underconsumption. The Russians instead subsumed these variants under disproportionality theory. Relations between consumption and production, just like relations between specific branches of industry, were subject to temporary disproportionality crises under capitalism. Socialist planning would change that.

A second stimulus to Marxist political-economic theory came from the economic crash that began in Germany and elsewhere in 1929–1930. In the United States, it generated Roosevelt's New Deal policies. In Germany, although the depression went even deeper than America's, no revolution resulted. The message, at least for some Marxist intellectuals, was new: there would be no automatic collapse of capitalism even in the midst of severe depressions (cf. Marramao 1975: 66).

In the late twenties and early thirties a group of political economists, including Friedrich Pollock, Kurt Mandelbaum, and Gerhardt Mayer, gathered at the Institut für Sozialforschung (the Frankfurt school). The experiences of the depression in Germany, the American New Deal, and the Russian planned economy led these theorists to consider economic planning in the capitalist countries and its impact on crises and upon socialist movements. In a series of essays in the institute's journal, *Zeitschrift für Sozialforschung*, these theorists discussed what were to become the dominant themes of post–World War II Marxism: the ability of monopolies to avoid disproportionality crises, and the use of government planning to manage or minimize crises (Marramao 1975).

The work of these individuals remains little known and appears to have had comparatively little impact on the postwar generation of Marxist political economists. But for our sociology of knowledge analysis they provide an interesting case, for they illustrate the practical concerns and the theoretical issues that have dominated more recent Marxist theory: namely, the rise of state economic intervention and the planned management of crises.

Radical Political Economy in the United States

1940–1970

In the sections above we have discussed the first fifty years or so of post-Marxian political economics. These developments were totally dominated by German and Russian theorists; American, British, and French intellectuals not heard from, with the possible exception of certain émigré Europeans living in America. The debates within Marxist economics appeared to be limited to a small world of Austro-German theoretical journals.

It is all the more remarkable, therefore, that one of the first treatments of Marxist political economy in America was also a major contribution to these debates. Paul Sweezy's *Theory of Capitalist Development* (1942) not only gave the first encyclopedic review of the European materials; it also laid the foundations for his own distinct school of Marxist political economy. The book first presents a review of Marx's own economic theory and then proceeds to analyze the various emendations of later Marxists: Bortkiewicz's solution of the transformation problem, the breakdown debates, and so on. While describing these theories, Sweezy also offers his own analytic perspective, which will be the focus of our discussion.

What may at first appear to be an expositional device turns out to be one of Sweezy's more important contributions. He separates crisis theory into two distinct types of crises: those associated with the falling rate of profit versus those having to do with realization problems (i.e., problems of selling goods). On the surface this approach may seem insignificant. But Sweezy was pointing out what had remained obscured in the eclecticism of European theory: namely, that there existed two quite distinct Marxist crisis theories with totally separate logics of action.

Sweezy's review of the falling rate of profit argument is basically critical. Although he couched the discussion in very guarded terms, stating, for example, that "there has been no thought of denying the existence or fundamental importance of such a tendency" (1942: 106), Sweezy showed that the then standard exposition of the law was untenable. He concluded that, given the variety of counter-tendencies that can negate the impact of a rising organic composition upon profit rates, there is no reason to believe that the profit rate must fall (1942: 104). The actual long-term impact of the law consequently becomes indeterminate.

Having denied, however circumspectly, what was previously considered by numerous Marxists as the guarantor of the fall of capitalism, Sweezy turns to the second theme permeating post-Marxian crisis theory: realization crises. Regarding these, Sweezy relegates simple disproportionality crises à la Tugan-Baranowski to a "position of secondary importance" and focuses on underconsumptionism.

The crux of underconsumptionism is that capitalism restricts workers' wages and hence consumption while simultaneously increasing production capacity via the never-ending cycle of reinvestment of accumulated surplus. Sweezy sees two possible manifestations of this contradiction: either excess productive capacity will be utilized, leading to commodity gluts, falling prices, and hence crises; or there will be a tendency to leave productive capacity underutilized, resulting in chronic stagnation rather than cyclical crises (1942: 180). An important issue is whether such underconsumption crises actually manifest themselves or whether (just as for the rising organic composition/ falling rate of profit argument) there are counter-tendencies that offset or negate the underconsumption effect. Sweezy points to two counter-tendencies. First, certain short-run phenomena slow the increase in productive capacity that results from new investment (these we shall skip). Second, new sources of demand may in principle augment the relatively restricted consumer demand of workers. These sources include population growth, unproductive consumption, and state expenditures. The first is an echo of Otto Bauer's population theory, mentioned previously. Sweezy argues that this counter-tendency is indeed potent, especially in newly developing countries, where rural populations boost the labor force and where birthrates are high. In contrast, the trend among the working class in the industrialized nations is to have smaller families and hence a higher standard of living, so this counter-tendency is absent. In a section reminiscent of Luxemburg, Sweezy points out that capitalist expansion into Third World countries is effectively equivalent to adding new consumers (1942: 225–226).

More significant for Sweezy is the capacity of unproductive consumption and state spending to offset the restricted demand of the working classes. Sweezy includes the commercial sector (all those involved in selling rather than producing goods) as well as service workers in the category of unproductive consumption. According to orthodox Marxism, unproductive workers are paid out of the surplus value produced by other workers, so their wages are a drain on the pool of surplus value available for investment. A large unproductive sector works against underconsumptionism in two ways. It diverts money away from investment, thereby preventing a further increase in productive capacity. Unproductive workers also buy goods and therefore boost consumer demand. Similarly, to the extent that state expenditures drain money from the surplus destined for investment and shift that money into consumption, they act to counter underconsumptionism. On balance, Sweezy sees state activity as capable of providing a counterweight to overproduction/underconsumption. But will it actually do so?

At this point it is important to inject a comment. I suggested earlier that the emergence of monopolies challenged Marxist theorists of the generation preceding Sweezy. Similarly, after the New Deal and the involvement of the state in ameliorating the problems of the 1930s depression, German theorists (Pollock, Bauer, and others) discussed the state's role. On the whole, that earlier generation had analyzed monopolies and the state as potential managers of disproportionality. Thus they focused on planning the output of economic sectors. Sweezy, facing the same new events—the role of the state, the role of monopolies, the role of imperialism—views them in terms of underconsumption crises. Hence, although analyzing the same institutions, Sweezy looks to those facets related to consumption rather than disproportionality/planning.

To the extent that monopolies can gouge a higher rate of profit than competitive companies, Sweezy argues that they exacerbate underconsumption, for they shift income from consumers to investors (1942: 277). However, a second feature of monopoly acts in the reverse direction. In place of price competition, monopolies or oligopolies try to tempt consumers to buy their products rather than those of others, and they do so by spending large amounts of their own money on advertising, sales, and distribution. Thus monopoly capitalism creates a mass of advertising and sales workers who are unproductive in the strict sense but who provide a strong source of extra consumer demand.

Similarly the state aids consumption at the expense of capital accumulation if it takes from the rich to give to the poor. But when the state is dominated by capitalist interests, it tends to favor accumulation over consumption, and its fiscal efforts will simply redistribute buying power from one group of consumers to another rather than make real inroads into the capitalists' accumulated surplus. To the extent, then, that the state aids consumption by taxing capital, it slows investment and brings consumption up to par with productive capacity. To the extent that it acts in capital's favor, investment booms, productive capacity grows, and, for Sweezy, underconsumption crises and/or stagnation loom.

Sweezy's conclusion in 1942 seems very dated today. He argued that capitalism's tendencies toward stagnation would assert themselves, thus slowing economic growth, while the socialist nations, undeterred by underconsumption, would boom:

> We must conclude that, because of the differences in their underlying economies, the socialist sector of the world would quickly stabilize itself and push forward to higher standards of living while the imperialist sector would flounder in the difficulties with which we are already sufficiently familiar. . . . Once socialism has had an opportunity to demonstrate its superiority on a large scale and under reasonably favorable conditions, the effect not only on the working class but also on the great majority of the middle class still living under capitalist conditions can be counted upon to be unprecedently powerful. The adherents of socialism will multiply by leaps and bounds; the small oligarchy whose social existence is bound up with the old order will be weakened, deprived of its international support and eventually rendered impotent. (Sweezy 1942: 361–362)

As one can see from this quotation, Sweezy's work predated the next phenomenon with which Marxist political economy had to deal: namely, the extraordinary postwar boom in the capitalist countries. Yet, despite the work's dated political conclusions, it was and is a seminal work in several respects. Sweezy was among the first Marxists to dispute the falling rate of profit argument in theoretical terms. Hence his work set the tone of American political economy for several decades. Problems of underconsumption, not falling rates of profit, were to lie at the heart of American Marxist theory. Sweezy also emphasized the state and monopoly as crucial features of modern capitalist economies, each having an important impact on the balance of consumption-demand versus investment. These issues also continue to dominate Marxist thought.

Sweezy's attempt to turn Marxist crisis theory away from the falling rate of profit argument and toward underconsumptionist themes was not unique. Indeed, it is striking that in the period after the 1930s depression several young left-wing academic economists in Britain and the United States came to similar conclusions: the organic composition of capital/falling rate of profit logic did not lead to a determinate result (Robinson 1942: 50–51; Dobb 1937: 96–129). The next logical step was to go beyond deductive logic to measurement, and that is what the young economist Joseph Gillman did in his book *The Falling Rate of Profit* (1957).

Gillman's work should be better known, for in it one finds many of the arguments that Sweezy later put forward in his *Monopoly Capital*. After reviewing the rising organic composition/falling rate of profit argument, Gillman attempts to examine its accuracy statistically. Does organic composition rise in actuality, and does the rate of surplus value fall? In brief, he finds that, up to World War I, statistics on American industry show a rising organic composition and a falling rate of surplus value, as the theory predicts. After World War I, however, organic composition seemed to flatten. and the rate of surplus value and profit rose. This postwar data contradicted the law of the falling rate of profit. (We should add here that all attempts such as Gillman's to examine Marxist value categories in the light of census data present technical problems of measurement. Adherents of the falling rate of profit argument can and do dispute these findings.) To explain these findings, Gillman proposes that the law of the falling rate of profit was *historically specific*: "While Marx's law of the falling tendency of the rate of profit applies to capitalism in its stages of rapid development and mechanization, it gradually ceases to apply and asserts itself but feebly as industry becomes fully developed and fully mechanized" (Gillman 1957: 59). Gillman, like Sweezy, looks to the nature of monopoly capitalism to account for this historical shift. He argues that modern technology boosts productivity without requiring enormous inputs of capital because scientific-technological advances involve changes in the quality and kind of machinery rather than the quantity or cost (Gillman 1957: 74–81). Thus organic composition need not climb in order to achieve higher productivity.

In addition, Gillman sees a second crucial feature of monopoly capital: a rise in realization costs. We earlier noted Sweezy's description of the problems of the sales effort and its expense under monopoly capitalism. These costs of realization, according to Gillman, counter what would otherwise be a ruinous underconsumption problem. For if monopolists really reversed the falling rate of profit and reinvested their ever-increasing profits, there would be a massive excess of production capacity in relation to demand. However, the added costs of realization lower profits, boost unproductive demand, and curb this tendency. For Gillman, then, monopoly balances the tendency of profits to fall and the tendency of production to exceed consumption. Such a balance is only temporary: the capitalist's interest is to boost profits at the expense of consumption, while the consumer's is the reverse. Once again we have an image of monopoly capitalism as a tug of war between balanced consumption and rising profits.

In 1966 Baran and Sweezy's celebrated *Monopoly Capital* appeared. Noteworthy as a collaborative effort between Baran, an émigré economist and one-time student at the Frankfurt school, and the American Sweezy, the book displays its origins: the first section is a technical analysis of accumulation problems under monopoly conditions, whereas the later section is a trenchant critique of the low quality of life under monopoly capitalism and its irrationalities. The core argument of the book is that the rise of giant corporations in the contemporary economy represents a radical break with the previous era of competitive capitalism. Baran and Sweezy use the term "monopoly capitalism" rather loosely. They are really referring to the fact that in each major industry a small clique of giant firms dominates the market (oligopoly). Instead of indulging in self-destructive price cutting, these monopolies allow prices to float up to near-monopoly prices via a mechanism known as "price leadership." For example, U.S. Steel raises its prices, Bethlehem Steel follows suit, and soon the whole industry is enjoying higher prices. For such oligopolized industries, wage increases are not threatening, since higher costs can be passed on to consumers. The fundamental notion is that the proliferation of monopoly means that profitability goes *up*. Instead of a fall in the rate of profit, one sees a rise. But this increasing surplus presents problems. First and foremost, how will this surplus be invested?

If the surplus is invested in new plants, capacity will soon exceed consumer demand, resulting in stagnation. If the surplus is *not* invested, another crisis will develop even faster if capitalists hold their surplus in money form (Keynes's "liquidity preference"). The demand for investment goods is rapidly curtailed, again leading to underconsumption and stagnation. The crisis of monopoly capitalism is therefore a glut of investment capital and a chronic tendency to underconsumption.

Several arenas can potentially absorb this surplus. Foreign investment, however, is not one of them, since the short-term outflow of surplus is rapidly reversed as the profits made from it flow back. The state, especially via military spending, mops up a large amount of surplus, considered both in terms of investment and surplus goods. According to Baran and Sweezy, the sales effort also has the unintended effect of raising aggregate demand. When monopolies choose not to compete via price cutting, they resort to advertising in order to shift consumer demand away from others' products. Consequently, huge numbers of unproductive workers have to be employed in advertising, and the constant need for new products, packaging, and design engages some of the investment surplus.

The overall image of the book was particularly suited to the height of the postwar boom. America was seen to suffer not from too little capital but from too much. Within the logic of capitalism, this situation led to excess productive capacity, excess funds seeking opportunities for investment, and limited consumer demand. The solution was a massive program of unproductive effort, which boosts aggregate demand and opens arenas for investment in socially useless areas such as armaments, luxury goods, and the sales effort. Marxist theory had finally caught up with postwar consumerist America.

A final figure in this progression of American underconsumptionist theorists is Victor Perlo, whose book *The Unstable Economy: Booms and Recessions in the United States Since 1945* was published in 1973. Perlo represents the orthodox line in American political economy. He did not reject the organic composition/falling rate of profit position; nor did he hold to most of the monopoly capital notions (1973: 109–110). And he used Marxian value categories for his analyses, rather than Baran and Sweezy's heterodox notion of surplus. His work is important for exactly these reasons, for in Perlo we see the impact of underconsumptionist theory even in the midst of orthodox crisis theory.

Perlo's book is concerned with cyclical crises in America, in contrast to Baran and Sweezy's image of secular stagnation. His purpose is to show that business cycles remain endemic to American capitalism. This may seem an unnecessary point to make, but one should remember that in the postwar era the boom/bust cycle appeared to have vanished. Never before had American capitalism shown an ability to expand for so long without crises, and never had the downturns seemed so mild. Thus Perlo's aim to prove the inevitability of crises was a reaction to the spectacular expansion and relatively mild downturns that dominated post–World War II economic performance until 1970.

It is significant that in analyzing the business cycle in contemporary capitalism, Perlo chose not to emphasize the falling rate of profit argument (although he did mention it). Instead he saw a "basic contradiction" between stagnating consumer demand and increasing productive capacity (Perlo 1973: 33)—in short, underconsumptionism. The statistical data he derived from the census showed a steady rise in the rate of surplus value. In other words, the surplus accruing to the capitalists had increased throughout the postwar era, while labor's share of production had fallen (Perlo 1973: 27–33). This finding led him to predict a problem of underconsumption, for the extra surplus would prove unusable in the face of restricted consumer power.

Like Gillman and Baran and Sweezy, Perlo subsequently looked for countervailing trends. The expanding sectors of salaried bureaucrats and sales and distribution workers helped but did not erase the underconsumption/rising surplus problem, according to Perlo's data. Hence he looked to state expenditures, as well as to militarism, credit, and inflation, for other factors that might mitigate the impact of underconsumptionism. His materials represent probably the best attempt to evaluate the various ways in which underconsumptionism can be managed by government and other sources. But he argued that these measures had limits. Since many were already exhausted, he concluded: "While there will be no repetition of 1929–32, the developing economic contradictions make increasingly likely the eruption of crises that will be considerably more severe than any of the postwar period" (Perlo 1973: 208).

We have discussed three major works by American authors who formulated Marxist positions on political economy in the postwar period. It is significant that these individuals were not collaborators or members of one school; on the contrary, they do not mention one another's books in their works, and they seem to hold quite different political positions. Collectively, their works demonstrate the almost unchallenged hegemony of underconsumptionist theories in American circles in the period up to the early 1970s. In each case, the works cite economic data that indicate a rising rate of surplus value in the American economy. The theorists took this evidence as proof for an underconsumptionist theory of post–World War II crises and viewed the expansion of state sector activity and of unproductive workers as corroboration for their views.

It is also noteworthy that the underconsumptionist view, at least insofar as it stresses insufficient consumer demand and stagnation through idle excess productive capacity, has influenced even those Marxist scholars whose views would appear inimical to underconsumptionism. For example, the European theorist Ernest Mandel, who holds to the falling rate of profit theory, nevertheless largely adopts the underconsumptionists' view of state expenditures and the permanent arms economy.

The overwhelming acceptance of the view that postwar capitalism is stagnationist and that the state can counter this tendency, principally by means of military spending, has brought charges from opponents to the effect that American Marxists are solidly left Keynesians. This label (it is intended as an epithet) is accurate so long as it is not understood to refer to the origins of these Marxists' positions. As we have seen, an underconsumptionist theme is evident in Marx's own work. It became explicit in Kautsky's writings in 1902 (Kautsky 1910), in Luxemburg's work, and so on. Indeed, it inspired a young Polish socialist, Michael Kalecki (1933), to develop a theory of crises of effective demand (including a notion equivalent to that of liquidity preference) and publish it several years before Keynes's celebrated *General Theory of Employment, Interest, and Money*. Thus we find parallels between Marxist and Keynesian theories of underconsumption. But whereas Keynes's disciples have in the main attempted to apply his work toward ameliorating the business cycle, Marxists continue to see state involvement as a temporary or limited counter-tendency to crisis. These Marxists argue that Keynesian state spending and deficit financing can put off crises only at the cost of exacerbating other economic contradictions.

A similar position has been adopted since by the New Right, monetarists, "balanced budgeters," and others.

Crisis Theory Since 1970

The underconsumption theorists discussed above are the "old guard" of American Marxist political economy, the courageous individuals responsible for the continuity of Marxist scholarship through the repressive Cold War years. With the upheavals of the sixties, however, a new generation of left scholars came into prominence. The field of political economy boomed, the Union for Radical Political Economics was founded, and an amazing variety of radical political economic analyses was published. Much of this work was very different from and in some cases actually in opposition to the tradition of Sweezy et al. Moreover, with the expansion of radical activity in British and Continental universities, the new academics in America found themselves in contact with similar movements elsewhere. American political economy began to lose some of its distinctive aspects, giving way to an internationalized neo-Marxist economics.

The author whose work most closely resembles the earlier genre is James O'Connor, a central figure in the attempt to bridge American and German Marxist scholarship during the early seventies. In 1973 O'Connor published his celebrated book, *The Fiscal Crisis of the State*. Its central theme is the relationship of the state to the larger economy, the various functions the state attempts to perform, and the ways in which the role of the state becomes increasingly contradictory. O'Connor used a tripartite model of the economy encompassing a monopolized, capital-intensive, unionized, high-wage sector ("the monopoly sector"); a competitive, labor-intensive, comparatively non-unionized, low-wage sector ("the competitive sector"); and a state sector that includes federal, state, and local administration, government services such as education, welfare, and health, and the military. Included as part of the state sector are private enterprises totally dependent on government for their existence, such as the armaments industry. The U.S. work force, O'Connor stated, is split fairly evenly between these three sectors.

Unlike some theorists who see the competitive sector as marginal or dying off, O'Connor believes that it plays a complementary, almost symbiotic role with regard to the monopoly sector. It provides cheap inputs for the monopolies and acts as a sales conduit (retailing) for monopoly-produced goods. However, the relationship is all one-sided, since the monopolies dominate the competitive sector both commercially and politically.

O'Connor argues that the state has two functions. First, it guarantees the ability of the private sector to make a profit. The state is responsible for manipulating the economy such that accumulation of capital proceeds as smoothly as possible. This responsibility goes well beyond the obvious economic activities, such as regulating taxation, the currency, and credit. The second function of the state is "legitimation." By this term O'Connor seems to mean the maintenance of social harmony. He stresses that any specific activity of government simultaneously serves both functions. For example, schools both provide trained labor (accumulation function) and educate, indoctrinate, or simply corral youths (legitimacy function).

One goal of O'Connor's analysis is to explain the state budget in terms of this dual function model. Analytically, state expenditures fall into one of two categories: "social capital" or "social expenses." Social capital is money spent to aid the accumulation function of the state; it involves expenditures that enhance the profitability of private enterprise and that therefore indirectly expand surplus value. When government builds roads, dams, and oil pipelines or pays for developing communications satellites, it is investing social capital where private capital would otherwise have been required. Similarly, by paying for education, work training, and workmen's compensation, government removes a potential expense from the private sector. This section of state expenditures aids industry in its accumulation efforts by lowering its costs.

The other aspect of government spending, social expenses, does not aid accumulation in any way; such expenditures do not even indirectly help to produce surplus value. Social expenses perform the legitimacy function of government. Looking after the unemployed, maintaining the legal system, and so on are largely social expenses. However, as O'Connor points out, almost any given government activity involves partly the expenditure of social capital and partly the expenditure of social consumption: the accumulation and legitimation functions intermingle.

In this view government, far from being a burden on the private sector, performs crucial services that sustain the profitability of capitalist enterprises. However, such services are not equally distributed. According to O'Connor, *the expenditures of the state benefit the monopoly sector much more than the competitive sector*. Monopolies generate more social problems than the competitive sector: their high degree of mechanization keeps pushing workers onto unemployment. In addition, the monopoly sector consumes the lion's share of social investment: it needs huge power sources, roads, oil piplines, high-technology research, highly educated personnel, and foreign aid contracts more than the competitive sector does. Thus, for O'Connor, the growth of the state sector in contemporary capitalist nations is intimately bound up with the growth of the monopoly sector, for the deleterious effects of monopoly are solved and paid for by the state, and state expenditures guarantee the profitability of monopolies.

We can now turn to the crisis aspects of O'Connor's theory. O'Connor takes a view very similar to that earlier described for Sweezy. The state can opt for policies that maximize profitability and accumulation, thereby risking overproduction/underconsumption, or it can maximize consumption, thus mitigating crises. But it can achieve the latter goal only at the expense of accumulation, by squeezing capitalists. Thus O'Connor writes:

> On the one hand, social capital outlays indirectly increase productive capacity and simultaneously increase aggregate demand. On the other hand social expense outlays do not increase productive capacity, although they do expand aggregate demand. Whether the growth of productive capacity runs ahead or behind the growth of demand thus depends on the composition of the State budget. (1973: 8)

In O'Connor's model, as in Sweezy's, the state acts in a Keynesian way only when it denies capitalists what they want: increased profits.

O'Connor's larger purpose is to show that the growth of the state, while it solves some of monopoly capital's problems, simply shifts or transmutes economic contradictions into political ones. O'Connor argues that government takes responsibility for alleviating the problems generated by the monopoly sector but that the cost of these government services is not paid for by the monopoly sector. Instead workers in all three sectors and businesses in both the monopoly and the competitive sector pay. If anything, the monopoly sector pays least, since it can more easily pass on taxes via increased prices. The result is a fiscal crisis, as government expenses tend to outrun government income:

> The socialization of costs and private appropriation of profits creates a fiscal crisis, or "structural gap," between state expenditures and state revenues. The result is a tendency for state expenditures to increase more rapidly than the means of financing them. (O'Connor 1973: 9)

The fiscal crisis becomes a political crisis when interests battle over which services to cut or over where to raise taxes. The legitimacy of the state also suffers as the fiscal crisis worsens. This logic has led many Marxists away from economic theory and considerations of accumulation and crisis considered in isolation and taken them into the area of the political and organizational sociology of the state. This trend is most marked in Germany but is also widespread in America (cf. Wolfe 1977; Habermas 1975).

One can view O'Connor's work as a bridge between underconsumptionism and the new political economy. However, other schools of crisis theory evidence a distinct antipathy toward the underconsumptionist thesis. One of these perspectives, profit-squeeze theory, is our next subject.

I have discussed three phenomena that have engaged the energies and interest of post–World War II Marxist theorists: monopolies, the economic boom from 1945 to 1970, and the increased role of the state. To these should be added a fourth: inflation. Until about 1965, consumer prices in the advanced countries rose by about 2 percent annually. This amount was not considered very significant, and Marxist theoretical works of that period usually did not consider the topic. Between 1965 and 1972 inflation rose to about 5 percent per annum; by 1973 it was 8 percent and increasing (Jacobi et al. 1975). Inflation rapidly loomed as an undertheorized area in Marxist political economy.

There are now numerous works that probe the problem. But before dealing with these, let us consider an offshoot or byproduct of the interest in inflation: theories of profit squeeze. The period after 1964 in Britain was characterized by high employment, a very serious balance-of-payments problem, and rising inflation. One cause widely discussed in the business press was unionized workers, whose insistence on wage hikes was denounced for fueling inflation and undermining the soundness and profitability of British industry. Government propaganda soon supported this view, and economic data were provided to show that wages had increased faster than productivity, hence exacerbating profitability and inflation problems.

In one of the more remarkable results of this campaign, several Marxist economists in Britain accepted and indeed extended this analysis. In 1972 Andrew Glyn and Bob Sutcliffe published *British Capitalism, Workers and the Profit Squeeze*, in which they argued that British enterprises were caught in a dilemma. Relatively full employment and unionization allowed workers to bargain successfully for wage increases in excess of productivity raises. Since foreign competition prevented British companies from recouping these losses through price increases, company profits were being "squeezed" out of existence. The rate of profit was falling, not because of a rising organic composition of capital, but because workers had the power to lessen the degree of exploitation and to demand a larger share of their product than previously.

This theory proved popular among several American intellectuals associated with the Union for Radical Political Economics (URPE), who reapplied profit-squeeze theory to the United States (cf. Gordon 1975; Zimbalist 1975; and Wycko 1975). In particular, Raford Boddy and James Crotty (1975; 1976a; 1976b), two members of URPE, have extended it into a comprehensive critique of underconsumptionist theory.

In a 1976 paper Boddy and Crotty (1976b) listed their objections to Baran and Sweezy's version of underconsumptionism. At the most general level, they expressed their dissatisfaction with the underconsumptionist view of post–World War II economic expansion. Since underconsumptionism views monopoly capitalism as essentially stagnant, it is forced to regard the postwar boom as exceptional, the result largely of wars and epoch-making innovations. Otherwise, stagnation would have been worse. In contrast, Boddy and Crotty wish to portray monopoly capitalism as expansionist and dynamic, though they grant Baran and Sweezy's point that for much of the postwar era, and especially between 1956 and 1963, the empirical reality seemed to conform with the stagnation theory. But Boddy and Crotty attribute this period of stagnation more to restrictive government policies than to the stagnationist tendencies of capitalism per se.

Their most intense disagreement with underconsumption theory involves the present period. The last twenty years have seen the rise of competition between American products and those from Germany, France, and Japan. Such international competition has become particularly fierce in those industries that epitomize monopoly/oligopoly (e.g., cars and steel). In such an internationally competitive environment, Baran and Sweezy's image of monopoly firms that are able to raise prices with impunity seems not to apply. Indeed, argue Boddy and Crotty, labor costs in these industries have risen since the 1960s, while their profit rates have declined. Consequently, we are witnessing an era of competition and profit squeeze rather than one of monopoly, rising surplus, and stagnation.

This perspective is detailed further in Boddy and Crotty's study of cyclical economic crises, "Class Conflict and Macro-Policy: The Political Business Cycle" (1975). The authors draw on empirical data that show that, since World War II, the profit share of income has *fallen* during the latter half of each economic expansion, while labor's share has increased. In other words, each economic downturn is preceded by a period in which labor appears to be squeezing profits. According to Boddy and Crotty, the economic downturn following the squeeze should not be considered an autonomous readjustment of economic processes but should be viewed as a conscious and planned effort to reverse labor's inroads into profits (Boddy and Crotty 1975: 2–3).

One should note the contrasting implications of this view with regard to government policy. In underconsumptionist theory, government is balanced precariously between efforts to maintain accumulation and attempts to cure the problem of insufficient demand via spending for full employment. Boddy and Crotty see government economic policy as aimed solely at maintaining accumulation by aiding business profitability. They point out that U.S. postwar unemployment rates have remained comparatively high and that cyclical downturns are not avoided by government action.

Much of Boddy and Crotty's 1975 article is devoted to an empirical demonstration that the ratio of wages to profits increases as economic expansions progress, thus cutting into profits. They argue that it is therefore in the interest of capitalists as a class to reverse this trend. Unemployment, achieved especially by laying off workers, serves as an antidote to claims for wage increases and allows capitalists to reestablish profit margins.

But how do capitalists accomplish this goal? Boddy and Crotty (1975: 11) argue that the most significant actions take place on the political level of government macro-economic and monetary policy and by means of inflation. As a boom proceeds and as wages begin to climb, so do prices. Business leaders then appeal to government in the name of the national interest to curb inflation. What this actually entails is a decrease in government spending and a tightening of the money supply. In sum, government deliberately provokes an economic downturn (Boddy and Crotty 1975: 10–11). Boddy and Crotty note that in instances where inflation has not coincided with incursions of wages into profits, capitalists have not insisted on rapid government deflationary action. They cite high rates of inflation in Japan and Brazil as examples where weak labor movements do not threaten profits and where inflation is therefore tolerated. Similarly, inflation was allowed in America in 1972 and 1973, since controls were holding down wages but not prices or profits.

Two points in Boddy and Crotty's analyses bear closer discussion. First, the authors tend to adopt a functionalist perspective to explain government fiscal policy. They show that recession can be turned to the advantage of capitalists (i.e., made functional for them) and then argue that governments provoke recessions for this reason. Such an interpretation is a leap of faith unless Boddy and Crotty can demonstrate the mechanism by which capitalists accomplish this goal. Second, they gloss over the argument that recessions may also damage profits. Instead, they simply assert that capitalists are willing to suffer temporarily for the longer-term goal of curbing wage increases. Boddy and Crotty's work has drawn fire from several theorists for these and other weaknesses. Since government data are complex and the theory of the cycle is elaborate, there is much room for dissent and reinterpretation (cf. Perlo 1976; Sherman 1976a). Rather than follow this debate itself, we shall examine an alternative crisis theory proposed by Howard Sherman.

Sherman shares the view of Baran and Sweezy that monopoly market structures decisively change the nature of contemporary capitalism, and much of his work is aimed at developing a theory of monopoly capitalist behavior. In an early work (Sherman 1968), he documented the existence of elevated rates of profit in the monopoly/oligopoly sector compared with those in the competitive industries. His more recent work focuses primarily upon inflation as a product of monopoly power (Sherman 1976b).

In opposing the view of the falling rate of profit theorists and the profit-squeeze position, Sherman resorts to a complex array of post–World War II economic data. He concludes that over the long term profits, though fluctuating, show no downward trend (Sherman 1976b: 101–102). However, he accepts the notion that the downturns in the economic cycle are triggered by temporarily lowered profits, though, according to him, wage increases do not cause these lowered profits. Rather they are the result of increased costs for raw materials, lower demand, and tightened credit (Sherman 1976b: 100–104). Thus Sherman's image of cycles blends underconsumption and rising organic composition, rather than looking to profit squeeze.

Sherman's most innovative work centers on his analyses of inflation and stagflation. The Keynesian view of inflation, in which aggregate demand exceeds aggregate supply (known as "demand-pull"), accurately characterized inflations up to the 1950s, says Sherman, but during the recessions of 1958, 1969, and 1974 the old pattern broke down. In particular, prices continued to rise in these recessions, even though demand dropped drastically. As we have already mentioned, Sherman discounts the wage-increase version of cost-push inflation as a means of explaining this unusual combination of recession and rising prices, for wages lag behind prices during most inflations, and especially during inflationary recessions.

To account for the combination of falling demand, falling production, and rising prices (called "stagflation"), Sherman looked instead to disaggregated economic data and focused on the behavior of monopoly industries during recessions. Following institutionalist economists such as John M. Blair (1974), Sherman demonstrates that since 1958 prices in the monopoly sector have climbed even during the depths of recessions, despite falling demand. Their market power enables oligopolies to face recessions by cutting back production and raising prices (Sherman 1976b: 165–171). In effect, monopolies can ride out recessions by transferring the burden of their costs onto competitive sector customers and wage earners. Thus, although profits in the monopoly sector decline during recessions, they fall only about half as much as those in the competitive sector. Hence stagflation flows from the monopolies' evasion of the negative consequences of recessions by means of raising prices. During the subsequent upswing, inflation worsens as workers attempt to regain the buying power lost in the previous recession, the competitive sector tries to recoup its losses, and the monopoly sector just keeps raising prices slightly ahead of its costs.

Sherman goes on to elaborate this model and its connections to state policy, credit, and international trade. The important conclusion to be drawn here is that he reasserts the empirical relevance of the notion of monopoly capital and denies Boddy and Crotty's assertion that international competition reduces American oligopolies to the position of large but competitive firms. Sherman regards inflation as a special side effect of monopolistic crisis management, an unintended havoc that monopoly capitalist firms wreck as they attempt to avoid the loss of profits following a downturn.

In concluding this section on contemporary crisis theories, we must mention one additional school of thought that is technically American. The work of Paul Mattick has been very influential within theoretical Marxism. Born in Germany, Mattick came to America in 1926, worked with the IWW, and was editor and contributor to a theoretical journal in the thirties known variously as *International Council Correspondence*, *Living Marxism*, and *New Essays*. Although Mattick is an American, his work has had very little influence among left scholars in the United States; but it has many adherents in Germany and Britain (cf. Yaffe 1973). Paradoxically, then, Mattick's work is in a sense much more typical of crisis theory in Europe than of that in America.

Nevertheless, we shall summarize his views, for they stand in marked contrast to those we have discussed previously. Mattick is an intellectual follower of Henryk Grossman, whose breakdown theory, a variation on the rising organic composition/falling rate of profit theme, we mentioned earlier. Grossman's innovation was to argue that Marx should not have concentrated on the falling *rate* of profit so much as on the *mass* of profits (cf. Pannekoek 1977). For Grossman and for Mattick, the rising organic composition of advanced capitalist enterprises over time brings with it a new problem. The mass of surplus value required for investment increases, while the actual surplus value available stagnates or actually decreases. In contrast to Baran and Sweezy's image of late capitalism swimming in unusable surplus, Mattick sees an ever more severe capital shortage (Mattick 1934).

The lack of sufficient surplus for expansion generates unemployment, unused productive capacity, and so forth. Thus, for Mattick, underconsumption occurs as an effect of insufficient surplus, not as a result of excess surplus. State spending will indeed alleviate this shortage by setting industries to work and boosting unproductive consumption. But where Baran and Sweezy see such spending and waste as partial solutions to the crisis, Mattick and his followers argue that the state exacerbates the problem. Though addressing the political or legitimacy issue of setting people to work, state spending actually deducts (via taxation) from the pool of available surplus value. Since, according to Mattick, this pool is already insufficient to allow capitalist expansion at its normal rate, state expenditures further destabilize the system (Mattick 1969). Unable to find surplus for investment, more and more firms fail, further concentration of giant corporations occurs, and the economy staggers on toward its inevitable breakdown.

This argument concerning a chronic insufficiency of surplus capital has proven popular in Britain and elsewhere. Since it views Keynesian governmental policies as a form of cure that worsens the disease, its prognosis for capitalism is very bleak: worsening crises will lead to total economic collapse. The only solution for capitalism is to attack the standard of living of the working class, to raise its profits by cutting wages.

Long Waves and Crises

The 1975 publication of an English translation of Ernest Mandel's *Late Capitalism* resurrected the long-dormant theory of economic "long waves," first espoused by the Russian economist N. D. Kondratieff in the 1920s. Long-wave theory has caught on with several American theorists, and I shall briefly summarize its major tenets. Long-wave theory begins with the observation that the international capitalist economy seems to go through approximately fifty-year cycles of boom and stagnation. These are not typical business cycles, which usually last only four to ten years. Thus several business cycles are nested within each long wave. In the first twenty-five years or so of a long wave, the international economy expands. Short-term business cycles still occur, but they are modified such that their booms are strong and their contractions are shallow. The later twenty-five years of a long wave witness decline and relative economic stagnation. Business cycles in this period show weak upswings and long, severe downswings.

The causes of long waves are a matter of debate. Kondratieff believed that long waves result from an internal dynamic of capitalism. The beginning of a new wave is triggered by a pool of uninvested capital that accumulated during the previous twenty-five year downswing. In the early twenties Trotsky countered that the turning points in long waves are due to external shocks—wars, revolutions, and major inventions—impinging on the capitalist system and not to the internal dynamics of capitalism (cf. Day 1976). Kondratieff responded that wars, revolutions, and inventions are caused by the cycles of expansion and contraction, not vice versa.

This theory remained an esoteric curiosity among business cycle theorists for fifty years (Kondratieff 1935; Garvy 1943; Rostow 1975). Then Mandel (1975) revived it as an innovative way of explaining the long economic expansion since World War II, a boom that had confounded traditional Marxist crisis theory. Mandel borrowed various theoretical elements from Kondratieff and added others himself. He argued that during the downswing of a long wave large amounts of surplus value are not invested because of the stagnating condition of the economy and because of low profitability. But once these large pools of underused capital are invested, they produce an economic boom of major proportions. Mandel placed considerable reliance on major technological innovations as a trigger for investments at the beginning of each new long wave. New technologies dramatically restructure industry. They provide new investment outlets for the pent-up capital accumulated in the prior cycle. They also alter production processes, creating a demand for new machinery, and boost consumer demand as new products come to market. Mandel (1975: 113) identifies three "fundamental revolutions in power technology": steam-driven motors after 1848; electric and combustion motors since 1890; and electronic and nuclear-powered machines since the 1940s—each of which appeared at the beginning of a new long wave.

Yet, although technological breakthroughs trigger the upswing of a new long wave by releasing an avalanche of investment, they are not the original stimulus behind the wave (i.e., they are not exogenous causes). Instead, Mandel views technological innovation as itself a product (hence endogenous) of the capitalist economy. He therefore goes back one more step. What causes the investment in technology, which causes the breakthrough, which causes the new wave to begin? His answer draws long-wave theory back into orthodox Marxism. It is the relative movements of the rate of profit and the rate of exploitation that affect technological innovation. The rate of profit, in turn, is influenced by factors such as the rise or defeat of working-class militancy, the opening or closing of international markets, the balance of oligopoly and competition, and so on.

Mandel's treatment of the long wave is detailed and complex, but his reason for importing this theory into Marxism is simple. Both falling rate of profit and underconsumptionism were totally unable to explain the thirty-year economic expansion after World War II and the near disappearance of crises. However, if the 1945–1970 period coincided with the upswing of a long wave, then we can see why the boom was so strong and long and why business cycles experienced only shallow downturns. Also, since the upswing of the long wave was over, Mandel could predict that much worse crises were soon to strike the international economy.

This approach has delighted many American radical theorists, since it allows for a new periodization of economic history and a new linking of accumulation, class struggle, and technological innovation. As we saw in the previous chapter, Gordon and his colleagues (1982) applied it to their theory of economic segmentation and to the history of control types within the firm. Wallerstein and his followers have also incorporated it into their world systems analyses. Thus, even though long waves are not in themselves a theory of crises, they provide an explanation of the irregularity of crises that complements Marxist theory.

It will be the task of our conclusion to rise above the substance of these theories to the level of the sociology of knowledge, to raise questions about when new crisis theories arise, why there are so many variants of crisis theory, and why certain versions have achieved popularity in America but not elsewhere.

Conclusion: Crisis Theory and the Sociology of Knowledge

We now have a sense of the variety and number of crisis theories. I do not propose to assess specific theories or to discuss the complex debates between different positions. Instead, I want to use these materials to examine more general questions about Marxist theorizing. What can these theories as a group tell us about the purpose of Marxist theory? Under what kinds of circumstances do new varieties of crisis theory seem to appear? Why are there so many variants of the theory? Do different crisis theories express different political viewpoints? These are the concerns of the sociology of knowledge, to understand ideas by analyzing the conditions of their production.

The starting point is to consider at what periods and under what circumstances major bursts of activity in Marxist crisis theory have occurred. Two hypotheses come to mind: such theoretical activity might proliferate during economic crises themselves, or it might be stimulated by upswings in working-class revolutionary activity. The very obviousness of the first possibility—that crisis theory flourishes when there are crises—hides what is in fact a very complex issue. Marx and Engels's crisis theory, according to my characterization of it, was an attempt to grapple with crises as or shortly after they were happening. Following this initial theorizing, however, the pattern seems to have changed. The Bernstein and anti-Bernstein debates, far from occurring in the midst of a crisis, thrived during an economic boom. This period followed a twenty-year economic downturn that, according to Colletti (1972: 56), was so mild that commentators at the time did not even recognize it as such. Tugan-Baranowski's major works appeared during the expansion phase of early Russian capitalism. The post–World War I debates of Luxemburg, Bauer, and Grossman preceded the crash of 1929–1930 (Grossman's essay was published in 1929.) The work of Pollock and the other economic planners indeed immediately followed the thirties crash. The left Keynesians and American underconsumptionists wrote mainly during the long post–World War II boom (though Dobb's first work in 1937 coincided with the depths of the Depression). Contemporary U.S. and British theorists clearly did turn to crisis theory in response to the 1970 and 1973 downturns.

The conclusion I draw is that little relationship can be seen between the timing of theoretical innovation and the timing of economic crises. On the contrary, many, if not most, of the periods of theoretical innovation occurred during economic booms or lulls.

If the pattern of theoretical innovation does not fit a sequence of economic crises, perhaps we should instead consider it "within the context of revolutionary upsurges," as Russell Jacoby (1975: 47) suggests. Yet I would argue that the timing of crisis theory fits revolutionary upsurges even less successfully than it does economic downturns. The Bernstein debates were waged during the heyday of German social democracy (1895–1914), a period known for its reformism and peaceful political activity. Luxemburg's major book on crisis theory appeared during a period of relative quiet, "the prevailing mood in the German party being one of caution and marking time after the heady days of the Russian Revolution" (Tarbuck, in Luxemburg 1972: 4). The post–World War I theorists were most certainly surrounded by an upsurge of political activity, although the initiative came from Nazism rather than communism. Finally, most observers would agree that nothing in the context of post–World War II American or British political economy can by any stretch of the imagination be considered a "revolutionary upsurge."

The timing of crisis theory therefore defies a simple identification either with crises themselves or with revolutionary periods. Let us then recapitulate the apparent inspirations for the various movements in Marxist political economy up to the latest (post–1970) surge. (We shall deal with the post–1970 developments separately.)

The Bernstein debates of 1895–1900 followed a long but shallow depression of 1873–1895. Yet the theoretical context of the debate was precisely that capitalism had survived the crisis and was now booming. This observation "triggered" Bernstein's revisionism and the counter-attacks that asserted the valdity of crisis and breakdown theory despite the apparent ability of capitalism to survive. The Luxemburg-Bauer-Grossman debates of 1913–1929 and the contributions of Lenin and Bukharin centered on the logic of reproduction schema on the one hand, and the relationship of imperialism to the economy on the other. Pollock's studies after the 1930s depression similarly focused on the ability of capitalism to survive the crisis and on the role of state monopoly capitalism in mitigating the economic side of crises by means of planning (Marramao 1975: 66). The postwar work of the left Keynesians also dealt with state intervention, as did Baran and Sweezy and Gillman. The postwar boom produced a series of works, from Baran and Sweezy through Mattick, whose common theme was to show that, despite state intervention and despite the apparent boom, capitalism was still stagnation- or crisis-prone. Perlo's book, although published after the 1970 crisis, similarly attempted to demonstrate logically why the boom could not last. Mandel's *Late Capitalism* (1975), although predicting the slump of the seventies, was largely concerned with explicating the postwar boom.

The pattern revealed by these examples is the emergence of new versions of crisis theory when expected crises fail to occur or when capitalism shows its ability to survive and even thrive following severe economic downturns. Thomas Kuhn (1962) would call these situations "anomalies," occasions when theoretical predictions go astray, when reality seems not to fit the accepted theory. According to Kuhn, anomalies in the natural sciences do not result in theoretical innovation each time they appear. Instead, anomalies are left to one side while scientists pursue the positive explanatory power of their current theory. Only when numerous anomalies have accumulated does some group of scientists attempt to create a new paradigm or theory that can explain the anomalies. Evidently, Kuhn's model does not apply to the history of Marxist theory. Repeatedly, individual anomalies have led to immediate modifications in the theory and/or new theories of crisis.

We can specify in more detail how anomalies act as stimuli for theoretical innovation in crisis theory. In several instances only a few theorists responded to anomalous events by pointing out that the theory was wrong. However, these revisionist arguments called forth replies from orthodox theorists. Thus the survival of capitalism after crises has provoked revisionism, which has in turn forced orthodox theorists to defend crisis theory. In order to do so, they have had to elaborate or restructure crisis theory, creating theoretical innovations.

A second stimulus for innovation involves the emergence of new socio-economic phenomena that demand explanation in terms of accumulation theory. Each instance—the rise of imperialism, monopoly, state planning, and Keynesian fiscal management—has evoked new theoretical activity as left scholars attempt to integrate the new feature into the corpus of Marxist theory. It is also noteworthy that in almost all cases these new phenomena are read as countervailing tendencies. That is, they are explained in terms of how they counteract, avoid, or delay the tendencies toward crisis that would otherwise be manifest. Thus these new phenomena are used to neutralize anomaly. Without imperialism, monopoly state planning, and so on, the lack of severe crises would have cast crisis theory into doubt. But these new phenomena were integrated into Marxist theory as explanations of why breakdown was not occurring. Including them strengthened the Marxist paradigm by explaining away apparent anomalies.

The third stimulus for crisis theory seems to be internal debate. New versions of crisis theory provoke attacks or further developments from other theorists, as in the ongoing debate over how to read the implications of the reproduction schema for crisis theory. To the extent that internal innovation begets debate that begets more innovation, the history of crisis theory becomes independent of outside events.

In sum, the factors that seem to have provoked new developments in crisis theory are: challenges to crisis theory from outsiders, based on the ability of capitalism to recover from crises; the emergence of new socio-political phenomena that may potentially modify or reverse crises; and ongoing internal debate as a self-generating force. The first two factors are examples of the tension between the paradigm maintenance aspect and current events aspect of Marxist theorizing. Crisis theory is challenged when it appears not to fit the facts—when crises seem mild or when a boom persists. The theory must be modified to show why in each case the boom is only temporary. Likewise, the emergence of imperialism, state intervention, and similar phenomena is in tension with the body of accepted theory. The task becomes one of proving that the theory can explain why these phenomena had to emerge at this stage in history, how they modify crisis tendencies, and so on.

Thus we view crisis theory as an ongoing process of tension between the desire to maintain the orthodoxy of theory on the one hand and the need to account for new events on the other. Either the theory is modified, or the events are read as predicted by the old theory. In either case, the task of the theorist is to lessen or manage the ongoing tension between theory and unfolding events. This task is most urgent when current events seem to diverge totally from theoretical expectations, as during long booms, the apparent success of state intervention against crises, and so forth. Such high-tension periods lead to revisionism (i.e., defection from the theoretical system) or elaboration of theory to show how crises *will* manifest themselves but are temporarily masked or moderated by contemporary phenomena.

How does this tension management notion account for the post–1970 proliferation of crisis theory? Several points come to mind. There is no doubt that the surge of interest in crisis theory in the seventies was occasioned by the stagnation of 1970, by the spectacular downturn of 1973, and by subsequent recessions. Yet the model of tension between theory and events still holds, for one of the most notable features of this latest round of crisis theory is that the traditional explanation, the organic composition of capital/falling rate of profit argument, was not accepted. Such new events as stagflation, government intervention, unions, and monopoly instead inspired innovative crisis theories. Wage-induced profit squeeze, monopoly inflation, and fiscal crisis are testaments to the dissatisfaction felt by many late-twentieth-century Marxist economists with the explanations provided by 1930s Marxist political economic textbooks. But we also find a revival of the old orthodoxy as it attempts to assert that it can indeed explain the current scene. So we have Yaffe, Cogoy, Fine, and Harris insisting that the organic composition argument does hold and attempting to accommodate the new role of the state within the old theory. On balance, however, most left political economists do not believe that the old theory can adequately explain contemporary reality, which is why we find an extraordinary amount of innovative work occurring.

Having considered the issue of when crisis theory appears to flourish, we should also consider who the theorists are. In the classical period, prior to World War I, political economy was largely the domain of party intellectuals, who typically earned a living through the party journals and schools. Thus Luxemburg taught in the German Socialist party (SPD) Central School in Berlin while writing *The Accumulation of Capital*. Hilferding was working as a full-time journalist for *Vorwarts* when he wrote his *Finanzkapital*. Bukharin wrote economic expositions such as *Imperialism and the World Economy* while in exile, worked with Trotsky as a journalist in New York in 1916, and from 1917 on was the editor of *Pravda*. Otto Bauer led the secretariat of the parliamentary group of the Austro-Hungarian Social Democratic party prior to World War I. Kautsky edited *Die Zeit*, the SPD theoretical journal. Eduard Bernstein edited another SPD journal, the *Sozialdemokrat*. And the legal Marxist Tugan-Baranowski was a professor in Russia.

Sociologically, it is significant that the social democratic parties of pre–World War I Europe were able to sustain this small but high-powered stratum of intellectuals. It should also be added that these figures, despite their oft-expressed distain for *Katheder-sozialisten* (professor-socialists), were not uneducated. Most had academic backgrounds. Luxemburg held a doctorate from the University of Zurich. Bukharin attended Moscow University and while in exile studied marginalist economics in Vienna. Hilferding was a medical student, Otto Bauer a lawyer, and Kautsky a student of anthropology and other social sciences. Of all the prewar Marxist political economists, Eduard Bernstein alone had not gone to the *gymnasium* and on to the university. Thus, by the standards of their time, these Marxist intellectuals were highly educated individuals.

The academic bent of Marxist political economy became even stronger as Henryk Grossman, Friedrich Pollock, and Fritz Sternberg joined the interwar debates. Grossman was a professor of economics at Warsaw prior to moving to Frankfurt, where he became an assistant professor at the university in addition to his role in the Institut für Sozialforschung. Pollock had received a doctorate in economics before joining the institute.

The post–World War II American figures were typically university-trained economists (e.g., Baran, Sweezy, Perlo, Gillman). Most members of this older generation did not teach, however, due partly to McCarthyist pressures. Finally, the contemporary generation of post-sixties contributors to political economy consists of graduate students and professors of economics.

What is the importance of such factors of background, occupation, and education? Advances in crisis theory have typically been made by individuals of petit-bourgeois origins with good educations and while employed full-time in positions enabling them to devote their major efforts to Marxist intellectual work. This fact suggests that there are material underpinnings to movements of left thought. Generally, only individuals whose time is sufficiently unencumbered with the necessity of earning a living and whose intellectual backgrounds give them the facility and knowledge required to contribute to these topics will be found doing innovative work. This material basis for the existence of a professional left intelligentsia appears to have been a historical prerequisite for the development of theoretical Marxism—an interpretation that has major implications for how one conceptualizes the Marxist ideal of the "unity of theory and praxis."

It is clear that after World War I the primary occupation among left intelligentsia shifted from party journalist to academician. But it is not accurate to suggest, as Perry Anderson (1976) does, that pre–World War I Marxist political economy was spun out by party politicians who generated theory in the heat of current political events, whereas post-war work is the product of ivory tower intellectuals. Delightful as such an image of the prewar unity of theory and praxis may be, it is highly overdrawn, at least for Marxist political economy. Anderson himself notes the precocity of many political economic thinkers. What he does not allow for is that Bauer and Hilferding wrote their most celebrated political-economic works before taking up political positions; that Bukharin and Lenin wrote most of their economic works while in exile or before the revolution; that Luxemburg's economic writing took place in the relative isolation of the SPD school, and so on. This is not to say that active politicians produced no works of significance. Rather, many of the most important theoretical advances were made by individuals who were paid intellectual workers during early or time-out phases of their political careers. The unity of theory and praxis is temporally fragmented. Major intellectual advances in political economy have rarely been made by individuals immersed in revolutionary struggle on a daily basis.

Although political economy may not have met the criteria for the unity of theory and praxis in Anderson's sense—that is, a merging of theory in ongoing political activism—some alternative notions of this unity rest on different criteria. Such definitions are of importance to the present generation of left theorists and will therefore be discussed shortly.

For the moment, however, we shall turn from crisis theory and political economy at the general level to consider the specific varieties of crisis theory. Why is each produced? Jacoby (1975) attacks the notion that breakdown versions of crisis theory have some equivalent political or philosophical position within the left by showing that both adherents of political spontaneity and political reformism accept breakdown theory. Similarly, it is impossible to take the four varieties of crisis theory—disproportionality, underconsumptionist, organic composition/falling rate of profit, and wage-induced profit squeeze—and deduce some obvious class interest or political persuasion for each. Underconsumptionism was used by Malthus to justify the necessity of landowners' unproductive consumption, by the legal populists to argue for agrarian socialism, by Luxemburg to promote a spontaneous revolutionary movement, and by Baran and Sweezy to advocate democratic socialism in America. Disproportionality was held in favor among legal Marxists like Tugan-Baranowski, among revisionists like Hilferding, and among Bolsheviks like Lenin. Disproportionality theory does indeed accord with the perspective of a social planner (eliminate the contradictions of capitalism via planning), but the politics of planning have varied across the entire right-left spectrum. The organic composition of capital explanation in the present period has been adopted by most communist and Trotskyist parties, but it is not clear that this position derives from anything except the dogmatism and traditionalism of those sections of the left. In particular, it does not easily translate into political policy differences. Similarly, the wage-induced profit-squeeze theory appears to stress the active agency of working-class struggle, yet its adherents do not seem to represent any especially distinct left tendency.

If, I suggest, there is no simple equivalence of theory and politics regarding these theories, no determinate political tendency or class faction upholding each version, an explanation for their variety and timing must be sought elsewhere. I would argue for an explanation that considers the empirical circumstances represented by each version. *For it is striking that there is a variant of crisis theory for almost every empirical permutation.* Thus, if we take the rate of surplus value and the organic composition of capital as two basic dimensions by which Marxists consider the economy, we find that all possibilities are covered (see Table 2).

We appear to have one theory that captures the essence of those periods when companies are profitable, investment flows abroad, but stagnation crises occur (i.e., underconsumptionism); another theory for when wages boom while company profits appear to falter (wage-profit squeeze); and another theory for when wages do not appear to shift but profits appear to lag and companies seem to lack investment capital (falling rate of profit). To the extent that theorists observe a particular constellation of events, one would expect a rise and fall in the popularity of specific variants of crisis theory.

In particular, I believe this explanation accounts for the popularity of underconsumption theory in the United States and for the limited application of wage-induced profit-squeeze theory to cyclical issues. The power, profitability, and resilience of American capital over thirty-odd years has tended to undercut faith in the organic composition/falling rate of profit position. The critique of waste and of excess capacity appears to fit the American reality more closely than notions of failing profitability. By contrast, in Britain, plagued by twenty years of balance-of-payments crises, inflation, and so on, the falling rate of profit argument has more empirical appeal, as does profit squeeze, while the notion of a glut of surplus profits seems highly unrealistic.

Having linked kinds of crisis theory to different economic situations, I should stress that the state of an economy is not always clear in terms of Marxist variables. This observation leads us to the issues of data use and of measurement and verifiability of alternative versions of crisis theory. We have already noted that Marx, Engels, and Lenin did

TABLE 2. *Varieties of Marxist Crisis Theory*

Behavior of Rate of Surplus Value	Behavior of Organic Composition	Outcome	Theorists Associated with Each Position
Goes up	Relatively constant during period in question	Capital glut and underconsumption lead to stagnation	Baran and Sweezy; Perlo
Goes down	Relatively constant during period in question	Wage-induced profit squeeze	Glyn and Sutcliffe; Boddy and Crotty
Stagnates (becomes difficult to raise)	Rises	Falling rate of profit leads to collapse	Mattick; Yaffe; Cogoy

not hesitate to resort to empirical data in order to understand an economic tendency. Contemporary American radical theorists continue to follow this practice. Indeed, the existence of elaborate censuses of manufactures and of national income accounts imposes an increasing burden upon Marxist theorists to test their arguments. (I would also suggest that the academic position of most theorists, the desire to legitimate their work as science, and the need to delegitimate the anti-Marxist orthodoxy places an even stronger pressure on American Marxist economists to prove their theories empirically.)

Every major American work discussed above has employed empirical data, from Baran and Sweezy's demonstration of a rising surplus to Boddy and Crotty's argument for a falling one. Naturally, since Marxists are not vulgar empiricists, there is much debate over what categories should be counted and how. Thus Boddy and Crotty insist on slicing a business cycle into four, whereas Sherman cuts it into two; Wright conceives of state expenditures differently than do Baran and Sweezy, and so on.

It is noteworthy, however, that reliance upon empirical data has been especially characteristic of the "newer" versions of crisis theory, those other than the organic composition/falling rate of profit school. The organic composition orthodoxy has responded not by arguing over the accuracy of the data but by frequently going to the extreme of denying the possibility of measurement. Thus, whereas critics of the falling rate of profit thesis have examined it empirically (cf. Mage 1963; Gillman 1957; Hodgson 1974; Perlo 1973), only one of its supporters, Ernest Mandel, has come to its defense on similar empirical grounds (Mandel 1975). Mandel has also provided a withering critique of his fellow falling rate of profit theorists who contend that their theory is untestable (Mandel 1975: 19–20).

In Chapter One I suggested that different types of structural constraints on left academics produce different styles of left scholarship. How does this framework apply in the case of crisis theory? Once again we shall contrast the United States and Britain. Three features of contemporary American work set it off from its European counterparts: its theoretical eclecticism, its empirical emphasis, its orientation toward orthodox economics.

In the British debates much effort has been expended to show the logical weaknesses of opposing varieties of crisis theory, and theorists debate which is the one correct version. American work, on the other hand, is eclectic. Wright in his review (1975) and Boddy and Crotty in their critique of underconsumptionism (1976b) do not dismiss competing theories on logical grounds. Even the two most directly opposed approaches—Sherman's version of profit squeeze versus Boddy and Crotty's—grant partial validity to each other's viewpoint. Instead, arguments center on the relative empirical efficacy of the theories.

In Chapter One, we discussed the phenomenon of historicizing theory as one method of avoiding conflict. Instead of arguing the absolute incompatibility of two theories, which necessarily involves proving that one version is wrong, one adopts a theoretical position that allows each variant its due. One relegates certain versions to the past with the explanation that they correctly described a certain historical period but do not apply to the changed circumstances of the present. Each theory, rather than being right or wrong, has its place in some sequence of historical periods. This form of historical eclecticism is very common in American work and leads to some curious interpretations. For example, Erik Wright (1975) argues that falling rate of profit has given way to underconsumptionism. Boddy and Crotty (1976b) assert exactly the reverse: the falling rate of profit has replaced underconsumptionism.

This eclecticism reaches its pinnacle in Thomas Weisskopf's (1978) formulation, where the wage-induced profit squeeze, the organic-composition-induced profit squeeze, and the underconsumption position are simultaneously inserted in one equation. Weisskopf concludes:

> Three alternative models of capitalist cyclical economic crises were developed on the basis of different variants of Marxist crisis theory. Each of these models was found to be logically consistent and theoretically plausible, under an appropriate set of assumptions. Thus on purely theoretical grounds it is impossible to single out any one as the most valid model of cyclical crises in modern capitalist economies. Indeed it is quite possible that the mechanisms of two or three models could operate simultaneously. . . . The choice among these models . . . can therefore only be made with reference to specific historical circumstances, and by means of an analysis of the empirical evidence. (Weisskopf 1978: 256)

This evaluation stands in stark contrast to the British debates, which take place almost entirely on the level of high theory and assert the essential incompatibility of competing crisis theories. (See Fine and Harris 1976 for a description of the British debates.)

Contemporary crisis theory in the United States and that in Britain differ not only in their eclecticism and empirical analysis but also in their application of their findings. In addressing this issue, one cannot help but raise the larger issue of the place of crisis theory in Marxism generally. We have already pointed out that crisis theory—a theory of the collapse of capitalism and the consequent necessity of socialism— is silent on all the crucial questions. Is there an economic collapse or just serious crises? Do crises necessarily worsen? Does revolution take place because of the direct consequences of some severe crisis or because of the cumulative socio-political consequences of crises upon class behavior, irrespective of the state of the economy at the moment of revolution? The failure to answer these questions suggests that the real function of crisis theory, outside of some global assurance that capitalism cannot survive, does not involve any contribution to the theory of revolution. But if crisis theory offers no theory of revolution, does it nevertheless have practical utility as a guide for revolutionary activity? Is there a practical side to crisis theory, and, if so, what is it?

One eminent crisis theorist, Rosa Luxemburg, seems to have had a low opinion of its utility for political struggle. Jacoby, in his excellent essays on the politics of crisis theory, discusses and quotes Luxemburg to this effect:

> The reason Luxemburg offered to explain this situation [i.e., the lack of interest in volume three of *Capital* by the working-class movement] . . . was paradoxical, at least for a Marxist; Marxist economic theory was neglected because it was impractical to the actual working class movement. The theory "remains unused because it greatly transcends the needs of the working class in the matter of weapons for the daily struggle." In particular, the problems of *Capital* III, "however important from the outlook of pure theory, are comparatively unimportant from the practical outlook of class war." (Jacoby 1975: 44, quoting Luxemburg)

If one accepts Luxemburg's formulation (elsewhere she takes a different view), Marxist political economy becomes a strange exercise. We could adopt Antonio Gramsci's cynical view that a mechanistic crisis theory is essential to keep up the faith of revolutionaries that capitalism must end:

> When you don't have the initiative in the struggle and the struggle itself comes eventually to be identified with a series of defeats, mechanical determinism becomes a tremendous force of moral resistance, of cohesion and of patient and obstinate perseverance. "I have been defeated for the moment, but the tide of history is working for me in the long term." (Gramsci 1971: 336)

Though there is clearly some truth in Gramsci's observation, for intellectuals crisis theory is something more than a guarantor of capitalism's demise. I suggest that the larger import of crisis theory among left academics is its practical utility, not as a theory for political strategy or tactics, but as a central part of a left Weltanschauung. The essence of a world-view is its ability to predict and render sensible emerging events. To the extent that Marxists have understood history, especially at moments of upheaval and economic crisis when others saw only confusion, the former gained authority for their actions. Indeed, along with the moral idealism of Marxism, its powerful Weltanschauung has been a major factor in its appeal.

If we accept this view of crisis theory, we can understand the differences in emphasis between British and American versions of crisis theory. Both nationalities use crisis theory as part of an intellectual Weltanschauung concerning capitalism, but their applications of such a world-view differ. The tension between maintaining an orthodox paradigm and explaining ongoing events offers an especially clear contrast, which may be understood in terms of the different structural positions that American and British theorists occupy.

In the United States left theorists most often employ crisis theory to attack orthodox economics and hence defend the appropriateness of a Marxist economics in academia. The introduction to virtually every American work on crisis theory includes a preamble to the effect that neoclassical economics cannot and has not dealt with the empirical reality of the present crisis. Neoclassical economics cannot explain crisis because its models of equilibration and harmony ignore any possibility of contradiction and systematic conflicts of interest. It must therefore resort to ad hoc explanations of crises, depending on exogenous factors like weather, governmental irresponsibility, or the Federal Reserve. By contrast, Marxist political economy successfully predicts crises and accounts for them as systematic endogenous features of capitalism (cf. Union for Radical Political Economics 1978: 5; Frank 1978; Alcaly 1978: 16; Weisskopf 1978: 241; Wright 1975: 5).

The implicit message is that Marxist political economy is a more scientifically valid enterprise than the apolitical orthodoxy. One sees here the institutional insecurity of the American left in academia. As I argued earlier, academic leftists find themselves attacked as ideologues, as persons involved in politics rather than science. The response of American Marxist economists, who are highly dependent upon acceptance by their apolitical colleagues for tenure and advancement, is to reverse the accusation: Marxism is *more scientific*; ideological conservatism prevents the neoclassical orthodoxy from admitting the systematicity of crises.

But by endorsing empirical inquiry as a means of legitimating their enterprise, Marxists become caught in its criteria of evaluation: they must prove the scientific rigor of their work. This need explains the empirical bias of American political economy, its effort to demonstrate the hard facts of its case to skeptical non-Marxist colleagues or audiences. In such a context the relative emphasis between maintaining the Marxist paradigm and explaining unfolding events shifts to the latter.

Thus the work of American crisis theorists is theoretically eclectic, empirically detailed, and directly oriented toward professional peers, especially as an attack on orthodox economics.

Contemporary British crisis theorists of course share the general desire to sustain a Marxist Weltanschauung and to render ongoing events intelligible in terms of theory. But the relative importance given to paradigm maintenance and to explaning ongoing events is much different. The empirical emphasis is not so apparent; as we have seen, one whole school (the falling rate of profit position) even argues that its theory does not have to hold up to empirical verification. Conversely, the emphasis on purity of Marxist doctrine, the correctness of one's theoretical and methodological position vis-à-vis Marxist orthodoxy, is much stronger in Britain. In the place of eclecticism one finds sectarian struggle. Those who revise Marx and place the goal of explanation above that of maintaining orthodox categories are dismissed as "neo-Ricardians." By contrast, the "fundamentalists" see the crucial issue as improving their understanding of Marx's position on the topic and of his methodology as the only successful way to solve the problem (cf. Fine and Harris 1976). Thus, in the absence of a dependency upon orthodox economics (or upon orthodox economists), British Marxist political economy does not orient itself in competition with orthodox economics but tends to develop internally as a debate among already committed socialists over the correct methodological and theoretical reading of Marxist texts.

In this sociology of knowledge analysis I have examined why crisis theory appears when it does, what functions the theory fulfills, and how a model stressing three goals of Marxist theory and the tensions between them allows us to understand national variations in the predominant style of crisis theory. I have identified several ways in which the tension between paradigm maintenance and the analysis of current events has been handled: by revisionism, by identifying tendencies that appear to neutralize anomalies, and by assigning crisis theories to different historical periods.

In the next chapter I intend to show how the historical development of imperialism theory reflects other tensions within Marxist theory and how these tensions have been resolved in the process of theoretical innovation.

Chapter Five

IMPERIALISM AND DEPENDENCY

TO THE CONTEMPORARY READER, the term "imperialism" conjures up images of global inequality, of malnourished children in Asia or Africa contrasted to affluence or excess in Europe and North America. The fact that these images are juxtaposed, that one implies the other, testifies to our culture's widespread familiarity with radical critiques of imperialism. This preconception poses a problem for us, since imperialism has not always had this connotation in Marxist theory. At one time the term evoked images of wars between European powers or of the economic advance of colonial nations. In short, the nature of imperialism has changed, and we can find accompanying transformations in Marxist analyses of its causes and consequences.

Consequently, I shall use "imperialism theory" as a generic term to refer to the various theories of colonialism, neocolonialism, dependency, and underdevelopment. All of the theories consider economic and, to a lesser extent, political relationships between the industrialized capitalist nations of Europe, North America, and Japan on the one hand and the relatively less industrialized nations of the Third World. Marxist analyses generally characterize these relationships as exploitative, although the nature of the exploitation varies from writer to writer.

One purpose of this chapter is to review the major figures in radical imperialism theory and to outline their analyses. My second goal is to examine the dynamics of this body of scholarship, to develop a sociology of knowledge that accounts for the evolution of imperialism theory.

Earlier I argued that contemporary Marxism is simultaneously an analytical scientific project and a moral critique. Tensions emerge between the goal of maintaining a traditional paradigm and the goal of developing a moral critique when the Marxist approach is applied to imperialism, and all too often theorists have found themselves unable to achieve both goals. This particular tension explains several developments in imperialism theory. Typically, theorists have responded by strengthening the critique at the expense of modifying or breaking with the orthodox paradigm. We illustrate this argument by following imperialism theory from Marx and Engels to the present, emphasizing at each stage the correspondence between analysis and critique.

Marx and Engels: Exploitation and Imperialism

The theory of exploitation that lies at the center of Marxist thought derives from the labor theory of value. Labor power is a commodity like any other, but it also possesses certain unique properties. Specifically, "the value of labor power and the value which that labor power creates in the labor process are two different magnitudes" (Engels 1970: 226). In other words, the value that a worker creates during a day's work exceeds his/her own wage. The difference constitutes an unpaid "surplus value" that accrues to the capitalist class. The ratio of this surplus value to the value paid as wages is what Marx termed the "rate of exploitation."

Although Marx and Engels used the term "exploitation" for this process, they refused to moralize about it. Specifically, they never asserted that this arrangement was "unjust" or that the surplus "belonged" to the workers. Speaking of theorists who used Ricardo's labor theory of value to argue that surplus value was stolen from workers, Engels wrote:

> The above application of the theory of Ricardo, which shows to the workers that the totality of social production, which is their product, belongs to them because they are the only real producers, leads direct to Communism. But it is also, as Marx shows, false in form, economically speaking, because it is simply an application of morality to economy. *According to the laws of bourgeois economy, the greater part of the product does not belong to the work-*

ers who have created it. If, then, we say, "That is unjust, it ought not to be"; that has nothing whatever to do with economy, we are only stating that this economic fact is in contradiction to our moral sentiment. That is why Marx has never based upon this his Communist conclusions, but rather upon the necessary overthrow, which is developing itself under our eyes every day, of the capitalist system of production. He contents himself with saying that surplus-value consists of unpaid labour; it is a fact, pure and simple. (Engels 1900: vi; my emphasis)

Elsewhere Engels suggests that this surplus value is "a piece of especially good luck for the buyer [the capitalist], but on the basis of the laws of exchange of commodities by no means an injustice to the seller [the worker]" (Engels 1970: 226). Similarly Marx (1972) objected to those who took from his theory of exploitation the idea that capitalism's extraction of surplus unpaid labor is theft. In sum, the core theory of exploitation in Marxism involves the unpaid element of surplus labor, but Marx and Engels eschewed the opportunity to read it as a swindle, theft, or otherwise unjust practice: by the laws of commodity production, workers are paid the full value of their labor power.

How, then, did Marx and Engels relate their theory of exploitation to colonialism and imperialism? They viewed economic relationships between colonizing and colonized countries as going beyond straightforward capitalist exploitation of the native work force (although that too occurred), and they identified at least three mechanisms of this extra exploitation. First, the initial phase of colonialism was characterized by plunder and theft of the colony's riches. Second, super-profits were extracted from colonies insofar as those countries purchased commodities at above normal prices from monopoly industries in England. Third:

Two nations may exchange according to the law of profit in such a way that both gain, but one is always defrauded. . . . One of the nations may continually appropriate for itself a part of the surplus labour of the other, giving back nothing for it in exchange, except that the measure here [is] not as in the exchange between capitalist and worker. (Marx 1973: 872)

In this fragment of the *Grundrisse* lies the germ of a theory of unequal exchange, which we shall review later.

Despite these mechanisms of exploitation, it is clear that Marx and Engels expected the imperialist relationship to result ultimately in the industrial development of colonized nations. Marx and Engels wrote about the deliberate destruction and subsequent prohibition of native manufactures in British India. They also knew of the underdevelopment of Ireland that resulted from its relationship to Britain; it regressed into the role of an agricultural exporter to England. Yet their general position seems clear: imperialism ultimately leads to the industrial development of the colonized nations, despite the havoc it wrecks in the interim:

> Modern industry, resulting from the railway system, will dissolve the hereditary division of labour, upon which rest the Indian castes, those decisive impediments to Indian progress and Indian power.
>
> All the English bourgeoisie may be forced to do will neither emancipate nor materially mend the social condition of the mass of the people, depending not only on the development of the productive powers, but on their appropriation by the people. But what they cannot fail to do is to lay down the material premises for both. Has the bourgeoisie ever done more? Has it ever effected a progress without dragging individuals and peoples through blood and dirt, through misery and degradation? (Marx, in d'Encausse and Schramm 1969: 118)

As we shall show, this view that imperialism and colonialism lead to industrialization of Third World nations, albeit at the cost of human suffering, was the orthodox Marxist position up to 1928.

Classical Theories of Imperialism

The topic of imperialism did not excite the interest of Marxist writers until the period between 1900 and World War I. Two factors seem responsible for bringing the subject to the fore. First, the successful recovery of the European economies from recessions in the last quarter of the nineteenth century cast doubt upon the notion that capitalism would fall apart economically. As described in the last chapter, this anomaly resulted in a wave of innovative and revisionism in Marxist crisis theory. Several Marxists, faced with the need to explain the resilience of the capitalist system, turned to imperialism as a factor that had temporarily staved off the crisis of the advanced capitalist nations. This position is clearly evident in Luxemburg's works and, less straight-forwardly, in Lenin's.

The second stimulus for analyzing imperialism derived from the po-litical tensions that arose between Britain, Germany, and other Euro-pean powers over the scramble for empire. Marxist political commen-tators needed to explain how imperialism had intensified competition between the European powers. The advent of World War I ("The Great Imperialist War") created a sense of urgency among theorists of impe-rialism, and several additional analyses appeared in the early years of the war.

The classical studies of imperialism either subsumed imperialism under the theory of economic crises or focused on imperialism as a cause of wars between European powers. They did not aim, in any large degree, to assess the prospects of Third World communism or Third World capitalism. In that sense we could reasonably call the early imperialist theories "eurocentric." They were primarily intended to serve as discussion documents for the Marxist intelligentsia or as popular pamphlets explaining the war. Since we have dealt with sev-eral of these theories at length in the last chapter, our review will be brief.

Hilferding, a young Austro-Marxist, revolutionized Marxist theory with his 1905 study of finance capital. His main concern was the cen-tralization of capital that had occurred over the prior quarter century, the development of the joint-stock company, and the fusion of banking and industrial capital (hence finance capital) in Germany. One aspect of this concentration of economic power was the rise of monopolies (actually oligopolies) and the formation of national industrial cartels. The cartels pushed for tariffs to protect their home markets against for-eign competition and to enable them to charge monopoly prices. They also encouraged their governments to expand the national markets by acquiring colonial territories and to exclude foreign sellers from those markets by imposing high tariffs. Colonies became important as mar-kets for goods, as sources of raw materials, and as favorable oppor-tunities for investment, given their low wages. Hence, capital export to the colonies became an important factor. Rivalries grew between im-perialist powers as each sought new territories for itself while trying to exclude competition from foreign concerns.

Rosa Luxemburg saw an even more basic cause for imperialism. Her *Accumulation of Capital* (1912–1913) was simultaneously a criticism of orthodox crisis theory, an affirmation of the chronic underconsumption theory of crises, and an explanation of imperialist expansionism. To reiterate her conclusion, imperialism was necessary because European capitalists faced a chronic problem of insufficient demand, which resulted in realization crises. Trade with the noncapitalist colonies provided additional markets for goods and thus temporarily mitigated or staved off this difficulty. Imperialism was pre-eminently a push for markets, and imperialist rivalries could be understood as the attempt to monopolize crucial markets:

> So long as we retain the assumption that there are no classes but capitalist and workers, then there is no way that the capitalists as a class can get rid of the surplus goods in order to change the surplus value into money, and thus accumulate capital. . . .
>
> . . . So there must develop right from the start an exchange relationship between capitalist production and the non-capitalist milieu, where capital finds the possibility of realizing surplus value in hard cash for further capitalization. . . .
>
> . . . The more capitalist countries participate in this hunting for accumulation areas, the rarer the non-capitalist places still open for the expansion of capital become and the tougher the competition; its raids turn into a chain of economic and political catastrophes: world crises, wars, revolution. (Luxemburg and Bukharin 1972: 58–60)

As we noted earlier, the conclusions in Lenin's pamphlet, *Imperialism: The Higher Stage of Capitalism* (1916), are similar in many respects to Hilferding's and J. A. Hobson's. Like Luxemburg as well, he viewed imperialism as a response to crisis tendencies in the advanced nations, but he concentrated on the lack of profitable investment opportunities in the advanced capitalist nations. Colonialism provided a focus for capital exports and investment and for the importation of cheap raw materials, both ensuring the continued prosperity of monopolies at home. Lenin shared Marx's conclusion that this process would result in the industrialization of the colonies:

> The export of capital influences and greatly accelerates the development of capitalism in those countries to which it is exported,

while, therefore, the export of capital may tend to a certain extent to arrest development in the capital-exporting countries, it can only do so by expanding and deepening the further development of capitalism throughout the world. (Lenin 1969: 76)

Nikolai Bukharin, who shared Lenin's exile in Switzerland, wrote two treatises dealing with imperialism: *Imperialism and the World Economy* (1915) and *Imperialism and the Accumulation of Capital* (1924). In some ways Bukharin's treatment of imperialism is unoriginal; he borrows heavily from Marx and from Hilferding. His contribution lies in his identification of many of the logical pitfalls of Luxemburg and others and in his ability to avoid the functionalist teleology that sees imperialism as a solution to crisis problems. For Bukharin (in Luxemburg and Bukharin 1972: 243-247), the causes of imperialism are to be found in the seach for profits, and especially in the higher rates of profit to be found in the colonies. These higher profits occur, in part, because of the harsh exploitation of colonial labor. In addition, since colonial industries are relatively backward and inefficient, many goods cost more to produce in the colonies. When goods produced relatively efficiently in Europe are sold at colonial prices, they make a higher than normal rate of profit (a surplus profit).

One does not have to invoke underconsumptionist crises to explain imperialism. The normal desires of individual capitalists to maximize profits will lead to trade with and investment in colonial countries and to the expansion of imperialism. Bukharin admits that the extra markets afforded by the colonies will be helpful during what he views as temporary crises of overproduction, but he argues that underconsumption is not the central cause of imperialism that Luxemburg believes it to be.

Taking these classical theorists together, we find an array of mechanisms underlying imperialism: markets for goods (Luxemburg); investment opportunities and raw materials (Lenin); higher profits from trade and investment (Bukharin); cheap labor (Bauer); and all of the above (Hilferding). Despite their different emphases, all these theorists agree that the net effect of imperialism is to develop the productive capacities of the colonial countries. The reversal of this belief was the turning point of Marxist imperialism theory, and it occurred first in the political realm.

The Communist International

Following World War I, an entirely new forum opened up for Marxist debate with the establishment of the Communist International (Comintern) in March 1919. This body of international socialist and communist parties concerned itself with the practical and intellectual task of defending the recent Russian revolution and extending revolution abroad by planning the strategy of communist movements. It was also preoccupied with the split in the international socialist movement: the various social democratic organizations had backed their respective countries during World War I while Bolshevik parties had opposed the war.

In a series of congresses from 1919 to 1928, major figures of the world's communist movements met to discuss strategy, the political and economic struggles of their various proletariats and peasantries, the world economic situation, and the struggles of the USSR against the capitalist powers. Imperialism theory played a role in the Comintern because communist parties from colonized countries demanded that their struggles be given consideration. These nationalist anti-imperialist struggles took on a dual importance, first as sources of strategic allies for the Soviet Union in its strained relations with the capitalist powers, and later as arenas of revolutionary activity when the expected revolutions in the advanced Western countries failed to appear. (The potential "weak link" of capitalism might be in the colonies.)

However, in assessing the theoretical pronouncements of the Comintern regarding imperialism, it is important to consider a point made by H. C. d'Encausse and S. R. Schram (1969). The theory of imperialism took a back seat to the political interests of Russian diplomacy, to Soviet Russia's stance regarding the ethnic minorities within its own borders, and to the aspirations of Third World communist parties in colonized countries. Because these practical matters dominated the discussions, there were flip-flops on the issue of theoretical interest to us: whether or not the colonized nations would develop economically, given their relationship to the central capitalist powers.

When this question was raised, it was linked to the tactical question of whether or not Third World communist parties should ally themselves with their local bourgeoisies in national independence struggles against the colonial powers. At the first congress, a few Comintern members, most notably an Indian delegate, M. N. Roy, tried to answer this question with the following logic: to the extent that colonial powers frustrated or reversed capitalist development in the colonies, the objective interests of local bourgeoisies were to ally with the communists in a national liberation struggle against imperialism. However, if imperialism industrially developed its colonies, the local bourgeoisies were likely to back the imperialists against communism and national liberation movements. This argument did not receive much attention at the time.

At the second congress of 1920, Lenin introduced his celebrated notion that the world was divided into oppressor and oppressed nations (as distinct from classes). Communists in the colonies were therefore to ally themselves with bourgeois national independence movements in the fight against imperialism. It is noteworthy that Roy argued that rapid industrial development was occurring in India and that the domestic class struggle between peasantry, proletariat, and bourgeoisie was therefore equally as important as that of national liberation. Roy's development notion coincided with the pre-1918 writings of Marx, Lenin, Luxemburg, and others and was formally accepted by the second congress. However, J. Degras (1960: 138–139) argues that it was essentially ignored by the Comintern after this period.

The reversal on the issue of whether imperialism developed or underdeveloped colonial economies came on the occasion of the sixth Comintern congress of 1928. Roy, extending his previous line of reasoning that imperialism was resulting in the rapid economic development of India, suggested that the colonies were becoming "decolonized." It followed that the Indian bourgeoisie, who gained from local industrial development, were moving against local communists and against the independence movement. It would therefore be foolish for the Comintern to order an alliance between Indian communists and the Indian bourgeoisie. For the first time, the International came out against such a claim. Otto Kuusinen, who prepared the counter-position, argued: "If it were true that British imperialism had really turned to the industrialization of India, we would have to revise our entire conception of the nature of imperialist colonial policy" (Degras 1960: 527). The congress adopted Kuusinen's theses to the effect that imperialism "retarded the development of native industry" (Degras 1960: 531), that this was imperialism's policy, and that imperialism seeks "to preserve and perpetuate all those pre-capitalist forms of exploitation" (Degras 1960: 534).

We therefore find that in 1928 the Comintern switched from a view that imperialism developed colonies, albeit with much attendant human suffering, to a view that imperialism retarded or destroyed the possibility of colonial development. This latter position was to become the essence of Marxist underdevelopment theory. According to the theses adopted by the Comintern in 1928:

> In its function as a colonial exploiter, the ruling imperialism is related to the colonial country primarily as a parasite, sucking the blood from its economic organisms. . . .
>
> Real industrialization of the colonial country, in particular the building up of a flourishing engineering industry which would promote the independent development of this productive forces, is not encouraged but, on the contrary, is hindered by the metropolis. This is the essence of its function of colonial enslavement: the colonial country is compelled to sacrifice the interests of its independent development and to play the part of an economic (agrarian raw material) appendage to foreign capitalism. (Degras 1960: 534)

To the extent that this new theory examined the causal mechanisms underlying economic retardation in the colonies, it seized upon two factors. One was the extraction of monopoly super-profits by metropolitan-owned enterprises. These companies drained the colonial economies, removing potentially investable surplus. Second, colonial administrators attempted to protect the products of metropolitan industries by prohibiting colonial industrialization. Instead, they encouraged the production of raw materials to complement rather than compete with the metropolis (Degras 1960: 535).

The new Comintern theory exhibits two weaknesses that concern us here. First, emphasis on the political policy of colonial administrations as a crucial factor in the lopsided economic development of the colonies limited the theory's scope. Specialization on raw materials production combined with little basic industry was a pattern characteristic of the politically independent nations of Latin America as well as of colonial countries. This kind of economic organization appeared to reproduce itself long after the end of the colonial administration. The issue of postcolonial development therefore remained unclear. Second, the Comintern continued to emphasize the validity of Lenin's characterization of imperialism as involving capital exports to the colonial areas. But this interpretation raised the question of why such a steady influx of capital nevertheless kept the colonies so backward. Both of these theoretical weaknesses were addressed in the post–World War II period.

Post–World War II

A variety of changing circumstances after World War II indirectly caused a wave innovation in the theory of imperialism. Perhaps the most dramatic events were the independence struggles that resulted in the disintegration of the British colonial empire and brought pressure to bear upon the French, Belgian, and Portuguese colonial systems. The newly independent nations joined the ex-colonies of Latin America in a bloc now known as the Third World. Though politically weak, one forum in which those nations did have some influence was the newly created United Nations. Through the U.N. a considerable amount of funds was channeled into studies of the problems of these underdeveloped nations, and U.N. economic surveys provided much of the data upon which the next generation of scholars based their theories of development.

An additional stimulus to the development of theory was the failure of these Third World nations to match the performance of the industrialized powers in the postwar era. While the latter grew, the former's problems intensified. By the late 1950s the discrepancies were well documented and politically significant. The Cold War and ongoing national liberation struggles heightened the perceived dangers of economic and political instability in Third World countries.

The fifties saw a rapid expansion of academic disciplines, including development economics and the sociology of development, as an intellectual response to these postcolonial issues. Contributing to the boom in apolitical interest in the Third World was a series of left-wing analyses of the plight of the ex-colonies. Andre Gunder Frank cites Baran's *Political Economy of Growth* (1957), John Strachey's *The End of Empire* (1959), and Yves Lacoste's *Les Pays Sous-Developpes* (n.d.) as pioneering works in the new critical theory of underdevelopment.

A parallel school appeared in Latin America under the auspices of the United Nations Economic Commission for Latin America (ECLA). Raul Prebisch, Celso Furtado, and Osvaldo Sunkel emerged as its major theorists. From these early efforts the theory of underdevelopment and dependency took shape.

The new theorists of imperialism, neocolonialism, and dependency were almost all academic economists and sociologists. The first generation, especially, tended to be left-wing academics in the West. In the *Communist Manifesto* Marx and Engels predicted that elements of the bourgeois intelligentsia will defect to the cause of the proletariat. In an analogous fashion an important early sector of dependency theorists consisted of Western socialist academicians who took the position of the underdeveloped nations against that of the imperialist powers. To this group should be added some non-Marxist (but nationalist) Third World academicians who were also originators of the dependency approach.

The radical approach crystallized as an alternative to the orthodox theories of development, which were viewed as inadequate. Nonradical Western theorists typically located the origins or causes of economic backwardness in endogenous features of underdeveloped nations: attitudinal elements of Third World cultures; the ignorance, corruption, or backwardness of their political elites; their uneducated populaces, and so on. These theorists tended to view Western intervention in underdeveloped countries as progressive and beneficial. Third World countries' problems stemmed from barriers to the efficient penetration of Western influences or from misuse of Western inputs, owing to retarding factors generated within underdeveloped nations.

By contrast, the dependency theorists emphasized that the ills of underdeveloped nations were to be found in the historical relationships between these nations and the industrialized West. Also, the problems in question were viewed as structural, typically economic ones, not as attitudinal, psychological, or cultural ones. The external relationships regarded as harmful were summarized by the metaphor of "dependency." Though not clearly defined by many of its proponents, at the core of this term is the idea that dependent nations are unable to carry out autonomous or self-sustained economic development because of their unequal and excessive reliance upon relationships with the industrialized capitalist countries. Much of the history of dependency theory centers on the identification of mechanisms that perpetuate and/or extend this asymmetrical interdependence.

Dependent countries earn an unusually large proportion of their gross national product by exporting goods. Consequently, their domestic economies are singularly sensitive to perturbations in world trade. This dependency is intensified by the narrowness of their export base. Many Third World countries tend to concentrate on only one or two export products. Market fluctuations in these products will cause severe economic dislocations for underdeveloped nations in a way that would not occur in more diversified economies. This consideration further disrupts Third World countries' capacity to develop internally.

Third World countries are also said to be highly dependent on Western sources of investment capital. Capital, whether held inside the country by Western-owned multinational companies or obtained through International Monetary Fund loans or foreign aid, remains outside the control of Third World governments. Consequently, their attempts to stimulate investment require Western cooperation.

They are also dependent upon Western goods for many purposes, which brings us to the related concept of "disarticulation." The demand for many manufactured goods is not met domestically in many Third World nations. Many industrial parts of a Third World economy do not produce for and buy from one another (hence disarticulation). Instead, they buy manufactured goods from abroad, which exacerbates the problems of an already outward-oriented economy. The reasons for this inability to produce internally are complicated. At one level, dependency theorists invoke the notion of limited internal markets. Beginning with a small industrial sector means that the market for any given capital good is small. Founding a domestic facility to manufacture that product is often uneconomical, since the restricted market makes it hard to achieve economies of scale. Also, domestic production must face Western competition. Finally, the ability to produce capital goods is limited by technological dependency: foreign manufacturers hold the patents for necessary techniques. Disarticulation also affects consumer goods. The wealthy elite is small (a restricted market) and wants sophisticated Western luxury goods; the mass of the population is too poor to constitute much of a consumer goods market other than in food and necessities.

Taken together, these mechanisms of dependency add up to the image of Third World nations highly dependent on foreign commerce, tottering on the edge of bankruptcy, always having balance of payments crises, and unable to control their own economic destinies. Dependency is therefore said to cause Third World underdevelopment. However, the concept of underdevelopment, like that of dependency, has changed over time. At the core of the concept of underdevelopment are the facts of low gross national product, low per-capita economic growth rates, the peculiarities of a highly uneven income distribution, and a polarized class structure, militarism, and urban poverty.

Dependency theory as a radical moral-evaluatory critique has broadened its scope over time. Its goal is to document the systematic relationships between an enormously wide spectrum of Third World social problems and to show that each problem was ultimately caused by Western imperialism/neocolonialism.

Paul Baran

Baran's *The Political Economy of Growth* (1957) is a good example of the new theories of underdevelopment that appeared in the postwar era. The major portion of the book that is devoted to the industrialized nations does not concern us here, beyond noting that Baran sets his general context as an examination of the economic laws of monopoly capitalism. The later section of the book adapts the framework developed for mature capitalism to the particular circumstances of underdeveloped countries. Baran's general thrust is to reorient Marxist theory of underdevelopment away from Marx's dictum that "the country that is more developed industrially only shows to the less developed the image of its own future." Baran counters:

> That in reality things have not developed in this way, that Western Europe left the rest of the world behind, was . . . by no means a matter of fortuitous accident. . . . It was actually determined by the nature of Western European development itself. (Baran 1957: 140)

This is the crux of critical theories of underdevelopment. They all reject the view that Western European nations developed while Third World nations were simply left behind in some primordial state of underdevelopment. Instead, they assert that the development of the Western nations and the underdevelopment of the postcolonial world are opposite facets of the same basic process. The development of the Western European nations occurred because of the underdevelopment of the Third World nations, and vice versa.

Baran identifies three processes that were fateful for both the Third World nations and their imperialist rulers during the colonial period. The first, the restructuring of agriculture in the colonized nations, involved a shift from self-sufficient subsistence agriculture to commodity (cash) crops, the expulsion of numerous peasants from agriculture, and the development of an export economy based on the new crops. Baran views this first impact of capitalist penetration as potentially a positive step toward capitalist development of the Third World. However, it was rendered futile by the two other aspects of colonialism.

The second process was the drain of wealth out of the colonies back to the metropolis. This appropriation of wealth is understood both in terms of simple plunder, principally via taxation during the early colonial period, and in terms of exploitation of colonial workers. Taxation of colonial peoples afforded a huge shift of capital to the Western nations, thus financing their development while simultaneously depriving the colonies of their indigenous capital.

The third major effect of imperialist domination was the destruction of native manufactures in the colonies and their replacement by exports from the metropolitan nation. This process initially took place by political means—by selectively taxing Indian textiles, for example. The resulting new market for goods stimulated development in England. With the subsequent introduction of power machinery in British textile mills, simple competition took the place of political tools. In the end, colonial industry was destroyed, leaving Britain better off and India a step less developed (Baran 1957: 144–147).

In sum, colonialism—the removal of potential investment surplus from the colonies and the destruction of native industry by competition—led to the simultaneous development of the colonizing nation and the underdevelopment of the colonized. Baran documents this process historically for the case of India and points to the contrasting example of Japan, where the failure of Western penetration allowed local accumulation and subsequent development to take place.

We now come to Baran's theoretical system for conceptualizing the basis of underdevelopment in the Third World. Baran is well-known (or infamous) for breaking with traditional Marxist categories, such as surplus value, and substituting his concepts of the "economic surplus" and "potential surplus" of a society:

> *Actual* economic surplus, i.e., the difference between a society's *actual* current output and its *actual* current consumption. It is thus identical with current saving or accumulation. . . .
> *Potential* economic surplus, i.e., the difference between the output that *could* be produced in a given natural and technological environment with the help of employable productive resources, and what might be regarded as essential consumption. (Baran 1957: 22–23)

Neither of these notions is equivalent to Marx's concept of surplus value. Actual economic surplus is but one part of surplus value, the part that is accumulated. Potential surplus is a critical concept that goes well beyond Marx in that it juxtaposes the amount of surplus that would be available for investment (and hence growth) if society were rationally organized, compared with the much smaller amount actually accumulated/invested, given capitalist class relations. By moving beyond orthodox Marxian categories, Baran enabled himself to provide a more trenchant critique of imperialism than would otherwise be possible.

The gap between the potential economic surplus of underdeveloped nations and their actual economic surplus is large: Third World nations generate substantial income above subsistence needs and, given a reorganization of their societies, could generate more, but the actual amount of surplus used for investment is small. The dearth of invested surplus condemns these countries to underdevelopment and poverty. Four elements account for the difference between the potential and the actual surplus: potential surplus is reduced by excess or unnecessary consumption (e.g., the luxury goods consumed by the wealthy); surplus is lost as a result of unproductive labor (e.g., the military, parts of the state bureaucracy, the commercial sector, etc.); surplus is lost because production itself is inefficiently organized; and unemployment brings the actual surplus below its potential. In the case of Third World nations one can add a fifth element: direct transfer of profit out of these nations lowers the actual surplus.

Baran argues that growth is hindered because the actual amount of investable surplus is well below what it could be. The specific losses from potential surplus can each be traced to capitalist socio-economic relations. In the context of imperialism, the largest single cause of the discrepancy between actual and potential surplus is the withdrawal of profit by foreign capital (Baran 1957: 226–229). Even when underdeveloped nations become independent, their economies remain based upon Western capitalist ownership of Third World industries. The loss of capital is so serious that the actual surplus available for reinvestment, and hence growth, drops to almost nothing. Thus Baran's notion of capital flow is the reverse of Lenin's: capital flows out of the underdeveloped world into the industrial capitalist nations. Even the initial investments by Western corporations in underdeveloped nations were typically financed by borrowing local funds and not by exporting capital from the metropolis (Baran 1957: 178).

Baran also points to other elements causing underdevelopment. The export orientation of agriculture creates massive unemployment, which widens the gap between actual and potential surplus. The peculiar class structure of underdeveloped nations also absorbs more surplus. Baran discusses the coalition of landowners, merchants, and comprador bourgeoisie that dominates these nations. The authority of these unproductive classes, which exhibit extravagant consumption patterns and low rates of capital investment, is predicated upon Western military and political support, as numerous American military interventions into such countries demonstrate (cf. Baran 1957: 172–195; and Baran 1973).

Finally, Baran's concept of surplus allows him to indict imperialism and neocolonialism as exploiters of Third World resources. Plantation agriculture ruins the soil, mineral extraction deprives Third World nations of their own future sources of these materials, and so on. One should note that such a notion goes well beyond the concept of exploitation as unpaid labor and evokes an idea of property quite different from that employed by Marx. For Baran, the use of Third World resources by developed countries is exploitation of the Third World's future potential surplus, irrespective of legal ownership or the dialectics of labor time. Baran concludes: "Thus to a number of underdeveloped countries what little they receive at the present time for the raw materials with which they are endowed may well turn out to be the mess of pottage for which they are forced to sell their birthright to a better future" (Baran 1957: 188). In such passages one sees the moral-evaluatory power of a critique that breaks with the limitations of Marx's theory of exploitation.

ECLA and Its Theorists

The United Nations Economic Commission for Latin America (ECLA) has stimulated research and writing on the problems of the Latin American economies since the late 1940s. Its theorists, most notably Raul Prebisch, Aldo Ferres, Celso Furtado, Antonio Barros de Castro, Maria de Conceicao Tavares, Jose Mayobre, Horacio Flores de la Pena, Anibal Pinto, and Osvaldo Sunkel, are non-Marxist economists. However, their work has provided the theoretical basis of a critique of imperialism, and, through such reports as the Economic Survey of Latin America, makes available the detailed statistical censuses of Latin American economies upon which many contemporary dependency theorists found their writings.

ECLA theorists often refer to themselves as "structuralists." Their explanations of dependency and development are opposed to both the psycho-social theories generated by Western social scientists and to Marxism (cf. Sunkel 1969: 4; Furtado 1964), and to various orthodox economic theories, such as monetarism. ECLA theorists tend to stress the historical particularism of the various American nations and argue that the barriers and paths to development will vary according to the structural circumstances of each nation. Thus they oppose the type of universal models of economic development made popular in the 1960s by individuals such as W. W. Rostow (1960).

ECLA theorists have advanced a general theory of Latin American underdevelopment that, in Raul Prebisch's early formulation, stresses two factors: the dependency of Latin American economies upon trade with the West, and the secular tendency for the prices of Third World exports to decline. Prebisch coined the now commonplace terminology of the "center" (meaning the industrialized capitalist nations) and the "periphery" (meaning the underdeveloped countries). The major factor in the relationship between center and periphery is their relative specialization in production—the center in industrial products and the priphery in raw materials. According to the classical economic theory of comparative advantage (cf. Emmanuel 1972), such an arrangement should benefit both parties. Prebisch's contribution to dependency theory is to show that, on the contrary, such a situation of mutual advantage has never existed. Instead, the specialization of the underdeveloped economies on raw materials exports drains capital out of the periphery, thereby retarding its development.

In emphasizing the loss of capital, Prebisch's argument sounds like Paul Baran's. The crucial difference is that Baran locates the cause of the capital transfer in foreign ownership of Third World businesses, whereas Prebisch focuses on the terms of trade (i.e., relative prices) of center-produced and periphery-produced goods. The key to Prebisch's position is the empirical observation that the prices of the periphery's exports have declined historically while the prices of the center's exports have risen. Thus the Latin American countries pay more for what they import from the center and receive less and less for the raw materials they export in return.

The declining terms of trade for the periphery vis-à-vis the center can be explained by the different structures of demand for raw versus finished products and by the distribution of productivity gains in the center and periphery. Prebisch argues that the income elasticity of demand for imports at the center is low (Baer 1969: 205–206), which means that the demand in the center for raw materials from the periphery tends to remain fairly static even when the income of the center goes up. Equally, the price elasticity of demand for the center's imports is low: if the periphery lowers the prices of its exports, sales to the center do not go up much. Such inelasticities are associated with raw materials and foodstuffs. The important point is that the center's need for peripheral goods does not change very much over time.

The opposite is true of the periphery's demand for the center's exports. The latter are typically industrial goods and luxury products. As the economies of the peripheral nations grow, their demand for such goods rapidly increases. Indeed, the increase in demand tends to outstrip the rate of growth of the periphery's economies.

This situation would lead one to predict that as peripheral economies expand, their need for center goods shoots up, but their ability to pay for such goods via increased exports to the center is impeded by lack of demand. The result would be chronic balance of payments problems, and such is indeed the case in most of Latin America. However, Prebisch's argument goes beyond the problem of imbalance in demand and stresses the price consequences of this disparity.

Prebisch suggests that the productivity of the export sectors in both the center and the periphery is high and rises over time. In the center nations the fruits of productivity increases are captured either by unionized workers in the form of higher wages or by productive enterprises themselves as higher profits. Because center enterprises and center labor tend to be monopolistic, productivity gains are not reflected in reduced prices. Hence Third World and other consumers of center-manufactured goods do not gain at all from the increasing productivity of center industry. The ability of center firms to keep prices high is aided by the burgeoning demand for such products in the periphery.

By contrast, wages in the periphery remain low irrespective of productivity increases in the periphery because of the supply of excess labor available from high urban unemployment and migration from rural areas. Periphery enterprises are not able to hold on to the benefits of their productivity increases. First, there tends to be intense competition between periphery nations to sell their raw materials, which drives down prices. Second, and most important, the stagnant demand for periphery goods in the center discourages price increases. Hence the fruits of increased productivity in the periphery's export sectors tend to be passed on to their consumers via lowered prices. Since these consumers are center companies, a profound imbalance develops. The center benefits from productivity gains made both at home and in the periphery. The periphery loses in both cases. This situation is apparent in the steady decline in the balance of trade of periphery and center goods. For some seventy years (from about 1870 to 1940) the prices of the periphery's goods fell relative to those from the center. The trend resumed after 1950. The shift in the balance of trade results in a drain of capital out of the periphery due to high import prices and low export prices.

The policy conclusions that ECLA theorists drew from this theory were that the Latin American nations should shift away from dependency on raw materials exports and away from dependency on Western imports and instead attempt to industrialize internally, using protectionism if necessary. Given the terms of trade model, the most profitable place to start is import substitution: produce in the home economy those finished goods previously imported at exorbitant cost from the center. Such a policy was implemented in many Latin American countries during the late 1930s, when the slump in demand for Latin American products during the Great Depression had thrown those economies into chaos. But it was after World War II that this policy was most vigorously pursued at the urging of ECLA economists. Despite these efforts, the Latin American economies began to falter by the late 1950s. Economic growth rates declined, inflation and the balance of payments worsened, and unemployment soared (Bianchi 1973: 99).

The next wave of dependency theory appeared after the ECLA's policies were seen to fail. This time the proponents were Marxists of one stripe or another.

The Radical Dependency Theorists

Since the early 1960s a new version of dependency theory has been articulated, this time by predominantly Marxist or radical academics. The *dependistas*, as they are known, include Andre Frank, Theontonio Dos Santos, Fernando Cardoso, Enzo Faletto, Ruy Marini, and Anibal Quijano. The work of the first three provides a sense of how the radical dependency position differs from the earlier ECLA school and the range of variation within the radical position.

Andre Gunder Frank is probably the best known of this group. Unlike the others, however, he is not a native Latin American. A German émigré, he grew up in the United States, trained as an academic economist at the University of Chicago, and subsequently became involved in Latin American economics through his research on Chile and Brazil. His major contributions were published in the late 1960s and early 1970s. Most non-Latin commentators focus their discussions of dependency theory on Frank, in part, no doubt, because his work is regularly translated into English. Yet Frank also merits attention because he is the most outspoken (possibly the most extreme) of the *dependistas* on a variety of issues. Frank's work is typically critical and polemical. This is not to say that it is unscholarly or unscientific, but simply to note that he deliberately constructs his own position in debate with those of others. Rather than beginning with what Frank stands for, we shall therefore discuss what he argues against.

Frank's first animus is with those who see Latin American underdevelopment as stemming from the survival of powerful feudal landowning classes and of feudal relations of agrarian production. Once widespread among Latin American scholars, this position implies that the backward sector of an underdeveloped country has been untouched by capitalism and that the modern sector is separate from the feudal sector—an enclave within a basically feudal social structure. This position is linked to a notion of dualism within Latin American economies: the idea that two quasi-independent sectors coexist (modern manufacturing versus backward agrarian), each with its distinctive class structure (bourgeois and feudal, respectively).

A wide variety of political views accept the feudalism/dualism thesis and consequently conceive of the process of modernization in Latin America as a struggle between the progressive bourgeois elite (representing the modern sector) and the reactionary feudal oligarchy (representing the agrarian interests). This outlook appears in the work of ECLA theorists, but probably more importantly for Frank, the feudalism and dualism theses have guided the policy of the communist parties of the Latin American nations. Following the Comintern line, communists regard their nations as dualistic economies, dominated by feudal oligarchies that have been sustained in power by imperialist interests. Since the feudal class was hostile to local capitalist development, the communists saw an area of common interest with the local bourgeoisie. Two conclusions followed: first, communists should form alliances with the local bourgeoisie in democratic struggles against the feudal oligarchy/foreign imperialist coalition; second, the dualism thesis implied that any socialist revolution in Latin America could only follow upon the yet-incomplete bourgeois revolution against feudalism and after a basically capitalist economy superseded the feudal one (Frank 1974: 92−93).

Frank believes the feudalism and dualism theses to be erroneous both in theoretical and in political terms. But before describing his alternative, we need to discuss another animus. In an essay entitled *Sociology of Development and Underdevelopment of Sociology* (Frank 1971), and in other works (Frank 1967, 1972; Cockcroft et al. 1972), Frank repeatedly attacks Western academics' non-Marxist explanations of underdevelopment. He views the entire spectrum of Western theories, from David McClellend's psychological studies through W. W. Rostow's stages of economic growth model, as sharing the underlying assumption "that underdevelopment is an original state which may be characterized by indices of traditionality, and that, therefore, development consists of abandoning these characteristics and adopting those of the developed countries" (Frank 1971: 5). Theorists who adopt this assumption believe in diffusionism: Western ways must diffuse into underdeveloped nations, undermining and transforming their traditionalism. There is a direct parallel between the feudalism/dualism theses and the diffusionist position. Both view underdeveloped nations as precapitalist; both see progress in terms of the penetration of capitalism (or modernity) into the precapitalist sectors or into the traditional culture of Third World nations.

To counter these approaches, Frank suggests that they lack empirical (especially historical) validity and hence lead to quite erroneous conclusions regarding the progressive nature of Western contact with Third World nations. In fact, he totally reverses both arguments: the Third World is underdeveloped because it has been capitalist for centuries. Its socio-economic structure is not in some primordial, traditional, or feudal state but was created and molded by a centuries-long process of interaction with the capitalist West. Consequently, there is no dualism in the sense of separate capitalist and noncapitalist sectors of underdeveloped countries. The most important conclusion from this argument is that further capitalist involvement is unlikely to bring underdeveloped nations into a state of economic independence; on the contrary, it will intensify the dependency and underdevelopment that it has already created.

We can best see the basis for Frank's conclusion in his historical case studies of Chile and Brazil (Frank 1967). On the issue of feudalism, Frank asserts that Latin American countries do not have feudal systems, if by the term "feudalism" one means a form of production that predated Western influence, mercantilism, and capitalism. Whatever one chooses to call the Latin American rural economy, it must be seen as the product of Western penetration, as an effect of capitalist relations of trade (Frank 1975: 47–51). Moreover, the Latin American rural economies do not display the usually cited characteristics of feudalism as understood in its original European sense, nor do they match some ideal type of "modern capitalist agriculture" (Frank 1967: 230). In terms of such analytic dimensions as landholding size, extensive/intensive production, labor/capital intensiveness, and so on, Latin American agriculture shows a distinct pattern of its own. Most important, one does not find, as both Marxist and modernization economists would predict, a spectrum from advanced capitalist agriculture in the export/cash crop sectors to feudalism in the subsistence and local commodity sectors. The export sectors and the non-export sectors show very similar structures of rent, mobility of labor, type of production (sharecropping, wage labor), and so forth. Variations are better understood in terms of the kind of crop than in terms of export versus domestic consumption (Frank 1967: 223–254). The penetration of capitalist export-oriented (commodity) production does not cause the system of agriculture to shift from one form to another. (There is no "diffusion.") Rather, according to Frank, both the forward and the backward areas of agriculture undergo the same economic processes, just as development and underdevelopment are opposite poles of one process:

> My argument with the feudalism thesis in a word comes down to this: It is not feudalism which has produced or maintains the features and consequences of much of rural underdeveloped society, however feudal seeming some of the forms may be, but it is the operation of the same forces in the same system which produced the modern developed parts. Since the latter is usually called "capitalist" I prefer to use that term for the underdeveloped feudal effects as well. (Frank 1975: 51)

It follows from Frank's analysis that Latin American societies are not dualistic, if by this one understands two isolated sectors—a modern sector resulting from Western influence and a backward one historically untouched by the West. Obviously, there are differences between sectors, but not in this dualistic sense (Frank 1969: 353).

Frank's position regarding feudalism and the dualistic economy becomes clearer when one understands his critique of diffusion—the idea that development has and will occur to the extent that capitalist investment and capitalist mores succeed in penetrating the basically feudal underdeveloped sectors. Frank marshals evidence for the opposite view: the periods of greatest industrial development in Latin America have occurred when the links between the metropolitan and Latin American powers have been weakened or interrupted. Conversely, Latin American underdevelopment and stagnation characterize the periods of most intense metropolitan-satellite interaction. (Frank uses "metropole" and "satellite" in a fashion analogous to ECLA's "center" and "periphery.")

As proof, Frank (1972: 3–18) offers a historical periodization of Latin American economic development. During periods of economic crisis or war in the metropolitan states, Latin American satellite nations are left in comparative isolation. Frank identifies five such periods: the European depression of the seventeenth century; the Napoleonic wars; World War I; the 1930s depression; and World War II (Frank 1972: 10). During each of these periods of comparative isolation from metropolitan influence, "marked autonomous industrialization and growth" took place in Latin American economic production. When the metropolis recovers from wars and crises and resumes economic links to the satellites, "the previous development and industrialization of these regions is choked off or channelled into directions which are not self-perpetuating or promising. This happened after each of the five crises cited above" (Frank 1972: 12).

Frank's attempt to prove the empirical falsity of the diffusion thesis also gives us insight into why he declines to consider the backward parts of satellite agriculture to be feudal. He argues that those regions that now seem most feudal (where subsistence agriculture is predominant) were in fact vigorously engaged in export production in the past (Frank 1972: 13–14). These presently underdeveloped areas were previously exporters of raw materials, but through loss of markets and depletion of soil or raw materials they are now defunct, allowing subsistence production to dominate. This scenario is the exact opposite of what one would expect from the diffusion or feudalism thesis, for capitalist contact seems to spell backwardness not development.

It is from the experience of such agricultural sectors and from the destruction of local industry by international competition during periods of intense metropole-satellite contact that Frank draws his most pessimistic conclusion: Latin America cannot develop so long as it is linked to the capitalist West. Any apparent success in industrializing or progress in agrarian exports soon dissipates once their utility to the metropolis is over.

Frank regards the varying levels of development and underdevelopment within Latin American nations as an internal version of the metropole-satellite international structure. The two sectors (advanced and backward) are intimately connected through a process of exploitation of one by the other, simultaneously producing the development of one and the underdevelopment of the other. Within any given underdeveloped nation this process is ruled over by one class or elite—a bourgeoisie—that enjoys interlocking interests in industrial and agricultural exports, in imports, and in local commerce. This class's income derives from all sectors, and it is meaningless therefore to talk of feudal versus bourgeois elites.

Two crucial political conclusions follow. The communist parties' Comintern-inspired strategy of alliances with the (progressive) bourgeoisie against the feudal/imperialist alliance is bound to fail, since no such distinction between bourgeoisie and feudal holds. Second, the idea that socialist revolution will only follow the bourgeois-democratic revolution against feudalism is incorrect. Such a view is predicated upon the notion of separate feudal and bourgeois elite classes, and it also presumes that capitalist relations will wipe out feudal agrarian relations. If, as Frank argues, the underdevelopment of the agrarian sector is itself a product of capitalist contact, then no such agrarian development will occur. Hence Frank takes a Castroist position: socialist revolution can occur in the Latin American countries as presently developed; one need not wait until they are "fully capitalist."

Against the orthodox notions of feudalism, dualism, and diffusion, Frank in each case advances an opposed metaphor, that of dependency causing underdevelopment. But wherein does this dependency reside? What are the vehicles of exploitation that underlie dependency? Frank points to a mixture of mechanisms drawn from several sources. From Baran he accepts the notions of surplus and potential surplus. Exploitation is therefore a dual process. First, foreign ownership of economic enterprises draws investable surplus out of the Third World nations back to the metropolis. Second, the Third World class structure allows an irrational, wasteful use of the remaining resources. Potential surplus is lost both by depletion of nonrenewable resources (minerals and land) and by the wasteful consumption of the ruling groups in the satellite nations. Frank also accepts the ECLA hypotheses that the specialization of periphery economies upon raw materials exports leads to long-term deterioration in the terms of trade and hence a transfer of wealth from the periphery to the center. Further, the specialization or concentration upon export commodities makes the peripheral economies very unstable.

Over and above these mechanisms, Frank stresses the impact of monopoly upon trade. In their raw materials exports, periphery nations are often faced with monopsony—few buyers for the many competing sellers of raw materials. Similarly, when buying goods from the developed nations, periphery nations typically must deal with highly concentrated, giant corporations. Thus underdeveloped nations are forced to sell their products cheap to monopsonic commodity markets in the center and buy overpriced imports from the Western monopoly corporations. Beyond ECLA's notion of productivity gains, such a pattern results in a flow of surplus out of the Third World (Frank 1967).

As noted earlier, the Leninist and Comintern positions on imperialism, which predate Frank's contributions, resulted in an ambiguous moral-evaluatory position vis-à-vis imperialism. Leninist theory predicted that imperialism would develop the colonized nations. The

Comintern indicted imperialism as underdevelopment but regarded Third World bourgeoisies and their attempts to gain political power as progressive, while blaming feudal oligarchies and imperialism for backwardness.

Frank's work, and the dependency argument in general, provide a much more straightforward analysis of imperialism as inherently destructive for Third World countries. In particular, his position regarding dualism is an exemplar of the methodology of moral-evaluatory critique. In place of the notion that rural backwardness and poverty result from the isolation of such sectors outside of the capitalist system, Frank asserts that their poverty stems systematically from their integration within that system. (In many ways this formulation is reminiscent of the dual labor market theorists who claimed that poverty was due not to the poor being left outside the labor market but to their incorporation into the secondary sector.) Demonstrating that capitalism systematically leads to certain social ills is the essence of our characterization of moral-evaluatory critique. However, in order to arrive at this critique, Frank was forced to amend (some would argue break with) various aspects of the orthodox Marxist paradigm. Thus, in terms of our earlier argument concerning the strain between paradigm maintenance and evaluatory critique in Marxist theorizing, Frank clearly opts for strengthening the critique at the cost of the paradigm.

Frank revised orthodox Marxism primarily by periodizing Latin American history, by insisting that it has been capitalist for centuries, and by refusing to designate the backward rural sector as feudal. As numerous critics have pointed out (e.g., Laclau 1977; Fernandez and Ocampo 1974; and Brenner 1977), Frank insists on characterizing a society as capitalist because at the level of trade it is integrated with capitalist countries. Orthodox Marxist theory finds this formulation vexatious in several respects. First and foremost, orthodox Marxism places causal and conceptual priority on the system of production relations rather than on that of trade or exchange. An economy is capitalist if production is based on wage labor and capital. Frank turns this definition around by labeling as capitalist that which is exchanged with capitalist mercantilists. This reversal jeopardizes numerous Marxist theorems regarding the causes and date of origin of capitalism (cf. Laclau 1977: 23–41).

During the early years of the debate over these revisions of orthodox Marxism, Frank attempted to justify his use of "capitalism" by showing similar usages in Marx's own writings (cf. Laclau 1977: 25–27). In more recent comments, Frank answers such criticisms by stating that he has never claimed to be a Marxist (Frank 1974: 96). For Frank, his critique of capitalism is more important than his acceptance of an orthodox Marxist paradigm or the label of "Marxist."

This tension between the critique of imperialism and the maintenance of traditional Marxist categories is found to a greater or lesser extent in the work of other dependency theorists. Two of the best-known Latin American *dependistas* seem to try to combine Frank's attack on the dualism and feudalism concepts along with more orthodox Marxist characterizations of modes of production and development. Fernando Cardoso coined the term "colonial-latifundist" to describe the Latin American agricultural mode of production. He shares Frank's assertion that such agriculture is not feudal but avoids characterizing agriculture as capitalist. Cardoso also takes a position midway between Frank and orthodox Leninism in his analysis of the prospects for industrial development. He attacks Frank's belief that imperialist exploitation prevents industrialization of Third World nations (Cardoso 1973: 14). For Cardoso, imperialism does result in industrialization. However, this industrial development is *dependent development*. Links with the capitalist metropolis destroy the possibility of balanced growth and autonomous industrialization. Instead one finds that the fragility of Third World economies, their dependency upon capitalist markets and products of the center nations, increases. This dependent development results in the particular mélange of state enterprises, local companies, and multinational firms that one associates with contemporary Latin American economies. It also facilitates the political alliances that underpin Latin American capitalism (Cardoso 1972a: 93–95; Cardoso 1972b).

Cardoso and Theontonio Dos Santos (1970) emphasize that dependency takes different forms at different times. In the present period it is characterized by the presence of multinational corporations. They call this type of dependency "technological-industrial dependence," because many industrial goods and processes are patented or otherwise monopolized by multinational corporations. Third World industrialization can proceed only by paying enormous sums in licensing and patent fees for the new technology. Monopoly profits on technology may be added to the other forms of exploitation that direct the flow of capital out of Latin America, intensifying its dependency upon metropolitan aid and investment.

Theorists of Latin American dependency can be arranged along a spectrum. At one end, Frank and his collaborators argue that Latin America is capitalist in its entirety, and they juggle somewhat carelessly with Marxist categories. At the other end, individuals such as Fernandez and Ocampo (1974) stick rigidly to orthodox Marxism for their analyses of imperialism. Their Marxist traditionalism leads them to the conclusion that the ills of Latin America derive from not enough capitalism rather than from too much. Thus one sees the wide span of permutations and combinations of the goals of paradigm maintenance and evaluatory critique in left theory. Theorists stress one goal to the detriment of the other. Some individuals offer a "strong" critique of imperialism by escaping the orthodox Marxist paradigm, while others stick to the paradigm, forgoing the strength of the revisionist evaluatory critique.

Unequal Exchange

Some time after the development of dependency theory, a new school of imperialism theory came into being in the francophone world. The principal figures in this school are Arghiri Emmanuel, an expatriate Greek, now professor of economics at the Sorbonne, and Samir Amin, an Egyptian economist and long-time resident of France. In terms of our sociology of knowledge concerns, these individuals are significant for their attempt to recast the Marxist theory of imperialism in such a way as to strengthen the critical element of the theory, especially its explanation of the poverty of Third World nations, while using the framework of Marx's own value theory. They bolster the evaluatory critique of imperialism and insist that this can be done without revising the orthodox paradigm.

Emmanuel (1972) and Amin (1974; 1976) show their academic orientation by devoting long sections of their work to critiquing non-Marxist economic theories of development before offering their own alternative. Emmanuel attacks the theory of comparative advantage, which proposes that both advanced capitalist nations and Third World nations gain from producing different kinds of products. This theory, originally advanced by Ricardo, gives a "scientific" blessing to the mercantilist viewpoint that trade is good for everyone. Emmanuel (1972: xxvi–xxxi) also criticizes the ECLA school, mainly over Prebisch's views on the inelasticity of demand for periphery products. Amin (1974) takes to task the section of development theory that claims that Third World nations will "take off" into development once their westernization is sufficiently advanced.

The theory of unequal exchange developed by Emmanuel (1972) uses Marx's labor theory of value to demonstrate that international trade involves the super-exploitation of periphery nations by metropolitan ones. Consequently, the optimistic prognosis for Third World development, as propagandized by Western experts, is not likely to occur. At its core, unequal exchange theory hangs on this idea: one hour's work embodied in a commodity produced by an underdeveloped nation exchanges for less than one hour's work embodied in the product of an industrialized nation. Over time, such unequal exchanges result in a steady drain of value away from the underdeveloped nations and into the developed ones: one side consistently overpays; the other underpays.[1]

Emmanuel details the technicalities of this process. The mobility of capital ensures that profit rates are "essentially equal" in core and periphery countries (Emmanuel 1972: xxxiv).[2] The immobility of labor allows wages to diverge between different areas of the globe. The ori-

---

[1] There are strong similarities between Emmanuel's theory of unequal exchange and Prebisch's argument concerning the declining terms of trade of Third World goods. Both show that if center and periphery specialize in different products and wages are unequal, then goods will trade unequally. However, a central part of Prebisch's argument concerns the fact that Third World goods are raw materials that have a characteristic income inelasticity of demand. Emmanuel (1972) emphatically rejects this approach. Swedish lumber and Scotch whiskey are relatively raw materials, he points out, yet they are priced at center levels. What matters is not the type of product but where it was made (Emmanuel 1972: xxx). Emmanuel also attempts to develop his theory of unequal trade in the context of an equal rate of profit to both sides, which he deduces from his assumption of internationally mobile capital. By contrast, Prebisch's unequal trade occurs because periphery manufacturers are unable to hold on to productivity gains in terms of increased profits. Competition pushes their profits below those of center industry. Finally, Emmanuel is concerned to develop his theory within Marx's value framework, while Prebisch works with market prices. However, their conclusions are quite similar.

[2] This is quite unorthodox Marxism. Traditional Marxist imperialism theory is based on monopoly super-profits earned by trade with the Third World and therefore implies unequal rates of profit (Marx 1967a: 232–233). Mandel (1975: 351–352) builds a theory of unequal exchange on unequal rates of profit and criticizes Emmanuel's position.

gins of this divergence are historical. In particular, Emmanuel (1972: 116) views American wages as having been raised via "political and trade union factors." Goods are sold internationally at their prices of production, which are the sum of capital and raw materials costs, wages, and profits. Given that profit rates are equal and, for the sake of argument, that capital and materials costs are equal, one finds that a product sold by America is priced to reflect high American wages, whereas a product sold by a Third World country has a price reflecting its low wages. Goods are therefore exchanged unequally—that is, not in proportion to the value (hours of work) embodied in them. Third World work is consistently devalued; center work is overvalued. The result is a constant bleeding of value away from low-wage countries. Consumers of Third World products in the advanced countries therefore benefit from the low wages of periphery workers through cheap commodities.

Emmanuel goes to great lengths to embed his application of unequal exchange in Marxist orthodoxy. He uses Marx's numerical examples and quotes Marx in his support. Thus, on the face of it, Emmanuel provides Marxism with a much-needed addition. Without relying conceptually on colonial policy or upon foreign monopoly control of production to explain underdevelopment, Emmanuel shows how even free competition on a world market produces exploitation of the peripheral nations by the center.

The theory of unequal exchange has not been without its critics. Although it appears to build a strong critique of imperialism upon the orthodoxy of Marx's labor theory of value, it nevertheless produces strains within the Marxian theoretical framework, the most important of which involves Emmanuel's treatment of wage levels in center and periphery nations. He regards them as essentially independent variables, whereas, in the usual interpretation of Marx's work, wages are dependent. As Charles Bettleheim says in his appendix to Emmanuel's book (1972: 287–289), Emmanuel reverses the causal direction of Marx's analysis: a correct reading of Marx explains the low wages of the periphery as caused in part by the low level of the productive forces there.

In order to argue that high metropolitan wages cause unequal exchange and hence further the exploitation of the periphery, Emmanuel must ignore two tenets of Marxian value theory: that wages are determined in part by the level of development of the productive forces, and that costs of production (and hence exchange prices) of goods under capitalism reflect both the labor and the capital employed in their production. When one allows for the different organic compositions (capital-intensiveness) between center and peripheral nations' production and the productivity differentials that result, one arrives at a position very different from Emmanuel's. As Bettleheim (in Emmanuel 1972: 287–289) and Michael Kidron (1974: 95–123) point out, the classical Marxian definition of the rate of exploitation says that workers in the advanced countries are exploited more than those in the peripheral nations. Strict adherence to traditional Marxian definitions consequently clashes with the use to which Emmanuel and his followers put value theory. As Amin notes (1974, 2: 596), the orthodox reading, if true, undermines the entire basis of the unequal exchange argument, which depends on a higher rate of exploitation in the periphery. The orthodox position would therefore not support the assertion that Third World workers are more exploited.[3]

If we abstract from the technicalities of the debate over unequal exchange and go below the surface of the polemics over the correct reading of value theory, we find ourselves once again in a debate over evaluatory critique and paradigm maintenance. Emmanuel and others have sought to strengthen the critique of imperialism by developing a new theory of exploitation (unequal exchange). But the requirements of the evaluatory-critical task undermine the task of paradigm maintenance. The theorist must make a choice: Which matters more, the new critique or the maintenance of the old paradigm? Apparently one can rarely have both.

American and British Developments

Dependency theory was very much a Latin American school of thought, despite its debt to Baran and to Frank. Similarly, unequal exchange was developed in France and has subsequently been adopted by Africans like Samir Amin. Since the early 1970s, American and British radicals have taken on the roles of testers and critics of these theories,

---

3 De Janvry and Kramer (1979) offer a very persuasive critique of various flaws in the unequal exchange theory.

probing their empirical and logical deficiencies. Left-wing scholars in America, particularly, have concentrated on subjecting the various theories of dependency to quantitative testing. The most direct way to examine imperialism theory is to measure the direction and amounts of capital flows between imperialist countries and the periphery. Leninist theory predicts an outflow of capital from the center to the periphery, while dependency theories imply the reverse, a drain of capital out of Third World countries.

Albert Szymanski (1974) carried out such a study, examining capital flows between the United States and the Third World. He found that the direction of net capital flows was out of America and into the periphery. Thus Lenin's position was generally supported. Unfortunately, there are problems with Szymanski's analysis. His data were limited to direct investments in manufacturing and thus excluded capital flows from the important raw materials sector. An examination of total capital flows, including all branches of production, gives more support to dependency theory. (Cf. Magdoff 1969: 198, and debate among Miller et al. 1970, Murray 1976, Magdoff 1977, and Szymanski 1977.)

Data on international capital flows are incomplete and present intractable problems for Marxist analyses. An alternative approach—to study the outcomes of dependency—draws upon more reliable data and has therefore proved to be very popular among American academics. Although underdevelopment is a complex phenomenon, it should have measurable outcomes, such as low gross national product (GNP) per capita and low growth rates in GNP. Similarly, the various causal mechanisms identified by dependency theory can be tested. Dependence on exports is measured in terms of the value of exports as a percentage of a country's GNP. Dependence on raw materials is reflected in the share of raw materials in a nation's exports. The drain of surplus value should be related to the proportion of businesses owned by foreigners. The rate of foreign investment and foreign aid as a percentage of a country's total investment measures the degree of dependence upon foreign sources of capital, and so on.

Since the United Nations and other international agencies publish comparative statistics describing most of the world's countries in terms of these measures, it is a relatively straightforward task to test dependency theory using this data on a sample of the world's societies. One can ask whether countries with a high degree of dependence on raw materials exports also have low economic growth rates, or whether nations with high proportions of foreign investment also have low per-capita income.

Johan Galtung (1971) appears to have initiated this approach, and numerous studies have followed: Christopher Chase-Dunn (1975), Richard Rubinson (1976), Jacques Delacroix (1977), Volker Bornschier et al. (1978), Bornschier and Thanh-Huyen Ballmer-Cao (1979), David Snyder and Edward Kick (1979), Peter Evans and Michael Timberlake (1980), Delacroix and Charles Ragin (1981). Most of these studies have corroborated the dependency argument: the various mechanisms underlying dependency are related to growth rates and GNP in the manner predicted by the theory. However, the statistical procedures involved in such tests are fairly complicated. Robert Jackman (1980) points to some potential sources of statistical bias inherent in the first difference or panel analyses used by many of these researchers in cross-national research. Arthur Stinchcombe (1982: 1395) also objects that several of these studies exclude such ex-colonies as Australia, Canada, Israel, and the OPEC countries from their analyses, thus avoiding several prominent exceptions to the dependency argument.

A second development in imperialism theory, both in America and in Britain, has been the emergence of conceptual and empirical critiques of the newer versions of the theory. The revisions made by Baran, Frank, the *dependistas*, Emmanuel, and others have drawn more orthodox Marxists into a sustained analysis of contemporary imperialism. One important element in this critique involves using Marx's value theory to address underdevelopment, dependency, and unequal exchange. Kay (1975), Kidron (1974), and Mandel (1975) have thoroughly examined this issue. Two points are worthy of note.

Bill Warren (1973, 1980) offers a forceful theoretical and empirical argument against the position held by Frank and others that industrial development is impossible in the Third World. He returns to the traditional vision of Marxism, in which capitalism implies material progress and imperialism, for all its inhumane aspects, wrenches colonial nations from semibarbarism and sets them upon the road of historical progress (Warren 1980: 40–44). From this vantage point, Warren views underdevelopment as a "fiction" (1980: 112) and dependency theory as a "nationalist mythology" (1980: 157) unsupported by facts. Reviewing economic statistics on the Third World, he suggests:

Substantial, accelerating, and even historically unprecedented improvements in the growth of productive capacity and the material welfare of the mass of the population have occurred in the Third World in the postwar period. Moreover, the developing capitalist societies of Asia, Africa, and Latin America have proved themselves increasingly capable of generating powerful internal sources of economic expansion. . . . (1980: 189)

Capitalism develops, it does not underdevelop. Interestingly, in light of our sociology of knowledge analysis, Warren (1980: 189) identifies his own view as lying within "the scientific tradition of Marxism," in contrast to the Third World nationalist moralism of much postwar imperialism theory. His claims have provoked furious rejoinders from theorists like James Petras (1978) who argue that the apparent development of certain Third World nations (South Korea, Taiwan, Hong Kong, Singapore, Malaysia, Brazil, and Mexico) is atypical, that industrialization there is lopsided and cannot be sustained over the long term, and that the gap between the developed and underdeveloped blocs is not closing (cf. Landsberg 1979). The debate continues with no sign of resolution.

The theory of unequal exchange has also come under attack. The criticism here is not against unequal exchange per se but against the particular version put forward by Emmanuel and Amin. Kidron (1974), de Janvry and Kramer (1979), and Gibson (1980) have pointed out the ways in which the unequal exchange theorists have violated the models of orthodox Marxism, and they have demonstrated various flaws in the internal logic of Emmanuel's position. For example, de Janvry and Kramer (1979: 10) show that "equal rates of profit, perfect free trade, and differences in wages for the same conditions of production cannot logically co-exist." Yet all three are basic assumptions of Emmanuel's model. Such criticisms have provoked impassioned rebuttals, especially from Amin (1977, 1978), who accuses his critics of being Western Marxist apologists for imperialism. In my opinion, though, the criticisms have not been successfully answered. Despite its logical weaknesses, however, unequal exchange may still have some descriptive validity. Gibson, for example, corroborates Amin's estimates of a 15 percent capital drain from the periphery to the core. In these critiques and debates we see attempts to "police" the Marxist paradigm, to maintain its conceptual unity and consistency, and to force out revisions insofar as they damage or contradict the traditional framework.

Quantitative tests of imperialism theory and orthodox critiques of dependency and unequal exchange constitute important parts of contemporary work on imperialism. However, in America they are overshadowed by a third development, the rise of "world systems theory." Scores of left scholars work within this new area, and numerous studies have appeared since the publication in 1974 of Immanuel Wallerstein's *The Modern World System*.[4]

Wallerstein's book represents an innovative fusion of two themes within Marxist scholarship. From Baran, Frank, and others, Wallerstein adopted and modified the notion that the development of Europe and the underdevelopment of the Third World are opposite sides of the same process. He applied this framework to a hitherto relatively unrelated theme: the transition from feudalism to capitalism in Europe, and especially the rise of capitalist agriculture and mercantilism in sixteenth-century Europe.

The transition question goes back to Marx, but it inspired an important debate in the pages of *Science and Society* during the 1950s, when Paul Sweezy criticized Maurice Dobb's *Studies in the Development of Capitalism* (1946). On the surface, this debate concerned the decline of feudalism, the origins of towns, the shift from subsistence to commodity agriculture, the role of mercantile capital, and a host of European historical events. But it in fact represented an attempt to hammer out the basics of the Marxist analysis of economic development, especially to determine the relative position of several causal elements, including class structure and class conflict, international trade, technical innovation, and regional specialization. The details of this earlier debate need not concern us here (cf. Hilton 1978); we can jump straight to Wallerstein's contribution.

Wallerstein's model is an eclectic mixture of dependency theory, Marxism, and historical sociology. He analyzes the economic development of European countries in the context of the emergence of a "world system" during the sixteenth century. A world system is an international economy based upon capitalist commerce and the production of commodities for sale. This unitary world system is composed

---

4 See Kaplan (1978), Goldfrank (1979), Hopkins and Wallerstein (1980), Rubinson (1981), and Friedman (1982) for anthologies of this research.

of three sectors: the core, the semiperiphery, and the periphery. As these three sectors came under the influence of international trade and later colonialism, they began to specialize in certain economic activities—the core in capitalist agriculture and industry, the periphery in single-crop agriculture and/or mining for export. As specialization advanced, disparities developed in the relative strengths of European states. Strong states were able to bring to bear extra-economic pressures that altered the balance of commerce; surplus began flowing toward the core, further strengthening the core states. This drain left the periphery in a weakened condition, retarding state development there and ultimately leading periphery nations into economic and political dependence.

Thus far, Wallerstein's model is compatible with earlier dependency theory. He believes that the development of the core resulted in the underdevelopment of the periphery, and he mentions the same mechanisms of surplus transfer (unequal exchange, monopoly pricing, foreign ownership of capital) that dependency theorists favor. His originality is to be found in his argument that economic specialization also affected the class structures and systems of labor control of countries in the world system. According to Wallerstein, ruling classes in the core opted for free wage labor as a system of labor control; their counterparts in the periphery used serfdom or forced cash-crop labor. He also departs from dependency theory in his emphasis on the relative strengths of states, by which he seems to mean the political, military, and administrative capabilities of national government apparatuses.

If Wallerstein's model of the core and periphery is clear, his characterization of the semiperiphery remains murky. The semiperiphery lies between the core and periphery in terms of its industrial development and the strength of its states. In some unclear way it acts as an economic and political buffer between core and periphery. In the present period Wallerstein would assign countries like Brazil, Argentina, South Korea, and Taiwan to the semiperiphery. The semiperiphery has a dualistic economy, exporting raw materials to the core as well as manufactured goods to the periphery. A relatively skilled but poorly paid labor force allows for the transfer of some industrial jobs from the core to the semiperiphery ("runaway shops") and thus for some measure of economic development. Apparently, semiperiphery states can fully develop into core states, although Wallerstein does not spell out the process. Core states sometimes decline economically, turning into semiperiphery ones, and some periphery states climb up into the semiperiphery.

This synopsis leaves out the wealth of empirical detail with which Wallerstein fleshes out his model. However, the sketch allows us to understand the orthodox Marxist counterattack on world systems theory and some of the subsequent development of world systems theory in America.

Wallerstein's approach appears at first glance to be highly compatible with orthodox Marxism. He uses many of the same concepts—capital flows, modes of production, class conflict, the state, international specialization. However, orthodox Marxists have found fault with his work because, at almost every point, Wallerstein reverses the causal direction that traditional Marxism views as linking these concepts. This critique has been made most forcefully by Robert Brenner (1977).

In classical Marxism, class conflict molds the social relations of production and thus the type of labor process found in a society (e.g., slavery, serfdom, wage labor, or peasant subsistence production). Once formed, different class structures exhibit different proclivities for change. Capitalist production is technologically innovative because the capitalist's profit is directly dependent upon the productivity of his/her enterprise. Competition and the desire for extra profit lead capitalists to seek new methods of making commodities; if an object can be made with less labor, the capitalist reaps the profit. Thus capitalism is characterized by reinvestment in new means of production and new techniques. It is dynamic.

By contrast, in systems where a class gains its income through merchant activity (buying and selling), there is little incentive at the level of the individual merchant for technical innovation or investment. The merchant as middleman does not benefit from the efficiency of producers. S/he just adds a markup to the cost of goods. Similarly, independent subsistence producers (e.g., peasants) are likely to respond to higher prices for their goods by cutting back on their working hours rather than attempting to accumulate capital or increase their production. In feudal and similar agrarian class situations, landlords are also disinclined to invest or innovate. They do try to make their serfs work harder and longer, but increasing the productivity of serfs by investing in new techniques does not benefit the landlord directly. Thus, according to orthodox Marxism, class systems dictate the presence or absence of innovation and accumulation.

Again from the orthodox position, no particular influx of capital is required to get capitalism off the ground. Primitive accumulation, the earliest phase of European capitalism, involved the redistribution of surplus already in the country and, more important, the separation of peasants from their land, producing a landless proletariat that could then be hired as wage labor. Once the dynamic system of capitalism was under way, technical innovation changed the availability and cost of various products. International trade arose because of the availability elsewhere of cheaper or higher quality products (whether raw wool or manufactures), and international specialization began. The capacity of different modes of production to generate surplus and to innovate technically (especially in armaments) affected their ability to create powerful states. Profit gave an incentive for powerful states to dominate others and to monopolize trade, leading to imperialism and international exploitation.

The orthodox argument implies the following causal direction: class structure———►technical change———►strong states. Strong states plus trade———►imperialism. Wallerstein reverses this direction. For him, the rise of capitalism begins with the voyages of discovery and the beginnings of trade in the sixteenth century. "Natural" differences in products initiated the specialization process in trade: "The different [specialized] roles led to different class structures which led to different politics" (Wallerstein 1974: 157). The strength of core states enabled them to capture surplus from the weak states, and this surplus became a crucial factor in the ability of core states to take off economically.

Perhaps to an outsider the disagreement over whether trade changes class structures and brings about specialization or whether different class structures cause differential innovation, specialization, and trade is a matter of splitting hairs. But to those interested in maintaining a consistent Marxist framework, such differences are crucial for defining the paradigm and its analytic approach. Thus we find Brenner (1977) attempting to prove that trade intensified feudal relations in eastern Europe rather than changing the class structure; that systems of labor control are not chosen by ruling classes but are imposed on them via class struggle; and that the shift to capitalism occurred when it did not because trade opportunities appeared (they had existed often in the past) but because class structure had changed in Britain, opening a new technologically dynamic system. Brenner's critique restates the boundaries of the Marxist paradigm.

Wallerstein's world systems theory is therefore an unorthodox variant of Marxism that nevertheless shares numerous concepts and concerns with classical Marxism. For our purposes, the significance of Wallerstein's work is that it has focused a whole generation of left scholarship on social transformation cross-culturally and historically. By insisting on the world system frame of reference, Wallerstein has guaranteed that this new body of research will not return to isolated histories of nations but examine the relationship between one nation's economic and political development and its external activities in the global context. His stress on the importance of the state and its strength offers a path away from dependency theory's overemphasis on external capital flows. Instead he recommends looking at institutional structures (state, classes, the organization of the economy) within nations and their interaction with the external context. Finally, through his example of empirically detailed historical case studies of particular parts of the world system, he has set a style that eschews general or statistical economic models of development/underdevelopment. This research includes studies of contemporary nations and their economic development (cf. Evans 1979; Rubinson 1981) and studies of social movements and revolutions (Skocpol 1979; Goldfrank 1978). As an intellectual movement, world systems theory is barely a decade old, but it is clearly destined to play a major role in contemporary left theory and, more generally, in American social science.

Since the mid-1970s another movement within imperialism theory has shared certain interests with world systems theory, but it is much more committed to building a thoroughly Marxist framework for analyzing Third World nations. This school has no accepted name, but its adherents are indentifiable by their use of the concept of "articulation of modes of production." The journals *Economy and Society* and *Review of African Political Economy* publish articles of this school.

The reader will recall that imperialism theorists, faced with the complex array of economic relationships in Third World countries, used either a dualistic metaphor in which separate capitalist and feudal sectors coexisted, or they characterized the whole economy as capitalist (e.g., Frank, Wallerstein). Neither of these solutions is adequate from an orthodox Marxist perspective. The different kinds of social relations of production (e.g., sharecropping, peasant production, wage labor) do not occur in separate economic spheres, as the dualism thesis suggests. A capitalist farmer may use wage labor for some crops and rent out land to sharecroppers for others; peasant producers may also be involved in some wage labor, and so on. Nor, from an orthodox Marxist viewpoint, is it acceptable to label these systems capitalist simply because they exchange and sell their goods in a predominantly capitalist world market. This approach obscures the technical definition of capitalism as a system of production using wage labor and capital.

One solution to these problems is to elaborate the Marxist notion of "modes of production" in order to conceive of a particular country as having several articulated modes of production. This tradition draws heavily on the work of French theorists Louis Althusser and Etienne Balibar (1970). Simplifying somewhat, a mode of production can be regarded as a particular combination of one type of forces of production and one type of social relations of production. "Forces of production" refers principally to the technology of production. In agriculture, for example, alternative types of forces might be slash-and-burn horticulture, hoe horticulture, plough agriculture, irrigated terraced agriculture, and so on. "Social relations of production" refers primarily to systems of labor control and control over the means and fruits of production. Types of social relations include slavery, serfdom, independent peasant producers, and wage labor. For each kind of social relation, one also needs to specify which social class produces, which one owns and controls the means of production, and which one controls the sale of the product and the profits from that sale. A mode of production, then, is an analytical concept that describes a particular combination of forces and relations (e.g., a system of industrial production using wage labor and capital, or a hoe horticulture economy using slave labor).

The purpose of this theoretical exercise is to conceptualize a concrete national economy (a "social formation") in terms of a mixture of different modes of production. These modes are articulated: they are interdependent, since people, goods, and money flow from one mode of production to another; but they also affect one another in that the logic and laws of development of one mode may affect the workings of another mode. This relationship is described in terms of hierarchy and dominance between modes.

Several empirical studies have employed this approach (e.g., Rey 1971, 1973; Wolpe 1975; Lubeck 1983). However, by far the largest part of this school's work seems to be devoted to complex debates over conceptual issues. Does the concept of a mode of production include the conditions for its reproduction, or are the latter a separate issue? Does a mode of production refer only to the economy, or are types of polity and ideology necessary parts of a mode? When modes are articulated, is the logic of development of the ensemble a logic that emerges out of the interaction of different modes, or is it the logic of the single most dominant mode? These and other theoretical debates far outweigh the empirical studies. Aidan Foster-Carter (1978) and Harold Wolpe (1980) give useful summaries of what is one of the most jargon-ridden and labyrinthian of Marxist literatures.

The growing popularity of this European school among left-wing American scholars reflects the desire to ground studies of particular countries and regions in carefully elaborated Marxist frameworks. The framework of articulated modes of production allows Marxists to look at world systems without adopting Wallerstein's unorthodox theoretical formulations. As such, it represents, along with the critiques of underdevelopment reviewed earlier, a return to Marxist orthodoxy after several decades of revisionist imperialism theory.

Conclusion

In this chapter I have reviewed a century of Marxist theory of imperialism. In its early stages the theory served as an adjunct to other concerns: imperialism was used to explain the continued survival of European capitalism. Luxemburg's underconsumption theory and Lenin's notion of the labor aristocracy are the best examples of this interpretation. A second impetus to innovation in the theory came from the rise of monopoly capital, the scramble for colonies, and the intensification of conflict between imperialist powers. In terms of our model, these are fairly straightforward examples of the current events orientation—the need to incorporate new and potentially anomalous phenomena into a traditional theoretical paradigm.

With the Soviet revolution and the formation of the Comintern, imperialism theory developed its own relative autonomy in Marxist thought. Spurred by the exigencies of Soviet foreign policy, the theory became both a critique of colonial exploitation and rationale for a policy that encouraged collaboration between Third World communist parties and nationalist movements controlled by local bourgeoisies. In this setting the underdevelopment/dependency critique was conceived. However, there was little theoretical grounding for that moral critique in the traditional paradigm.

It took Baran and later Frank to articulate a theory that was apparently Marxist and also explained underdevelopment as a result of capitalism and neocolonialism. This innovation strengthened the moral critique immeasurably. Exported to the Third World, this American-made Marxist analysis became extremely popular. The radical *dependistas* elaborated Baran's approach until it became their own. Unequal exchange appears to have had an analogous history: exported from the Sorbonne, it critiques international trade as a giant swindle perpetrated on the Third World.

The postwar era produced theories that superficially maintained the Marxist paradigm while strengthening the moral-evaluatory critique of imperialism. But the amalgamation was forced. Contemporary Western critics have demonstrated beyond any reasonable doubt that the postwar innovations are based upon concepts of value and exploitation foreign to Marxism. For their part, the adherents of dependency and unequal exchange take little heed. They would like the imprimatur of Marx, but the strength and success of their critical theories matter more than correct genealogy. The goal of moral critique overwhelms that of paradigm maintenance.

This process can be understood with the help of Alvin Gouldner's concept of metaphors in Marxism. Gouldner suggests that basic metaphors underlie the critical aspect of Marxism and that the ability of Marxism to provide an appealing critique in such a wide variety of cultures and settings stems from the universal appeal of these metaphors. Gouldner identifies slavery as the basic exploitation metaphor. Instead, I would suggest that the basic metaphor in the theory of exploitation is theft. Ruling classes are viewed as parasites living off the fruits of the working class's labors. They steal, through high rents, taxes, and low wages, the products of the toil of the masses.

The development of imperialism theory can be interpreted as a series of shifts in the metaphor of exploitation. From simple exploitation through partially unpaid labor, we move to Baran's notion of the theft of the fruits of the Third World's potential labor (what might have been accumulated if the society were a rational one). The unequal exchange concept gives us imperialism as swindle—the exchange of objects at less than fair price. Finally, cross-cutting Baran, Frank, and Emmanuel, and most clearly seen in Eduardo Galeano (1974), various nationalist notions of property emerge that have little to do with a labor theory of value. For example, it is considered exploitation for the West to take the copper that "belongs" to Chile, thus removing Chile's future resources for growth.

The point here is not to assess the accuracy or inaccuracy of these critical-evaluatory metaphors but to realize that the shift in metaphor points to the ongoing tension between articulating a moral critique of imperialism and maintaining a consistent paradigm or theoretical framework. Clearly, critiques of imperialism that the later metaphors imply cannot be made within the context of Marxist value theory. They are logically incompatible with it. As a result, the critical element of theorizing has consistently produced innovations in theory at the expense of paradigm maintenance.

This trend is understandable in some ways when one remembers that the traditional Marxian value theory focuses on exploitation of labor by capital. By contrast, the theoretical object of these new critiques of imperialism has been the exploitation of one country by another through the removal of surplus. By concentrating on surplus transfer, and by viewing dependency as a barrier to Third World capitalist development, some neo-Marxist theorists unintentionally take the position of Third World capitalists in constructing their critiques. That is, they show how imperialist capitalists prevent periphery capitalists from retaining their surplus and from investing it in the Third World. When caught up in this logic, the notions of exploitation involved are bound to gravitate toward those current among capitalists. Thus the critique of Western finance capital and foreign aid is reminiscent of the complaints of eighteenth- and nineteenth-century manufacturing capitalists over the high rate of interest or the burden of rent. Similarly, the argument that the First World, in owning Chilean copper, is robbing Chile of its birthright, comes down to the assertion that the profits made from copper belong to Chile, not to the United States. Although this argument has relatively little to do with the exploitation of Chilean labor, it has a lot to do with which capitalists should own the franchise for monopolizing certain sources of profit.

The contrast is perhaps best seen in Dick Roberts's (1971) pamphlet on the oil crisis. According to this Marxist writer, the enormous profits that U.S. companies formerly made on Arabian oil prove how exploited the Arab people were. But this evaluation depends on the notion that whatever profit can be made from oil "belongs" to the native capitalist and derives only from the exploitation of Arab oil workers. By contrast, a labor theory of value analysis would proceed as follows. Since oil sells at something like ten times its cost of production, the profit made on oil is largely a monopoly profit deriving not from the surplus labor of the oil workers but from the extra-high prices paid for the oil by its consumers. Those exploited by high oil prices are in fact the working-class consumers in the Western nations and the Western capitalist consumers of oil who are forced to pay exorbitant profits to whoever owns the oil. The oil crisis followed the transfer of these monopolies to the Arabian capitalists who now own and exercise the right to secure monopoly profits off that oil.

The point here is not to make a substantive argument concerning OPEC oil but to demonstrate that different metaphors of property and theft underlie different theories of exploitation and yield different evaluatory critiques of imperialism. In postwar theories of imperialism the ascent of a variety of evaluatory critiques has been accompanied by a decline in the traditional paradigm of value and exploitation. This is what I meant by the tension between evaluatory critique and paradigm maintenance as a source of theoretical innovation.

After several decades of uncritical Third Worldism, a major element in Western left scholarship has returned to Marxist orthodoxy. Though not minimizing the travails of the Third World masses, these theorists are more skeptical of the theoretical claims of dependency and unequal exchange. Other left scholars in the United States still adhere to dependency theory, but try to draw it closer to Marxist conceptual frameworks, integrating analyses of the internal class structures of the underdeveloped nations, emphasizing the importance of state institutions, multinational corporations, and so on. The pendulum seems to have swung back toward paradigm maintenance.

CONCLUSION

AT THE BEGINNING of this book I set myself several tasks: to describe and analyze the intellectual work of the new political economists; to develop a sociology of knowledge analysis stressing the work's commitment to a radical stance and its institutional context in the university; and, finally, to consider the new political economy in terms of the history of radical thought in general. The exposition and discussion of the substantive materials is complete, and I shall not review them here. Areas not dealt with—most notably, theories of the state, theories of class structure, and culture and ideology, in which considerable intellectual progress has also been made—will be the subject of a future book. However, I feel sure that the extensive materials I have reviewed in political economy provide sufficient data for a sociology of knowledge analysis.

In this chapter I shall conclude the sociology of knowledge analysis, principally by locating the new political economy within the larger framework of Marxist intellectual history. In this task I am greatly aided by Perry Anderson's *Considerations on Western Marxism* (1976). Although I maintain important differences of opinion with the book's analysis, it provides a good starting point for locating the new political economy and its sociology of knowledge within the larger stream of intellectual Marxism.[1]

---

1 When the present work was first written as a doctoral dissertation, completed in 1978, Anderson's book represented the only substantial treatment of the sociology of

Anderson's work is an exceptionally lucid intellectual history of European Marxism. He describes each of the major theorists since Marx and Engels in terms of social origins, involvement in political movements, and intellectual contributions. The essay concentrates upon the so-called Western Marxism tradition, especially Georg Lukács, Karl Korsch, Antonio Gramsci, Walter Benjamin, Max Horkheimer, Galvano Della Volpe, Herbert Marcuse, Henri Lefebvre, Theodor Adorno, Jean-Paul Sartre, Lucien Goldman, Louis Althusser, and Lucio Colletti. One cannot fault Anderson's command of the details of the lives of these individuals; nor would I challenge his assessment of the importance of their intellectual contributions. However, I have many criticisms of Anderson's attempt to derive a sociology of Marxist knowledge from his historical portraiture.

At the center of his analysis is a distinction between Classical Marxism and Western Marxism. These two Marxisms are distinguished geographically and historically. Classical Marxism came from eastern Europe, Western Marxism from Germany, Italy, and France. Historically, the "Classical" prefix refers to the period from the mid-nineteenth century to World War II and the generations of Marxist intellectuals from Marx and Engels to the Austro-Marxists (Bauer, Hilferding, etc.) and the Russian Bolsheviks. Western Marxism refers to the period after World War II and includes theorists from Lukács to Colletti.

It is important to understand that, for Anderson, Classical and

---

knowledge that dealt with Marxism. In 1980 Alvin Gouldner published his *The Two Marxisms: Contradictions and Anomalies in the Development of Theory*. There are similarities between my approach and Gouldner's. He too is interested in identifying strains and tensions within Marxist theory and their implications for the development of theory (1980: 14). He also uses Kuhn's concept of anomalies as a way of examining theoretical crises and identifies, as I do, the survival of capitalism through the end of the nineteenth century as the major anomaly that sparked theoretical innovation at the turn of the century (1980: 136).

We differ, however, in our treatment of Marxist theory as a project. Where I argue that moral critique and (scientific) paradigm maintenance are integral goals of one Marxism that sometimes strain against each other, Gouldner views them as two distinct and contradictory Marxisms that separated historically. He then proposes contrasting characteristics for the two types: scientific Marxism is evolutionary, optimistic, focused on the party; critical Marxism is catastrophic, pessimistic, focused on ideals of rationality, and so forth.

Unfortunately, Gouldner's untimely death means that he was unable to work out the implications of his sociology of knowledge beyond the period of classical Marxism. There is no way of knowing how he may have viewed my assertion that the critical and scientific elements of Marxism are fused within Marxist political economy both in the contemporary period and among earlier Marxist economic theorists.

Western Marxism are not two phases of one historical tradition but are distinct and discontinuous traditions. He calls Western Marxism a "mutation," an "entirely new intellectual configuration within the development of historical materialism" (Anderson 1976: 25). Given this judgment, it is not surprising that Anderson's most common expositional device is bipolarity: at one extreme is Classical Marxism; at the other, Western Marxism. The bipolarity enables Anderson to chart the changes that took place as Classical Marxism mutated into its Western variant. He uses a series of dimensions, including the occupations of the theorists, their areas of intellectual specialization, their relationship to political parties, and so forth. His discussion may be summarized in the form of two lists (cf. Anderson 1976: 92–94):

Classical Marxism	Western Marxism
Unity of theory and practice	Separation of theory from practice
Theory as economics/politics	Philosophy and culture criticism
Intellectuals in Party political positions	Intellectuals as academicians
Simple language used	Esoteric jargon used
Marxist thought as self-contained	Marxist thought oriented toward bourgeois thought
Concrete analyses of the concrete situation	Grand theory or philosophy
Active revolutionary class	Defeated revolutionary movement; quiescent working class
International, intellectually universalistic	National, intellectually parochial, or specialized

Of these dimensions, the most important for Anderson is the unity of theory and practice. He prefaces his book with two contrasting quotations. The first, Lenin's dictum, serves as his only definition of the unity of theory and practice:

> Correct revolutionary theory assumes final shape only in close connection with the practical activity of a truly mass and truly revolutionary movement. (Lenin, in Anderson 1976: ix)

The second is a selection from Spinoza:

> The multitude, and those of like passions with the multitude, I ask not to read my book; nay, I would rather that they should

utterly neglect it, than they should misinterpret it after their wont.
(Spinoza, in Anderson 1976: ix)

Since Anderson expounds at some length upon the fact that Althusser
is a student of Spinoza, and since Althusser is portrayed as one of the
major figures of Western Marxism, it is no daring interpretation to suggest that the Lenin quotation represents the Classical tradition and the
Spinoza quotation that of Western Marxism. Thus Anderson's central
claim is that Western Marxists have forsaken involvement with the
masses and thus have shattered the unity of theory and practice.

Why did a separation of theory and practice occur? Anderson suggests that the shift from Party intellectuals to university academics has
led to a Marxism preoccupied with cultural criticism and philosophy, a
Marxism of narrowly specialized literatures written in esoteric jargon,
intellectually oriented toward bourgeois thought. He comes to this
conclusion by linking up the various dimensions on which Classical
and Western Marxism differ (summarized in the lists above). From a
list of a series of parallel shifts we are supposed to infer a causal relationship between the various dimensions.

Serious problems permeate such a method. When we study Anderson's dimensions or polarities more closely, we find that each is accurate when taken individually but that together they do not fit when
superimposed on historical time and real individuals. Let us take Anderson's most emphasized pair of dimensions as an example. Although
it is true that historically there occurred a shift from intellectuals holding important political positions in communist parties to left intellectuals as academicians and a shift in emphasis from the study of economics or politics to that of philosophy, the two are not really related.
Lukács and Korsch, whom he categorizes as Western Marxists because
they focus on philosophy, were active Party members with high-level
political positions. Further historical detail (much of which Anderson
himself mentions but discards) further undermines Anderson's identification of party activisim with economics/politics and political inactiv-
ism with philosophy and cultural analysis. Marx and Lenin's own
involvement with Hegel; Lenin's critique of neo-Kantianism in *Materialism and Empirio-Criticism*; the intermingling of political-economic
analyses and a Kantian ethical philosophy among Bauer, Hilferding,
Adler, and other Austro-Marxists—all are examples of the longstand-
ing relationship between politically active Marxist theorists and philosophical thought.

In fact, a large number of the Classical and Western Marxists do not fit Anderson's model. In addition to Lukács and Korsch, Gramsci was a political theorist oriented toward bourgeois thinkers (Machiavelli). The entire Austro-Marxist school, which Anderson categorizes as Classical because of the party positions of its members and hence presumed unity of theory and practice, should be reclassified as Western Marxists by virtue of their philosophical interests and self-admitted orientation towards bourgeois thought (cf. Bauer, in Bottomore 1978).

Most peculiar of all is Anderson's extraordinary assertion: "This constant concourse with contemporary thought-systems outside historical materialism, often avowedly antagonistic to it, was something unknown to Marxist theory before the First World War" (Anderson 1976: 58). Anderson argues that such a concourse leads to or flows from the disunity of theory and practice. One would imagine that Marx and Engels never read British (bourgeois) economics, French (non-materialist) socialism, or German (bourgeois) philosophy. One would have to purge Bolshevism of its use of Kant, Mach, Hegel, and Hobson, deny Bukharin's interest in marginalist economics, ignore the Austro-Marxists' engagement with bourgeois scholarship, and so on.

The success of Anderson's schema for other individuals is achieved at the cost of glossing over important biographical detail. For example, though aware that Marx's and Engels' major economic works were written during a period of relative isolation from practical political activity, he chooses to assert the unity of theory and practice in these works (Anderson 1976: 3). Similarly, for Anderson, Roman Rosdolsky reflects the unity of theory and practice because he was a Trotskyist militant in the Ukraine and produced a major interpretation of Marx's *Capital*. Yet Rosdolsky wrote twenty years after his activist period, while working at Wayne State University—a fact that Anderson ignores. He also fails to mention that many of Lenin's and Bukharin's important economic works date from their periods of exile, when they lacked close connection with a mass movement, and that Hilferding wrote his *Finance Capital* prior to his position in the party hierarchy (while a journalist).

These and other difficulties cast doubt on Anderson's thesis. One is left with the accurate observation that, as the revolutionary movements of the pre–World War I era subsided, left intellectuals typically became academics rather than party functionaries and that esoteric philosophical or cultural studies overshadowed economic and political concerns. To explain the shift from party to university, Anderson offers an excellent description of how Stalinist parties stifled creative scholarship. What really remains is the issue of why an upswing in philosophical and cultural theory took place simultaneously with a downswing in political-economic theory.

The answer is not to be found in Anderson's identification of academia with philosophy and activism with political-economic thought. The central subject of the present book—the emergence of a new Marxist political economics in American academia—and of similar bodies of work in Britain, France, and Germany shows that there is no necessary equation between academic Marxism and philosophy or culture criticism.

An explanation for the shifts in interest between political, economic, philosophical, and cultural theory within European Marxism can only be resolved by questioning Anderson's notion of the unity of theory and practice. His essay leaves out the important realization that Marxism consists of two kinds of thought: abstract theory, such as analyses of the laws of motion of capitalism, the nature of the state, epistemological issues of Marxist method; and strategic, tactical, or applied knowledge, understood as "concrete analyses of the concrete." Anderson (1976: 109–112) is forced to confront this issue in his afterword, as he realizes that historical knowledge (to which he has made several important contributions) is not the same as strategy and tactics.

If we accept that there are different kinds of Marxist knowledge— something that proponents of the unity of theory and practice are loath to do—many of the difficulties in Anderson's historical sociology of knowledge disappear. Theoretical texts, whether in economics, politics, or philosophy, characterized the period of Classical Marxism, from Marx and Engels themselves up to the exile period of the Bolsheviks. Typically, such work appeared in times of retreat from active revolutionary politics or in periods of relative political quiet, and it was often the effort of young intellectuals not yet in the thick of political work. Hilferding's *Finanzkapital*, Luxemburg's *Accumulation of Capital*, Lenin's *The Development of Capitalism in Russia*, and Bukharin's *Imperialism* all fit this mold. These intellectuals were obviously involved in revolutionary politics, but they were also periodically disengaged from full-time activism either by exile or through their jobs as party journalists, in party schools, and so on.

Thus, contrary to Lenin's assertion quoted earlier, the great works of *theoretical* Marxism were not forged in the tumult of mass revolution-ary activity. Nor have the writings of Marxist theory proved to be of much practical use in the day-to-day politics of mass movements. As Luxemburg noted, the publication of Marx's third volume of *Capital* had little impact upon European communism because it was not rele-vant to actual struggles.

The unity of theory and practice that Anderson elevates as an ideal is expressed in the political writings that Lenin and Trotsky wrote in the midst of the Russian Revolution. But by Anderson's own characteriza-tion, these works fit the category of strategy and tactics (Anderson 1976: 11). They focus on the means of overthrowing state power, how to deal with elections, alliances with other classes, and a host of simi-lar practical issues. However, Anderson misperceives these works as political theory. It took the relative isolation of Marx (in his theory of the Bonapartist state), of Gramsci (his prison writings), and of con-temporary academics such as Poulantzas, Offe, and O'Connor to build a Marxist theory of the capitalist state, a task that even today is far from completed.

If we make this distinction between theoretical and strategic knowl-edge, it follows that economics, politics, philosophy, and cultural analysis are all topics in Marxist theory. They are alternatives. If one wishes to ask why at some point in time one topic flourishes while an-other languishes, one must look elsewhere than to the notion of the unity of theory and practice. One alternative approach is to employ Kuhn's model, discussed earlier in this book. I suggested that one im-petus for theoretical innovation is the realization that the current para-digm cannot account for emerging events. We have already described the history of crisis theory in this light. The apparent economic sta-bility of late-nineteenth-century capitalism brought Bernstein's the-oretical revisionism and new developments in crisis theory; the sur-vival of the Western economies despite the thirties depression turned the focus to state planning. The post–World War II lull in economic theory, strongly emphasized by Anderson, can be explained by the de-tailed and powerful body of crisis theory bequeathed from the prewar era. It took the anomaly of extended postwar expansion to provoke new approaches, such as Baran and Sweezy's *Monopoly Capital* and Man-del's *Late Capitalism*. It is only because the traditional logic of the falling rate of profit fails to persuade many theorists that another wave of innovative crisis theory has recently swept America and Western Europe.

Similarly, for political theory the dominance of Leninism effectively halted Marxist political theory for half a century. Only now have Marxist intellectuals in the West come to doubt the capacity of Lenin's *State and Revolution* to speak to the nature of Western democratic polities. Consequently, a new Marxist political theory is being formulated.

A similar approach could be taken to the rise of cultural analyses and of epistemology in the Western Marxist tradition. It is clear that Classical Marxism had little to say on these issues. Anderson himself tells us that "the successive innovations of substantive themes within Western Marxism, just surveyed, reflected or anticipated real and central problems that history posed to the socialist movement during the half-century after the First World War" (Anderson 1976: 88). But after admitting that Western Marxism attempted to update theory to account for real events and problems, he is moved to dismiss it as a "prolonged winding detour" (Anderson 1976: 103). Why would Anderson evaluate Western Marxism so negatively, if, as he suggests, it dealt with "real and central problems"? The answer is that Western Marxism has not addressed the central political and economic issues of the *present period*. Anderson projects present lacunae in Marxist theory backward in time and indicts Western Marxism for ignoring them. However, these issues became apparent only with the failure of Leninism as a strategy and theory for Western Europe, the failure of crisis theory to explain the postwar boom, and the failure of the old imperialism theory to explicate contemporary dependency. The recognition of so many theoretical lacunae is a comparatively modern event and depends in part on the existence of a left intellectual elite sufficiently distanced from the established Leninist parties to critique the obsolete parts of the latter's theoretical armory. The questions that Anderson feels were neglected by Western Marxism have re-emerged in the last two decades and are generating large bodies of Marxist theory concerned with the state, class structure, political economy, and ideology. Ironically, in view of Anderson's analysis, this theoretical movement is led largely by academics and in the absence of mass movements.

I shall now leave Anderson's analysis in order to discuss my own characterization of the sociology of Marxist theory and to consider the place of the new political economy and its likely course. At the center of my characterization is the tripartite notion of Marxist theory as paradigm maintenance, moral-evaluatory critique, and analysis of current events. The principal dynamics of such a model derive from the strains between these three functions. Typically, we find considerable practical difficulty in maintaining the Marxist paradigm in the face of current events and in holding to the paradigm while articulating an evaluatory critique of social phenomena. The case of crisis theory illustrated the first of these alternatives. Theorists made a series of innovations or revisions in order to incorporate explanations for new economic realities (from monopoly capital to the postwar boom) into the classical paradigm, hence lessening the tension between paradigm maintenance and the explanation of current events. Similarly, imperialism theory has undergone considerable theoretical transformation in order to incorporate convincing explanations of the new aspects of neocolonialism. In particular, contemporary theorists have sought to add a convincing evaluatory critique of underdevelopment. In the tension between paradigm maintenance and the evaluatory-critical function, the latter appeared to carry more weight, producing marked revisions in the classical paradigm.

In addition to demonstrating the utility of this approach to Marxist theory, I included a more structural analysis of the manner in which the occupational circumstances surrounding contemporary left theorists influence their intellectual work. Unlike Anderson, I do not believe that the position of left intellectuals in academia precludes political or economic theory or furthers philosophical or cultural analyses to the exclusion of all else. On the contrary, I regard these disciplines as equivalent. However, my analyses suggest other ways that academic life has and will affect Marxism.

First and foremost, I agree with Anderson that academia severs the connection of theory and practice in Marxism. But whereas Anderson believes that any theory that is not produced by activists in revolutionary parties is ipso facto disunited in terms of theory and practice, I maintain that the academy encourages the separation of strategic, tactical, and applied theory from systematic, grand, or general theory. Academia will tend to discourage the former while supporting the latter type of intellectual work.

There are at least two reasons why such a shift in Marxist intellectual work occurs as leftists move into academia. The first derives from

Max Weber's observation that when practitioners of applied knowledge become teachers or full-time theorists there will occur an increase in systematization and rationalization of knowledge. The role of teacher promotes the interests of coherence, systematicity, abstract principles, and knowledge for knowledge's sake, compared with the position of the practitioner (cf. Weber 1954: 198–255). Applied to Marxist theory, this view leads one to expect that a hegemony of academic Marxists over Party functionaries leads to a rise in grand theory over strategic and tactical thought.

Another, more salient explanation for the modification of Marxist thought by academia focuses on the demands placed upon Marxist academicians by the culturally dominant conceptions of science and scholarship. The hegemony of natural science conceptions of knowledge and method have greatly affected both political and apolitical scholars in the social sciences and humanities. This hegemony makes itself felt as a preoccupation with scientific rigor, demonstrating that one's work is scientific or scholarly. This concern is common to apolitical and politicized academics. However, since the image of the dispassionate observer stands in greatest contrast to that of the politically partisan intellectual, the burden of proof is borne disproportionately by politicized academics. Thus academic leftists vigorously attempt to legitimate their work as "real science" or "quality scholarship" and counter criticisms that they do politics, polemics, or unscientific work.

Although the pressure to meet the canons of science is felt by left academics everywhere, the dilemma is most intense in countries like the United States, where left academics are particularly dependent upon nonleftist colleagues, especially where job tenure is concerned. It is in America, then, that the transformation of Marxism through academicization is most dramatically expressed. The psychological or attitudinal manifestation of this structural dilemma can be seen in the attempts of American left scholars both to demonstrate the rigor of their intellectual work and to retain its distinctive political commitment. There are a variety of adaptations to these cross-pressures. The use of specialized jargon and academic methods of presenting one's work, which Anderson noted, should be read as one way that left scholars announce their membership in the scholarly community and the scientific value of their work. The tendency to specialize and thereby fracture Marxist thought into discipline-specific studies is another such adaptation. But for our purposes, several more weighty effects of academic position impinge on the content of Marxist work and its methodology.

I argued earlier that the culturally dominant notion of science affects left scholarship by intensifying the division between strategic and theoretical scholarship and encouraging specialization in the latter. Theory (and empirical studies) are much easier to legitimate in terms of the dominant conceptions of science or scholarship because they come closest in form to standard academic work. However, for left scholars, dropping the more strategic aspects of left scholarship raises the question of the political relevance of their work. Left intellectuals have responded by shifting their focus, expressing political commitment in terms of topic. In history, this tendency can be seen in the number of left scholars working on economic history, labor or radical movements, and periods involving the transition from one set of class or productive relations to another. In sociology and economics, this approach has produced a genre of scholarship focused on the "social problems" of capitalism. Marxist economists and sociologists study racism, sexism, poverty, crime, poor health care, and mental illness. Using the data and methodology of the orthodox social sciences, they attempt to demonstrate in a scholarly way that these social ills are necessary products of capitalism as a system. They hope to recapture the synthesis of scholarship and politics by blending critical evaluation and systematic attribution of blame.

A second response has been to reverse the criticism of left scholarship as "ideological" and "unscientific" by demonstrating the flawed underpinnings of the nonradical paradigm. This kind of attack can be accomplished theoretically: leftist scholars show that the assumptions or models of apolitical orthodoxy lack logical consistency and argue that adherence to such models indicates the ideological biases of the dominant paradigm. The popularity of the (British) neo-Sraffian argument against standard neoclassical economics is an example of this approach. This critique shows how the neoclassical conclusion that the rewards to labor and capital are technologically given and that total welfare is maximized is logically untenable. Using all the tools of modern mathematical economics, Sraffian scholars advance a contrasting (left-wing) conclusion: that the incomes of capital and labor are in an arbitrary zero-sum relationship.

This second response can also be pursued empirically, as indicated by the statistical debates between dual labor market theorists and human capital theorists reviewed earlier. The purpose of both approaches is to engage in intellectual struggle against the dominant paradigm, to show that it does not constitute scientific knowledge and that the radical approach does.

These genres within left academic work all illustrate the attempt to maintain a radical political commitment in one's work while proving its scientific validity. They are efforts to develop a theoretical praxis. But they all share one difficulty. By entering this legitimation problem of left academic work, radical proponents become caught up in the pursuit of Marxist research according to the canons of science or scholarship in their non-Marxist disciplines. In particular, Marxism within academia takes on the methodology, and thereby the epistemology, of the various standard academic fields. Anderson (1976: 52–53) appeared puzzled by the preoccupation of Western academic Marxists with questions of method and epistemology. He noted that numerous theorists had returned to the study of Marx's method and to a historical materialist epistemology. I suggest that this issue derives in part from the great difficulty that academic Marxism experiences in maintaining its separation from orthodox academia because it lacks consensus on what Marxist method is or should be. Similarly, it lacks an epistemology to set against scientistic positivism. Several generations of eminent left scholars have addressed this issue, advancing critiques of the dominant epistemological traditions, but they have not yet created a convincing alternative. Until such time as an alternative is forged, Anderson may expect the ongoing obsession with method to continue, and the methodology of academic Marxism will progressively converge with that of its nonradical counterpart.

We have discussed several ways in which radical theory becomes altered in the university context and have considered two structural explanations for those changes. It is now appropriate to ask what these transformations in style, topic, and methodology imply for the future of Marxism as a body of critical social science. Over and above the changes just discussed, I see major revisions occurring at two levels in Marxism: causality and level of analysis.

The causal statements of Classical Marxism, particularly Marx and Engels's, tended to be dramatically phrased and were initially interpreted straightforwardly in terms of unidirectional causation. The steam mill "gave us" the capitalist, the economy determined the polity, and so on. These interpretations sufficed for seventy years of orthodox ("Diamat") Marxism. How things have changed! Drawing upon the authority of Engels (who wrote that he and Marx had never intended a crude unidirectional causality), contemporary Marxist theoreticians have turned the old causality on its head or replaced the economic- and technologically-determinist sounding phrases of Classical Marxism with multiple determinations. This transformation is clearly seen in three of the areas discussed in earlier chapters: in the relationship between forces of production and relations of production; in the role of economic laws in crisis theory; and in the relationship between economic infrastructure and the political-ideological superstructure.

The forces of production were once believed to determine the social relations of production. The largely technical forces of production were seen as the dynamic force driving social change. Social relations cohered around particular forces of production, only to be overthrown as the forces of production outdistanced obsolete social relations. Recent literature on the labor process reverses this simple causality. Social relations are now regarded as causing technology, not vice versa. Marglin concludes that "it was not the handmill that gave us feudalism but the feudal lord that gave us the watermill" (Marglin 1974: 57). Anderson (1976: 204) concurs: "In others words, the relations of production generally change *prior* to the forces of production in an epoch of transition and not vice versa." This is Braverman's view as well and has been repeated by Brenner (Braverman 1974: 19; Brenner 1977). The subtleties of modern scholarship provide us with a complex explanation of the impetus for social change. In place of technological determinism we have a pluralistic multicausal system with no clear-cut direction.

An equivalent change has occurred in crisis theory. Traditional Marxism interpreted the falling rate of profit as a developmental law of capitalism (cf. Yaffe 1973). It could be expressed as an algebraic equation that could be solved to give the determinate result. The rate of profit was "the independent variable" (Marx 1967a: 620) in the Marxian system, and it was destined to decrease over time. Not only have contemporary theorists challenged this law, but they have also restructured the very notion of such economic laws and their relationship to historical events. More and more the rate of profit becomes the dependent variable of the accumulation process. It is determined by fluctuations in wages, the rate of exploitation, organic composition of capital, and so on. These variables, in their turn, are considered to be *outcomes* of historically specific events, especially the state of class struggles. Even the archtraditionalist Ernest Mandel takes this approach:

> This method treats all the basic proportions of the capitalist mode of production [organic composition, rate of exploitation, etc.] simultaneously as partially independent variables. . . . The key task will be to analyze the effect that these partially independent variables have in concrete historical situations, in order to be able to interpret and explain the successive phases of the history of capitalism. (Mandel 1975: 41)

Such partially independent variables become totally independent under the pens of Emmanuel, Amin, and the profit-squeeze theorists. Again, the old causal determinism seems to have been reversed, giving way to a historicized, complex, indeterminate causation.

Finally, we see the process at work in recent studies of the relationship between the economy and the state. In Stalin's formulation, the former was the infrastructure and the latter the superstructure. It used to be clear which one determined which. With the increasing power of state intervention in the economy, however, the causal emphasis has shifted. Many theorists now believe that economic contradictions become "displaced" into the state. Such a terminology does not assign relative causal importance to either of the two realms. It simply suggests that the contradictions producing social change will be predominantly political rather than economic in form.

This change in emphasis has been taken to its logical conclusion by Althusser and his followers. They view polity, ideology, and economy as "relatively autonomous" spheres; the polity, not the economy, is dominant in contemporary capitalism. The once determinant economy is now relegated to a peculiar status (based on one ambiguous footnote in *Capital*). For Althusser, the economy, though no longer dominant, is still "determinant in the last instance." However, as he quickly adds: "From the first moment to the last, the lonely hour of the 'last instance' never comes" (Althusser 1970: 113). There is little point in penetrating Althusser's jargon here. The basic idea comes through clearly: economic determinism is replaced by relative causal autonomy in the realms of politics, economics, and ideology.

In these three areas (and I believe one could find more) one sees evidence of a massive transformation under way within intellectual Marxism regarding causality or determination. Some old formulations are now reversed; others are rendered more complex. One is tempted to ascribe this movement to the sophistication gleaned by contemporary Marxism from its university setting. This interpretation would be only partially true, for this restructuring flows equally, in my opinion, from the historical disillusionment with Classical Marxism. But we can conclude that academic Marxists dissatisfied with traditional Marxist orthodoxy are at the forefront of this intellectual transformation.

Needless to say, the participants in this transformation do not believe that they are revising Marx or developing an innovative approach. In keeping with paradigm maintenance, they go to great lengths to prove that their new ways of looking at things are really restoring Marx's original method. For example, Althusser and Balibar titled their pathbreaking book *Reading Capital* rather than "rewriting Capital." They ransack Marx for evidence that the Master really saw things their way, even when this attempt entails chopping Marx's work into the real Marx and the Hegelian Marx. They build a new theoretical edifice and then insist that it is only a correct reading of Marx's intentions as proved by one short and ambiguous footnote in *Capital*.

Alongside these innovations in the causal structure of intellectual Marxism are several developments concerned with the level of analysis. To understand this shift, we must make a short digression to discuss the issue of abstraction and analysis in Marx's own work. In *Capital*, Marx generally pursued his analysis of the capitalist mode of production at a very high level of abstraction: "capital in general." His unit of analysis was not the individual enterprise or even a branch of production, but the economy as a whole. This approach involved abstracting from (setting aside) differences in the capital intensiveness of different sectors of production, disregarding the effects of monopoly, and conceiving of labor as simple homogeneous labor rather than as multiple fragmented occupations. These instances in which labor and capital are treated as if they were undifferentiated we may call "homogeneity assumptions."

Most commentators treat these homogeneity assumptions as conceptual heuristics. Ronald Meek (1956) argues that Marx knew of the heterogeneity of labor skills and organic compositions in the real economy but abstracted from them because they were not germane to his argument. Marx was able to discover basic contradictions at a higher level of abstraction: the contradiction between labor and capital, and the tendency of the falling rate of profit.

I take a slightly different view. My reading of Marx suggests that he believed in the empirical validity of his homogeneity assumptions. Although he knew of the differences in skill levels of workers and of differences in capital intensiveness across industrial sectors, he believed that capitalism eradicates them over time. Deskilling and an ever finer division of labor steadily turns labor into a homogenized factor of production. Similarly, Marx conceived of the differences in capital intensiveness as temporary: in time capital would flow into labor-intensive branches of production and even things up. If this interpretation is correct, what we earlier called homogeneity assumptions should more accurately be regarded as "homogenizing processes," since they refer to empirical tendencies.

Looked at in this way, Marx analyzed a mode of production in terms of two kinds of processes: those that polarize or intensify existing differences over time, and those that lessen differences over time and homogenize previously distinct phenomena. The former type of process is the core of the Marxian notion of contradiction. Polarizing processes arrive at a point where they cannot continue; the ever intensifying polarization destroys the process itself. Such contradictions are identified as *the* dynamic of social change in the Marxian system and are therefore the central focus. In contrast, homogenizing processes may be abstracted from theoretically, since they describe boundaries or segments in the social structure that are not polarizing but slowly disappear as differences are evened up. They will not lead to major social change and may therefore be safely ignored.

Returning to contemporary research, we find that recent analyses are pitched at levels of abstraction immediately below Marx's. Instead of invoking homogenizing or equalizing assumptions at these lower levels, they discover new discontinuities between economic sectors and the impact of the immobility of labor and capital. Situations formerly considered to be characterized by homogenization, convergence, or "evening up" are now treated as polarizing. Hence contradictions are examined between monopoly and competitive sectors, between productive and unproductive sectors, between a high-wage metropolis and a low-wage periphery, between high organic composition industries and low organic composition industries, between primary and secondary labor forces, and so on.

By lowering the level of abstraction one notch and by taking previously homogenizing, noncontradictory processes and treating them as polarizing, contradictory ones, contemporary theorists have accomplished two objectives. Implicitly they have moved away from the level at which one fundamental contradiction between labor and capital provides a necessary and sufficient cause of crises (e.g., the falling rate of profit). Simultaneously, they have opened a wide field in the search for lesser contradictions between industrial, class, occupational, and geographical sectors—monopoly sector versus competitive sector, producers of surplus versus state workers, center versus periphery, and so on. However, new areas for study are opened at the cost of losing the previous theoretical clarity and sense of certainty. The danger here is pluralism. One sometimes gets a sense of multiple arenas of conflict, multiple levels of causality, without any theoretical basis for understanding how the parts can be combined or ranked in importance. The potential advantage is that Marxism will be reconstituted to provide an analysis that is empirically and theoretically stronger than before, that is relevant to contemporary capitalism, and that retains its critical core. We see the beginnings of this process in the new political economy.

In this chapter I have offered my analysis of the impact of academia upon left intellectuals. Anderson and I differ more on prognosis than on description of past figures. Where he sees a tragic separation of unity of theory and practice, I see a separation of strategic and tactical thought from Marxist theory. Where Anderson associates the lack of contact with mass movements with the diminished political relevance of academic Marxism, I perceive a variety of compensatory adaptations, which I have described above. Left intellectuals do continue to unify political and moral commitment with scholarship and science, descriptive analysis with critique. Thereby they maintain an important alternative to the hegemony of academic orthodoxy while attempting to chip away at its foundations.

BIBLIOGRAPHY

Aglietta, Michel.
  1979 *A Theory of Capitalist Regulation: The U.S. Experience*. London:
      New Left Books.

Alberro, Jose, and Joseph Persky.
  1979 "The Simple Analysis of Falling Profit Rates, Okishio's Theorem,
      and Fixed Capital." *Review of Radical Political Economics* 11 (Fall):
      37–41.

Alcaly, Roger E.
  1978 "An Introduction to Marxian Crisis Theory." Pp. 15–21 in *U.S.
      Capitalism in Crisis*. New York: Union for Radical Political
      Economics.

Althusser, Louis.
  1970 *For Marx*. New York: Vintage.

Althusser, Louis, and Etienne Balibar.
  1970 *Reading Capital*. London: Monthly Review.

Amin, Samir.
  1974 *Accumulation on a World Scale*. New York: Monthly Review
      Press.
  1976 *Unequal Development*. New York: Monthly Review Press.
  1977 "Commentary on Gerstein." *Insurgent Sociologist* 7 (Spring):
      99–103.
  1978 *The Law of Value and Historical Materialism*. New York:
      Monthly Review Press.

Anderson, Perry.
  1976 *Considerations on Western Marxism*. London: New Left Books.

Andrisani, Paul.
  1973   "An Empirical Test of Dual Labor Market Theory." Ph.D. disser-
          tation, Ohio State University.
Aronowitz, Stanley.
  1974   *False Promises: The Shaping of American Working Class Con-
          sciousness*. New York: McGraw-Hill.
Arrow, Kenneth.
  1973   "Models of Job Discrimination." Pp. 83–102 in *Racial Discrimi-
          nation in Economic Life*, edited by A. H. Pascal. Lexington,
          Mass.: D. C. Heath.
Attewell, Paul.
  1982   "The De-Skilling Controversy." Unpublished manuscript. Depart-
          ment of Sociology, State University of New York, Stony Brook.
Averitt, Robert T.
  1968   *The Dual Economy: The Dynamics of American Industry Struc-
          ture*. New York: Norton.
Babbage, Charles.
  (1832) 1963. *On the Economy of Machinery and Manufactures*. New
          York: Augustus M. Kelley.
Baer, Werner.
  1969   "The Economics of Prebisch and ECLA." Pp. 203–218 in *Latin
          America: Problems in Economic Development*, edited by Charles
          T. Nisbet. New York: Free Press.
Bailes, Kendall E.
  1977   "Alexei Gastev and the Soviet Controversy over Taylorism, 1918–
          24." *Soviet Studies* 29 (July): 373–394.
  1978   *Technology and Society under Lenin and Stalin*. Princeton:
          Princeton University Press.
Bakke, E. W. (ed.).
  1954   *Labor Mobility and Economic Opportunity*. Cambridge, Mass.:
          MIT Press.
Baran, Paul A.
  1957   *The Political Economy of Growth*. New York: Monthly Review
          Press.
  1973   "On the Political Economy of Backwardness." Pp. 82–93 in *The
          Political Economy of Development and Underdevelopment*, edited
          by Charles K. Wilbur. New York: Random House.
Baran, Paul A., and Paul M. Sweezy.
  1966   *Monopoly Capital: An Essay on the American Economic and So-
          cial Order*. New York: Monthly Review Press.
Baron, James N., and William T. Bielby.
  1980   "Bringing the Firm Back In: Stratification, Segmentation, and the

Organization of Work." *American Sociological Review* 45 (October): 737–765.

Barrera, Mario.
1976 "Colonial Labor and Theories of Inequality: The Case of International Harvester." *Review of Radical Political Economy* 8 (Summer): 1–18.

Bauer, Otto.
1936 *Zwischen Zwei Weltkriegen?* Bratislava: Eugen Prager.

Baxandall, Rosalyn; Linda Gordon; and Susan Reverby (eds.).
1976 *America's Working Women.* New York: Vintage.

Beck, E. M.
1980 "Discrimination and White Economic Loss: A Time Series Examination of the Radical Model." *Social Forces* 59 (September): 148–168.

Beck, E. M.; Patrick M. Horan; and Charles M. Tolbert II.
1978 "Stratification in a Dual Economy: A Sectorial Model of Earnings Determination." *American Sociological Review* 43 (October): 704–720.

1980a "Industrial Segmentation and Labor Market Discrimination." *Social Problems* 28 (December): 113–130.

1980b "Social Stratification in Industrial Society: Further Evidence for a Structural Alternative (Reply to Hauser)." *American Sociological Review* 45 (October): 712–719.

Becker, Gary S.
1962 *The Economics of Discrimination.* Chicago: University of Chicago Press.

Bell, Daniel.
1964 *The End of Ideology: On the Exhaustion of Political Ideas in the Fifties.* New York: Free Press.

1976 *The Cultural Contradictions of Capitalism.* New York: Basic Books.

Bell, Daniel, and Irving Kristol (eds.).
1971 *Capitalism Today.* New York: Basic Books.

Bendix, Reinhart.
1956 *Work and Authority in Industry.* New York: Wiley.

Bianchi, Andres.
1973 "Notes on the Theory of Latin American Economic Development." *Social and Economic Studies* 22 (March): 96–121.

Bibb, Robert, and William H. Form.
1977 "The Effects of Industrial, Occupational, and Sex Stratification on Wages in Blue-Collar Markets." *Social Forces* 55 (June): 975–996.

Birnbaum, Howard.
1975   "The Economic Effect of Career Origins." Pp. 151–171 in *Labor Market Segmentation*, edited by Richard C. Edwards, Michael Reich, and David M. Gordon. Lexington, Mass.: D. C. Heath.

Blair, John M.
1974   "Market Power and Inflation: A Short-Run Target Return Model." *Journal of Economic Issues* 8 (June): 453–478.

Blau, Francine D.
1975   "Sex Segregation of Workers by Enterprise in Clerical Occupations." Pp. 257–278 in *Labor Market Segmentation*, edited by Richard C. Edwards, Michael Reich, and David M. Gordon. Lexington, Mass.: D. C. Heath.

Blau, Peter M.
1955   *The Dynamics of Bureaucracy*. Chicago: University of Chicago Press.

Bleaney, Michael F.
1976   *Underconsumption Theories: A History and Critical Analysis*. New York: International Publishers.

Bloch, Marc.
1969   *Land and Work in Mediaeval Europe*. New York: Harper and Row.

Bluestone, Barry.
1968a   "The Poor who HAVE Jobs." *Dissent* 15 (September/October): 410–419.
1968b   "Low Wage Industries and the Working Poor." *Poverty and Human Resources Abstracts* 3 (March/April): 1–20.
1970   "The Tripartite Economy: Labor Markets and the Working Poor." *Poverty and Human Resources Abstracts* 5 (July/August): 15–36.

Bluestone, Barry; William M. Murphy; and Mary Stevenson.
1973   *Low Wages and the Working Poor*. Policy Papers in Human Resources and Industrial Relations, no. 22. Ann Arbor, Mich.: Institute of Labor and Industrial Relations, University of Michigan.

Blumberg, Rae Lesser.
1977   "The Political Economy of the Mother-Child Family." Pp. 93–163 in *Beyond the Nuclear Family Model*, edited by Luis Lenero-Otero. London: Sage.

Boddy, Raford, and James Crotty.
1975   "Class Conflict and Macro-Policy: The Political Business Cycle." *Review of Radical Political Economics* 7 (Spring): 1–19.
1976a   "Wage Push and Working Class Power: A Reply to Howard Sherman." *Monthly Review* 27 (March): 35–43.

1976b "Stagnation, Instability, and International Competition." *American Economic Review* 66 (May): 27–33.

Böhm-Bawerk, Eugen von.

1896 *Karl Marx and the Close of His System*. London: T. F. Unwin.

Bonacich, Edna.

1976 "Advanced Capitalism and Black/White Relations in the United States: A Split Labor Market Interpretation." *American Sociological Review* 41 (February): 34–51.

Bonilla, Frank, and Robert Girling (eds.).

1973 *Structures of Dependency*. Stanford: Institute for Political Studies, Stanford University.

Bornschier, Volker, and Thanh-Huyen Ballmer-Cao.

1979 "Income Inequality: A Cross-National Study of the Relationship Between MNC Penetration, Dimensions of the Power Structure, and Income Distribution." *American Sociological Review* 44 (June): 487–506.

Bornschier, Volker; Christopher Chase-Dunn; and Richard Rubinson.

1978 "Cross-National Evidence of the Effects of Foreign Investment and Aid on Economic Growth and Inequality: A Survey of Findings and a Reanalysis." *American Journal of Sociology* 84 (November): 651.

Bottomore, Thomas B.

1967 *Critics of Society: Radical Thought in North America*. London: Allen and Unwin.

1978 *Austro-Marxism*. New York: Oxford University Press.

Bould Van Til, Sally.

1974 "Poverty and Work: Beyond the Stereotypes." *Poverty and Human Resources Abstracts* 9 (June): 155–169.

Bowles, Samuel, and Herbert Gintis.

1976 *Schooling in Capitalist America: Educational Reform and the Contradictions of Economic Life*. New York: Basic Books.

Braverman, Harry.

1974 *Labor and Monopoly Capital: The Degradation of Work in the Twentieth Century*. New York: Monthly Review Press.

Brecher, Jerry.

1972 *Strike!* San Francisco: Straight Arrow.

Brenner, Robert.

1977 "The Origins of Capitalist Development: A Critique of Neo-Smithian Marxism." *New Left Review* 104 (July/August): 25–93.

Brody, David.

1960 *The Steelworkers in America: The Non-Union Era*. Cambridge, Mass.: Harvard University Press.

Brown, Martin.
1977   "Labor Market Segmentation and Farm Labor Unionism in Cali-
        fornia: A Research Essay." Mimeographed. Berkeley: Department
        of Agricultural Economics, University of California.
Bukharin, Nikolai.
1972   *Imperialism and the Accumulation of Capital*. New York: Monthly
        Review Press.
n.d.   *Imperialism and the World Economy*. London: Martin Lawrence.
Burawoy, Michael.
1978a   "Toward a Marxist Theory of the Labor Process: Braverman and
        Beyond." Mimeographed. Berkeley: Department of Sociology,
        University of California.
1978b   "Making Out on the Shop Floor: Changes in the Labor Process
        Under Monopoly Capitalism." Mimeographed. Berkeley: Depart-
        ment of Sociology, University of California. Revised version pub-
        lished as *Manufacturing Consent: Changes in the Labor Process
        under Capitalism*. Chicago: University of Chicago Press, 1979.
Bureau of Labor Statistics, U.S. Department of Labor.
1969   *Employment Situation in Poverty Areas of Six Cities, July
        1968–June 1969*. Urban Employment Survey, BLS Report no.
        370.
Cain, Glen G.
1975.   "The Challenge of Dual and Radical Theories of the Labor Mar-
        ket to Orthodox Theory." Discussion Paper no. 255. Madison,
        Wis.: Institute for Research on Poverty, University of Wisconsin.
        Revised version published in *Journal of Economic Literature* 14
        (1976): 1215–1257.
Cain, Pamela, and Donald Treiman.
1981   "The DOT as a Source of Occupational Data." *American So-
        ciological Review* 46 (June): 235–278.
Cardoso, Fernando H.
1972a   "Dependent Capitalist Development in Latin America." *New Left
        Review* 74 (July/August): 83–95.
1972b   "Industrialization, Dependency, and Power in Latin America."
        Berkeley Journal of Sociology 17: 79–96.
1973   "Imperialism and Dependency in Latin America." Pp. 7–16 in
        Structures of Dependency, edited by Frank Bonilla and Robert
        Girling. Stanford: Institute for Political Studies, Stanford
        University.
Caute, David.
1978   *The Great Fear: The Anti-Communist Purge Under Truman and
        Eisenhower*. New York: Simon and Schuster.

Chandler, Alfred D., Jr.
 1962   *Strategy and Structure: Chapters in the History of the Business Enterprise*. Cambridge, Mass.: MIT Press.
Chase-Dunn, Christopher.
 1975   "The Effects of International Economic Dependence on Development and Inequality: A Cross-National Study." *American Sociological Review* 40 (December): 720–738.
Chilcote, Robert H.
 1974   "Dependency: A Critical Synthesis of the Literature." *Latin American Perspectives* 1 (Spring): 4–29.
Chilcote, Ronald, and Dale Johnson.
 1983   *Theories of Development: Mode of Production or Dependency?* Beverly Hills, Calif.: Sage Publications.
Clark, Olivia; Jerry Lembcke; and Bob Marotto, Jr.
 1978   *Essays on the Social Relations of Work and Labor*. A special issue of *The Insurgent Sociologist*. Vol. 8, nos. 2 and 3 (Fall).
Clecak, Peter.
 1973   *Radical Paradoxes: Dilemmas of the American Left, 1945–1970*. New York: Harper and Row.
Cockroft, James D.; Andre Gunder Frank; and Dale S. Johnson.
 1972   *Dependence and Underdevelopment: Latin America's Political Economy*. New York: Doubleday.
Cogoy, Mario.
 1973   "The Fall of the Rate of Profit and the Theory of Accumulation." *Bulletin of the Conference of Socialist Economists* 8 (Winter): 52–67.
Colfax, J. David.
 1973   "Repression and Academic Radicalism." *New Politics* 10 (Spring): 14–27.
Colletti, Lucio.
 1972   "The Theory of the Crash." *Telos* 13 (Fall): 34–36.
 1974   *From Rousseau to Lenin*. New York: Monthly Review Press.
Collins, Randall.
 1976   *Conflict Sociology: Toward an Explanatory Science*. New York: Academic Press.
 1979   *The Credential Society: A Historical Sociology of Education and Stratification*. New York: Academic Press.
Commons, John R.
 1935   *History of Labor in the U.S.* New York: Macmillan.
Coombs, Rod.
 1978   "Labor and Monopoly Capital." *New Left Review* 107 (January/February): 79–96.

Crozier, Michel.
1964   *The Bureaucratic Phenomenon.* Chicago: University of Chicago Press.
Cummings, Laird.
1977   "The Rationalization and Automation of Clerical Work." M.A. thesis, Brooklyn College.
Davies, Margery.
1975   "The Woman's Place is at the Typewriter: The Feminization of the Clerical Labor Force." Pp. 279–296 in *Labor Market Segmentation,* edited by Richard C. Edwards, Michael Reich, and David M. Gordon. Lexington, Mass.: D. C. Heath.
Day, Richard B.
1976   "The Theory of the Long Cycle: Kondratiev, Trotsky, Mandel." *New Left Review* 99 (September/October): 67–82.
1981   *The "Crisis" and the "Crash": Soviet Studies of the West (1917–1939).* New York: Schocken Books.
Daymont, Thomas N.
1980   "Pay Premiums for Economic Sector and Race: A Decomposition." *Social Science Research* 9 (September): 245–272.
Degras, J.
1960   *The Communist International 1919–1943: Documents, Volume Two, 1928–1938.* London: Oxford University Press.
De Janvry, Alain, and Frank Kramer.
1979   "The Limits of Unequal Exchange." *Review of Radical Political Economics* 11 (Winter): 3–15.
De Kadt, Maarten.
1979   "Insurance: A Clerical Work Factory." Pp. 242–257 in Andrew Zimbalist (ed.), *Case Studies on the Labor Process.* New York: Monthly Review Press.
Delacroix, Jacques.
1977   "The Export of Raw Materials and Economic Growth: A Cross-National Study." *American Sociological Review* 42 (October): 795–808.
Delacroix, Jacques, and Charles C. Ragin.
1981   "Structural Blockage: A Cross-National Study of Economic Dependency, State Efficacy, and Underdevelopment." *American Journal of Sociology* 86 (May): 1311–1347.
D'Encausse, H. C., and S. R. Schramm.
1969   *Marxism and Asia.* London: Allen Lane.
Dobb, Maurice.
1937   *Political Economy and Capitalism.* London: George Routledge.

Dobb, Maurice, et al.
1978   *The Transition from Feudalism to Capitalism.* London: New Left Books.
Doeringer, Peter B., and Michael J. Piore.
1971   *Internal Labor Markets and Manpower Analysis.* Lexington, Mass.: D. C. Heath.
Doeringer, Peter B.; Penny Feldman; David Gordon; Michael Piore; and Michael Reich.
1972   *Low Income Labor Markets and Urban Manpower Programs: A Critical Assessment.* Research and Development Findings no. 12, Washington, D.C.: United States Department of Labor, Manpower Administration.
Dos Santos, Theontonio.
1970   "The Structure of Dependency." *American Economic Review* 60 (May): 231–236.
Draper, Hal.
1965   *Berkeley: The New Student Revolt.* New York: Grove Press.
Dunlop, John T.
1957   "The Task of Contemporary Wage Theory." Pp. 117–139 in *New Concepts in Wage Discrimination*, edited by George W. Taylor and Frank C. Pierson. New York: McGraw-Hill.
1966   "Job Vacancy Measures and Economic Analysis." Pp. 28–47 in *The Measurement and Interpretation of Job Vacancies*, edited by National Bureau of Economic Research. New York: Columbia University Press.
Edwards, Richard C.
1975   "The Social Relations of Production in the Firm and Labor Market Structure." Pp. 3–26 in *Labor Market Segmentation*, edited by Richard C. Edwards, Michael Reich, and David M. Gordon. Lexington, Mass.: D. C. Heath.
1978   "The Great Transformation Inside the Firm: Conflict and Control in the Reorganization of the Labor Process in the 20th. Century." Mimeographed. Amherst, Mass.: Department of Economics, University of Massachusetts.
1979   *Contested Terrain: The Transformation of the Workplace in the Twentieth Century.* New York: Basic Books.
Edwards, Richard C.; Michael Reich; and David M. Gordon.
1975   *Labor Market Segmentation.* Lexington, Mass.: D. C. Heath.
Edwards, Richard C., Michael Reich, and Thomas E. Weisskopf.
1972   *The Capitalist System: A Radical Analysis of American Society.* Englewood Cliffs, N.J.: Prentice-Hall.

278   BIBLIOGRAPHY

Emmanuel, Arghiri.
1972   *Unequal Exchange: A Study in the Imperialism of Trade.* New York: Monthly Review Press.
Engels, Frederick.
1900   Preface to *The Poverty of Philosophy*, by Karl Marx. Translated by Henry Quelch. Publisher not listed.
1962   *The Condition of the Working Class in England in 1844.* Moscow: Foreign Languages Press.
1970   *Anti-Duhring: Herr Eugen Duhring's Revolution in Science.* New York: International Publishers.
1972   "Socialism: Utopian and Scientific." Pp. 605–639 in *The Marx-Engels Reader*, edited by Robert C. Tucker. New York: Norton.
Ericson, Edward E.
1975   *Radicals in the University.* Stanford: Hoover Institution Press.
Etzioni, Amitai.
1961   *A Comparative Analysis of Complex Organizations: On Power, Involvement and Their Correlates.* New York: Free Press.
Evans, Peter.
1979   *Dependent Development: The Alliance of Multinational, State and Local Capital in Brazil.* Princeton, N.J.: Princeton University Press.
Evans, Peter B., and Michael Timberlake.
1980   "Dependence, Inequality, and the Growth of the Tertiary: A Comparative Analysis of Less Developed Countries." *American Sociological Review* 45 (August): 531–552.
Farley, Reynolds.
1977   "Trends in Racial Inequalities: Have the Gains of the 1960s Disappeared in the 1970s." *American Sociological Review* 42 (April): 189–208.
Fernandez, Raul A., and Jose F. Ocampo.
1974   "Latin American Revolution: A Theory of Imperialism, Not Dependence." *Latin American Perspectives* 1 (Spring): 30–61.
Feuer, Lewis S.
1969   *Marx and the Intellectuals: A Set of Post-Ideological Essays.* New York: Doubleday.
Fine, Ben, and Laurence Harris.
1976   "Controversial Issues in Marxist Economic Theory." Pp. 141–178 in *The Socialist Register*, edited by Ralph Milliband and John Saville. London: Merlin Press.
Finlay, William.
1983   "One Occupation, Two Labor Markets." *American Sociological Review* 48 (June): 306–315.

Firebaugh, Glenn.
   1983   "Country Size and Rate of Economic Growth, 1950–1977."
           American Sociological Review 48 (April): 257–269.
Fischer, George; Alan Block; John M. Cammett; and Richard Friedman
(eds.).
   1971   *The Revival of American Socialism: Selected Papers of the Social-*
           ist Scholars Conference. New York: Oxford University Press.
Flacks, Richard.
   1971   *Youth and Social Change.* Chicago: Markham.
Foster-Carter, Aidan.
   1978   "The Modes of Production Controversy." *New Left Review* 107
           (January–February): 47–78.
Frank, Andre Gunder.
   1967   *Capitalism and Underdevelopment in Latin America: Historical*
           Studies of Chile and Brazil. New York: Monthly Review Press.
   1969   "Destroy Capitalism not Feudalism." Pp. 350–361 in *Latin*
           America: Underdevelopment or Revolution, by A. G. Frank. New
           York: Monthly Review Press.
   1971   *Sociology of Development and Underdevelopment of Sociology.*
           London: Pluto.
   1972   "The Development of Underdevelopment." Pp. 3–8 in *Depen-*
           dence and Underdevelopment: Latin America's Political Economy,
           edited by J. D. Cockcroft, A. G. Frank, and D. L. Johnson. New
           York: Doubleday.
   1974   "Dependence is Dead, Long Live Dependence and the Class
           Struggle: A Reply to Critics." *Latin American Perspectives* 1
           (Spring): 87–106.
   1975   *On Capitalist Underdevelopment.* London: Oxford University
           Press.
   1978   "Mainstream Economists as Astrologers: Gazing Through the
           Clouded Crystal Ball." Pp. 9–14 in *U.S. Capitalism in Crisis*.
           New York: Union for Radical Political Economics.
Freedman, Marcia.
   1976   *Labor Markets: Segments and Shelters.* New York: Universe
           Books.
Freidson, Eliot.
   1982   "Occupational Autonomy and Labor Market Shelters." Pp. 39–
           54 in Phyllis Stewart and Muriel Cantor (eds.), *Varieties of Work*.
           Beverly Hills, Calif.: Sage Publications.
Friedman, Andrew L.
   1977   *Industry and Labour: Class Struggle at Work and Monopoly*
           Capitalism. London: Macmillan.

Friedman, Edward (ed.).
   1982   *Ascent and Decline in the World System.* Volume 5 in the series
            Political Economy of World System Annuals. Beverly Hills,
            Calif.: Sage Press.
Furtado, Celso.
   1964   *Development and Underdevelopment: A Structural View of the
            Problems of Developed and Underdeveloped Countries.* Berkeley:
            University of California Press.
Galeano, Eduardo.
   1974   *Open Veins of Latin America: Five Centuries of the Pillage of
            Continent.* New York: Monthly Review Press.
Galtung, Johan.
   1971   "A Structural Theory of Imperialism." *Journal of Peace Research*
            (September): 81–117.
Gans, Herbert J.
   1962   *The Urban Villagers.* New York: Free Press.
Garfinkel, Harold.
   1956   "Conditions of Successful Degradation Ceremonies." *American
            Journal of Sociology* 61 (March): 420–424.
Garson, Barbara.
   1975   *All the Living Day: The Meaning and Demeaning of Routine
            Work.* New York: Doubleday.
Garvy, George.
   1943   "Kondratieff's Theory of Long Cycles." *Review of Economic Sta-
            tistics* 25 (November): 203–220.
Gedicks, Al.
   1976   "The Social Origins of Radicalism Among Finnish Immigrants in
            the Midwest Mining Communities." *Review of Radical Political
            Economics* 3, no. 3: 1–31.
Gerstein, Ira.
   1977   "Theories of the World Economy and Imperialism." *The Insur-
            gent Sociologist* 7 (Spring): 9–22.
Gibson, Bill.
   1980   "Unequal Exchange: Theoretical Issues and Empirical Findings."
            Review of Radical Political Economics 12 (Fall): 15–35.
Giddens, Anthony.
   1973   *The Class Structure of the Advanced Societies.* New York: Harper
            and Row.
Gillman, Joseph R.
   1957   *The Falling Rate of Profit.* London: Dennis Dobson.
Gitelman, H. M.
   1967   "The Waltham System and the Coming of the Irish." *Labor His-
            tory* (Fall): 227–253.

Glenn, Evelyn Nakano, and Roslyn L. Feldberg.

1979 "Proletarianizing Clerical Work: Technology and Organizational Control in the Office." Pp. 51–73 in Andrew Zimbalist (ed.), *Case Studies on the Labor Process*. New York: Monthly Review Press.

Glyn, Andrew, and Bob Sutcliffe.

1972 *British Capitalism, Workers and the Profit Squeeze*. London: Penguin.

Goldfrank, Walter L.

1978 "Fascism and World Economy." In *Social Change in the Capitalist World Economy*, edited by Barbara H. Kaplan. Volume 1 in the series Political Economy of the World System Annuals. Beverly Hills, Calif.: Sage Press.

———— (ed.).

1979 *The World-System of Capitalism: Past and Present*. London: Sage Publications.

Gordon, David M. (ed.).

1971 *Problems in Political Economy: An Urban Perspective*. Lexington, Mass.: D. C. Heath.

1972 *Theories of Poverty and Underemployment*. Lexington, Mass.: D. C. Heath.

1975 "Recession is Capitalism as Usual." *New York Times Magazine*, April 27, p. 18.

Gordon, David M.; Richard C. Edwards; and Michael Reich.

1978 "Labor Market Segmentation in American Capitalism." Mimeographed. New York: Department of Economics, New School for Social Research.

1982 *Segmented Work, Divided Workers: The Historical Transformation of Labor in the United States*. Cambridge: Cambridge University Press.

Gorz, Andre.

1976 *The Division of Labor: The Labor Process and Class Struggle*. Atlantic Highlands, N.J.: Humanities Press.

Gouldner, Alvin.

1954 *Patterns of Industrial Bureaucracy*. Glencoe, Ill.: Free Press.

1974 "The Metaphoricality of Marxism and the Context-Free Grammar of Socialism." *Theory and Society* 1 (Winter): 387–414.

1980 *The Two Marxisms: Contradictions and Anomalies in the Development of Theory*. New York: Oxford University Press.

Gramsci, Antonio.

1971 *Selections from the Prison Notebooks*. Edited and translated by Quintin Hoare and Geoffrey Nowell Smith. New York: International.

Greenbaum, Joan.
 1976   "Division of Labor in the Computer Field." *Monthly Review* 28
        (July/August): 40–55.
Grossman, Henryk.
 1929   *Das Akkumulations- und Zusammenbruchgesetz der ka-
        pitalistischen Systems*. Leipzig: C. L. Hirschfeld.
 1977   "Marx, Classical Political Economy and the Problem of Dynam-
        ics." *Capital and Class* 2: 32–55.
Gutman, Herbert.
 1976   *Work, Culture and Society in Industrializing America*. New York:
        Knopf.
Habermas, Jurgen.
 1975   *Legitimation Crisis*. Boston: Beacon.
Harrington, Michael.
 1962   *The Other America: Poverty in the United States*. London: Penguin.
Harrison, Bennett, and Andrew Sum.
 1979   "The Theory of 'Dual' or Segmented Labor Markets." *Journal of
        Economic Issues* 13 (September): 687–706.
Hauser, Robert M.
 1980   "On 'Stratification' in a Dual Economy." *American Sociological
        Review* 45 (August): 702–712.
Hilferding, Rudolf.
 1923   *Das Finanzkapital*. Vienna: Wiener Volksbuchhandlung Ignaz
        Brand.
 1981   *Finance Capital: A Study of the Latest Phase of Capitalist Devel-
        opment*. Translated by Tom Bottomore. London: Routledge and
        Kegan Paul.
Hilton, Rodney (ed.).
 1978   *The Transition from Feudalism to Capitalism*. Verso Editions.
        New York: Schocken Books.
Hobsbawm, E. J.
 1973   *Revolutionaries: Contemporary Essays*. New York: Meridian.
Hodgson, Geoff.
 1974   "The Theory of the Falling Rate of Profit." *New Left Review* 84
        (March/April): 55–80.
Hodson, Randy.
 1977   "Labor Force Participation and Earnings in the Core, Peripheral,
        and State Sectors of Production." Mimeographed. Madison, Wis.:
        Department of Sociology, University of Wisconsin. Reprinted in
        Politics and Society 8, nos. 3, 4 (1978): 429–480. 1978.
Hodson, Randy, and Robert L. Kaufman.
 1981   "Circularity in the Dual Economy: A Comment on Tolbert, Horan,
        and Beck 1980." *American Journal of Sociology* 86: 881–887.

1982   "Economic Dualism: A Critical Review." *American Sociological Review* 47 (December): 727–739.

Hopkins, Terence K., and Immanuel Wallerstein (eds.).
1980   *Processes of the World System.* Volume 2 in the series Political Economy of the World System Annuals. Beverly Hills, Calif.: Sage Press.

Horan, Patrick M.
1978   "Is Status Attainment Research Atheoretical?" *American Sociological Review* 43 (August): 534–541.

Horan, Patrick M.; E. M. Beck; and Charles M. Tolbert II.
1980   "The Market Homogeneity Assumption: On the Theoretical Foundations of Empirical Knowledge." *Social Science Quarterly* 61 (September): 279–292.
1981   "The Circle Has No Close." *American Journal of Sociology* 86: 887–894.

Hultgren, Thor.
1965   *Costs, Prices, and Profits: Their Cyclical Relations.* New York: National Bureau of Economic Research.

Jackman, Robert W.
1980   "A Note on Measurement of Growth Rates in Cross-National Research." *American Journal of Sociology* 86, no. 3: 604.

Jacobi, Otto; Joachim Bergman; and Walther Mueller-Jentsch.
1975   "Problems in Marxist Theories of Inflation." *Kapitalistate* 3 (Spring): 107–125.

Jacoby, Russell.
1975   "The Politics of Crisis Theory: Toward the Critique of Automatic Marxism II." *Telos* 23 (Spring): 107–125.

Jalee, Pierre.
1968   *The Pillage of the Third World.* New York: Monthly Review Press.

Kalecki, Michal.
1933   "An Essay on the Theory of the Business Cycle." Originally published in Polish. Subsequently published in English as "Outline of a Theory of the Business Cycle" in Michal Kalecki, *Studies in the Theory of Business Cycles 1933–1939.* Oxford: Basil Blackwell, 1966.

Kalleberg, Arne L., and Aage B. Sorensen.
1979   "The Sociology of Labor Markets." *Annual Review of Sociology* 5: 351–379.

Kalleberg, Arne L.; Michael Wallace; and Robert P. Althausser.
1981   "Economic Segmentation, Worker Power, and Income Inequality." *American Journal of Sociology* 87: 651–683.

Kaplan, Barbara H. (ed.).

1978   *Social Change in the Capitalist World Economy*. Volume 1 in the series Political Economy of the World System Annuals. Beverly Hills, Calif.: Sage Press.

Kaufman, Robert L., and Thomas N. Daymont.

1981   "Racial Discrimination and the Social Organization of Industries." *Social Science Research* 10 (September): 225–255.

Kaufman, Robert L.; Randy Hodson; and Niel D. Fligstein.

1981   "Defrocking Dualism: A New Approach to Defining Industrial Sectors." *Social Science Research* 10 (March): 1–31.

Kautsky, Karl.

1910   *The Class Struggle*. Chicago: C. H. Kerr.

Kay, Geoffrey.

1975   *Development, Underdevelopment and the Law of Value: A Marxist Analysis*. New York: St. Martin.

Kerr, Clark.

1954   "The Balkanization of Labor Markets." Pp. 92–110 in *Labor Mobility and Economic Opportunity*, edited by E. Wright Bakke. Cambridge, Mass.: MIT Press.

Kessler-Harris, Alice.

1975   "Stratifying by Sex: Understanding the History of Working Women." Pp. 217–242 in *Labor Market Segmentation*, edited by Richard C. Edwards, Michael Reich, and David M. Gordon. Lexington, Mass.: D. C. Heath.

Kettler, David.

1971   "The Vocation of Radical Intellectuals." *Politics and Society* 1 (May): 23–49.

Kidron, Michael.

1974   *Capitalism and Theory*. London: Pluto.

Kondratieff, N. D.

1935   "The Long Waves in Economic Life." *Review of Economic Statistics* 17 (November): 101–115.

Korsch, Karl.

1970   *Marxism and Philosophy*. London: New Left Books.

1974   "The Crisis of Marxism." *New German Critique* 3 (Fall): 3–11.

Kraft, Philip.

1977   *Programmers and Managers: The Routinization of Computer Programming in the United States*. New York: Springer Verlag.

1979   "The Industrialization of Computer Programming: From Programming to 'Software Production.'" Pp. 1–17 in Andrew Zimbalist (ed.), *Case Studies on the Labor Process*. New York: Monthly Review Press.

Kuhn, Thomas S.
   1962   *The Structure of Scientific Revolutions*. Chicago: University of
            Chicago Press.
Kusterer, Ken.
   1978a   "Working Knowledge and Work Control Among 'Unskilled'
            Workers." Paper presented to the Conference on New Directions
            in the Labor Process, State University of New York, Binghamton,
            May 5–7.
   1978b   *Workplace Know-How: The Important Working Knowledge of
            "Unskilled" Workers*. Boulder, Colo.: Westview.
Laclau, Ernesto.
   1977   *Politics and Ideology in Marxist Theory*. London: New Left Books.
Lacoste, Yves.
   n.d.   *Les Pays Sous-Developpes*. Paris: Presses Universitaires de France.
Ladd, Everett Carl, and S. M. Lipset.
   1975   *The Divided Academy: Professors and Politics*. New York:
            McGraw-Hill.
Landsberg, Martin.
   1979   "Export-Led Industrialization in the Third World: Manufacturing
            Imperialism." *Review of Radical Political Economics* 11 (Winter):
            50–63.
Larson, Magali Sarfatti.
   1977   *The Rise of Professionalism: A Sociological Analysis*. Berkeley:
            University of California Press.
Laslett, John H. M., and Seymour M. Lipset (eds.).
   1974   *Failure of a Dream: Essays in the History of American Socialism*.
            New York: Doubleday.
Lebowitz, Michael A.
   1976   "Marx's Falling Rate of Profit: A Dialectical View." *Canadian
            Journal of Economics* 9 (May): 232–254.
   1982   "The General and the Specific in Marx's Theory of Crisis." *Stud-
            ies in Political Economy* 7 (Winter): 5–25.
Leftwich, Richard H.
   1955   *The Price System and Resource Allocation*. New York: Holt,
            Rinehart and Winston.
Lenin, V. I.
   1935   *State and Revolution: Marxist Teaching About the Theory of the
            State and the Tasks of the Proletariat in Revolution*. New York:
            International.
   1967   *The Development of Capitalism in Russia*. 2nd ed. Moscow:
            Progress.
   1969   *Imperialism, The Highest Stage of Capitalism: A Popular Outline*.
            Peking: Foreign Languages.

Liebow, Elliott.
  1967   *Tally's Corner*. Boston: Little Brown.
Lifshultz, Lawrence S.
  1974   "Could Karl Marx Teach Economics in America?" *Ramparts* 12 (April): 27–52.
Lord, George F. III, and William W. Falk.
  1980   "An Exploratory Analysis of Individualist Versus Structuralist Explanations of Income." *Social Forces* 59 (December): 376–391.
  1982   "Dual Economy, Dual Labor, and Dogmatic Marxism: Reply to Morrissey." *Social Forces* 60 (March): 891–897.
Loveridge, Ray.
  1983   "Sources of Diversity in Internal Labour Markets." *Sociology* 17 (February): 44–62.
Loveridge, Ray, and A. L. Mok.
  1979   *Theories of Labour Market Segmentation*. London: Martinus Nijhoff Social Sciences Division.
Lubeck, Paul.
  1983   "Islam and Urban Labor: The Making of a Moslem Working Class." Unpublished manuscript. Department of Sociology, University of California, Santa Cruz.
Luxemburg, Rosa.
  1951   *The Accumulation of Capital*. With an introduction by Joan Robinson. New York: Monthly Review Press.
  1966   *Social Reform or Revolution?* Colombo, Ceylon: Young Socialist Press.
  1977   *The Industrial Development of Poland*. New York: Campaigner.
Luxemburg, Rosa, and Nikolai Bukharin.
  1972   *The Accumulation of Capital—An Anti-Critique*. Edited by Kenneth Tarbuck. New York: Monthly Review Press.
McCall, J. J.
  1971   "Probabilistic Microeconomics." *Bell Journal of Economics and Management Science* 2 (Autumn): 403–433.
Magdoff, Harry.
  1969   *Age of Imperialism*. New York: Monthly Review Press.
  1977   "How to Make a Molehill out of a Mountain: Reply to Szymanski." *Insurgent Sociologist* 7 (Spring): 106–112.
Mage, S. H.
  1963   "The Law of the Falling Tendency of the Rate of Profit." Ph.D. dissertation, Columbia University.
Maltese, Francesca.
  1973   "Notes for a Study of the Automobile Industry." Pp. 27–84 in *Labor Market Segmentation*, edited by Richard C. Edwards, Mi-

chael Reich, and David M. Gordon. Lexington, Mass.: D. C.
Heath.

Mandel, Ernest.
1968   *Marxist Economic Theory.* New York: Monthly Review Press.
1970   *Europe vs. America: Contradictions of Imperialism.* New York:
Monthly Review Press.
1971   *The Formation of the Economic Thought of Karl Marx.* New
York: Monthly Review Press.
1975   *Late Capitalism.* London: New Left Books.

Marcuse, Herbert.
1964   *One-Dimensional Man.* Boston: Beacon.

Marglin, Stephen A.
1974   "What Do Bosses Do?: The Origins and Functions of Hierarchy
in Capitalist Production." *Review of Radical Political Economics*
6 (Summer): 33–60.

Marramao, Giacomo.
1975   "Political Economy and Critical Theory." *Telos* 24 (Summer):
56–80.

Marx, Karl.
1967a   *Capital: A Critique of Political Economy.* Volume I: *The Process
of Capitalist Production.* Edited by Frederick Engels. New York:
International.
1967b   *Capital: A Critique of Political Economy.* Volume II: *The Process
of Circulation of Capital.* Edited by Frederick Engels. New York:
International.
1967c   *Capital: A Critique of Political Economy.* Volume III: *The Process of Capitalist Production as a Whole.* Edited by Frederick
Engels. New York: International.
1969   *Theories of Surplus Value.* (Volume 4 of *Capital.*) Moscow:
Progress.
1972   "Marginal Notes on Adolph Wagner's Textbook on Political Economy." *Theoretical Practice* 5 (Spring).
1973   *Grundrisse: Foundations of the Critique of Political Economy.*
Translated with a foreword by Martin Nicolaus. London: Penguin.

Marx, Karl, and Frederick Engels.
1972   *Selected Works.* New York: International.

Matthiessen, Francis Otto.
1941   *American Renaissance: Art and Expression in the Age of Emerson
and Whitman.* New York: Oxford University Press.

Mattick, Paul.
1934   "The Permanent Crisis: Henryk Grossman's Interpretation of
Marx's Theory of Capitalist Accumulation." *International Coun-*

cil Correspondence 2 (November): 1–20. Reprinted in *New Essays*, Vol. 1: *1934–1935*. Westport, Conn.: Greenwood, 1970.

1969   *Marx and Keynes: The Limit of the Mixed Economy*. Boston: Porter Sargent.

Meek, Ronald.

1956   *Studies in the Labour Theory of Value*. London: Lawrence and Wishart.

Merton, Robert K.

1968   *Social Theory and Social Structure*. London: Collier-MacMillan.

Miller, S. M.; Roy Bennett; and Cyril Alapatt.

1970   "Does the U.S. Economy Require Imperialism?" *Social Policy* 1 (September/October): 13–19.

Montgomery, David.

1979   *Workers' Control in America: Studies in the History of Work, Technology, and Labor Struggles*. Cambridge: Cambridge University Press.

Monthly Review.

1976   *Technology, the Labor Process, and the Working Class*. A special issue of *Monthly Review*. Vol. 28, no. 3 (July/August).

Morrissey, Marietta.

1982   "The Dual Economy and Labor Market Segmentation: A Comment on Lord and Falk." *Social Forces* 60 (March): 883–890.

Murdock, George, and Suzanne F. Wilson.

1972   "Settlement Patterns and Community Organization: Cross Cultural Codes 3." *Ethnology* 11 (July): 254–295.

Murray, Martin.

1976   "International Capital Flows and the Meaning of Capitalist Expansion." *Review of Radical Political Economics* 8 (Summer).

Nicolaus, Martin.

1973   "The Professional Organization of Sociology: A View from Below." Pp. 45–60 in *Ideology in Social Sciences: Readings in Critical Social Theory*, edited by Robin Blackburn. New York: Vintage.

Noble, David F.

1977   *America by Design: Science, Technology and the Rise of Corporate Capitalism*. New York: Knopf.

1979   "Social Choice in Machine Design: The Case of Automatically Controlled Machine Tools." Pp. 18–50 in *Case Studies on the Labor Process*, edited by Andrew Zimbalist. New York: Monthly Review Press.

O'Connor, James.

1973   *The Fiscal Crisis of the State*. New York: St. Martin's.

Osterman, Paul.
  1975   "An Empirical Study of Labor Market Segmentation." Mim-
         eographed. Department of Urban Studies and Planning, Massa-
         chusetts Institute of Technology.
Pannekoek, Anton.
  1977   "The Theory of the Collapse of Capitalism." *Capital and Class* 1
         (Spring): 59–82.
Parcel, Toby L., and Charles W. Mueller.
  1983   *Ascription and Labor Markets: Race and Sex Differences in Earn-
         ings.* New York: Academic Press.
Perlo, Victor.
  1973   *The Unstable Economy: Booms and Recessions in the United
         States Since 1945.* New York: International.
  1976   "The New Propaganda of Declining Profit Shares and Inadequate
         Investment." *Review of Radical Political Economics* 8 (Fall):
         53–64.
Petras, James.
  1978   *Critical Perspectives on Imperialism and Social Class in the Third
         World.* New York: Monthly Review Press.
Phelps, E. S.
  1972   "The Statistical Theory of Racism and Sexism." *American Eco-
         nomic Review* 62 (September): 659–661.
Piore, Michael.
  1970   "The Dual Labor Market: Theory and Implications." Pp. 90–94
         in *Problems in Political Economy: An Urban Perspective*, edited
         by D. M. Gordon. Lexington, Mass.: D. C. Heath.
  1975   "Notes for a Theory of Labor Market Stratification." Pp.
         125–150 in *Labor Market Segmentation*, edited by Richard C.
         Edwards, Michael Reich, and David M. Gordon. Lexington,
         Mass.: D. C. Heath.
Pomer, Marshall I.
  1981   *Intergenerational Occupational Mobility in the United States: A
         Segmentation Perspective.* Gainesville: University Presses of
         Florida.
Reich, Michael.
  1971   "The Economics of Racism." Pp. 107–113 in *Problems in Politi-
         cal Economy: An Urban Perspective*, edited by David M. Gordon.
         Lexington, Mass.: D. C. Heath.
  1981   *Racial Inequality: A Political-Economic Analysis.* Princeton,
         N.J.: Princeton University Press.
Rey, P. P.
  1971   *Colonialisme, neo-colonialisme, et transition au capitalisme.*
         Paris: Maspero.

1973   *Les alliances de classes*. Paris: Maspero.
Roberts, Dick.
1971   *Mideast Oil and Imperialism*. New York: Pathfinder.
Robinson, Joan.
1942   *An Essay on Marxian Economics*. London: Macmillan.
Roemer, John.
1979   "Divide and Conquer: Microeconomic Foundations of a Marxian Theory of Wage Discrimination." *Bell Journal of Economics* 10 (Autumn): 695–670.
Rosenberg, Samuel.
1975   "The Dual Labor Market: Its Existence and Consequences." Ph.D. dissertation, University of California, Berkeley.
Rostow, W. W.
1960   *The Stages of Economic Growth, A Non-Communist Manifesto*. Cambridge: Cambridge University Press.
1975   "Kondratieff, Schumpeter, and Kuznets: Trend Periods Revisited." *Journal of Economic History* 35 (December): 719–753.
Rowthorn, Bob.
1976   "Late Capitalism." *New Left Review* 48 (July/August): 59–83.
Rubinson, Richard.
1976   "The World-Economy and the Distribution of Income within States: A Cross-National Study." *American Sociological Review* 41 (August): 638–659.
———— (ed.).
1981   *Dynamics of World Development*. Volume 3 in the series Political Economy of the World System Annuals. Beverly Hills, Calif.: Sage Press.
Ryan, Mary P.
1975   *Womanhood in America: From Colonial Times to Present*. New York: New Viewpoints.
Sale, Kirkpatrick.
1974   *SDS*. New York: Vintage.
Schlatter, Richard.
1977   "On Being a Communist at Harvard." *Partisan Review* 44: 605–615.
Schlessinger, Arthur M., Jr.
1946   *Age of Jackson*. Boston: Little Brown.
Schroyer, Trent.
1972   "Marx's Theory of Crisis." *Telos* 14 (Winter): 106–124.
Selznick, Phillip.
1969   *Law, Society, and Industrial Justice*. New York: Russell Sage Foundation.

Sherman, Howard.
  1968   *Profit Rates in the United States*. Ithaca, N.Y.: Cornell University
          Press.
  1976a   "Inflation, Unemployment, and Monopoly." *Monthly Review* 27
          (March): 25–35.
  1976b   *Stagflation: A Radical Theory of Unemployment and Inflation*.
          New York: Harper and Row.
Skocpol, Theda.
  1979   *States and Social Revolutions*. Cambridge: Cambridge University
          Press.
Smith, Adam.
  1937   *The Wealth of Nations*. New York: Random House.
Smith, D. Randall.
  1983   "Mobility in Professional Occupational-Internal Labor Markets."
          American Sociological Review 48 (June): 289–305.
Smuts, Robert W.
  1971   *Women and Work in America*. New York: Schocken.
Snyder, David, and Edward L. Kick.
  1979   "Structural Growth Position in the World System and Economic
          Growth, 1955–1970: A Multiple-Network Analysis of Transna-
          tional Interactions." *American Journal of Sociology* 84, no. 5: 1096.
Spenner, Kenneth.
  1979   "Temporal Changes in Work Content." *American Sociological
          Review* 44 (December): 965–975.
Stark, David.
  1978   "Class Structure, Class Struggle, and the Labor Process: A Cri-
          tique of Braverman's *Labor and Monopoly Capital*." Paper pre-
          sented at the Conference on New Directions in the Labor Process,
          State University of New York at Binghamton, May 5–7.
Stinchcombe, Arthur.
  1982   "Review Essay: The Growth of the Modern World System."
          American Journal of Sociology 87, no. 6: 1389–1395.
Stokes, Randall, and David Jaffee.
  1982   "Another Look at the Export of Raw Materials and Economic
          Growth." *American Sociological Review* 27 (June): 402–407.
Stolzenberg, Ross M.
  1975   "Occupations, Labor Markets and the Process of Wage Attain-
          ment." *American Sociological Review* 40 (October): 645–665.
  1978   "Bringing the Boss Back In: Employer Size, Employee School-
          ing, and Socioeconomic Achievement." *American Sociological
          Review* 43 (December): 813–828.

Stone, Katherine.
  1974   "The Origins of Job Structures in the Steel Industry." *Review of Radical Political Economics* 6 (Summer): 61–97.
Stromberg, Anne H., and Shirley Harkess (eds.).
  1978   *Women Working: Theories and Facts in Perspective.* Palo Alto, Calif.: Mayfield.
Sunkel, Osvaldo.
  1969   "The Structural Background of Development Problems in Latin America." Pp. 3–40 in *Latin America: Problems in Economic Development*, edited by Charles T. Nisbet. New York: Free Press.
Sweezy, Paul M.
  1942   *The Theory of Capitalist Development.* New York: Monthly Review Press.
Szymanski, Albert.
  1974   "Marxist Theory and International Capital Flows." *Review of Radical Political Economics* 6 (Fall): 20–40.
  1976   "Racial Discrimination and White Gain." *American Sociological Review* 41 (June): 403–414.
  1977   "Capital Accumulation on a World Scale and the Necessity of Imperialism." *Insurgent Sociologist* 7 (Spring): 35–53.
  1978   "White Workers' Loss from Racial Discrimination: Reply to Villemez." *American Sociological Review* 43 (October): 776–782.
Thompson, James D.
  1967   *Organizations in Action.* New York: McGraw-Hill.
Thurow, Lester C.
  1969   "Poverty and Human Capital." Pp. 85–90 in *Problems in Political Economy: An Urban Perspective*, edited by David M. Gordon. Lexington, Mass.: D. C. Heath.
Tolbert, Charles M.
  1982   "Industrial Segmentation and Men's Career Mobility." *American Sociological Review* 47 (August): 457–477.
Tolbert, Charles M.; Patrick M. Horan; and E. M. Beck.
  1980   "The Structure of Economic Segmentation: A Dual Economy Approach." *American Journal of Sociology* 85 (March): 1095–1116.
Tucker, Robert C. (ed.).
  1972   *The Marx-Engels Reader.* New York: Norton.
Tugan-Baranowski, Michael.
  1901   *Studien zur Theorie und Geschichte der Handelskrisen in England.* Jena: G. Fischer.
  1905   *Theoretische Grundlagen des Marxismus.* Leipzig: Dunker and Humbolt.
Tyler, Gus.
  1961   "Marginal Industries, Low Wages, and High Risks." *Dissent* 8 (Summer): 321–325.

Union for Radical Political Economics.

1978   *U.S. Capitalism in Crisis.* New York: Union for Radical Political Economics.

Unwin, George.

1957   *Industrial Organization in the Sixteenth and Seventeenth Centuries.* London: Cass.

Van Parijs, Philippe.

1980   "The Falling-Rate-of-Profit Theory of Crisis: A Rational Reconstruction by Way of Obituary." *Review of Radical Political Economics* 12 (Spring): 1–16.

Villemez, Wayne J.

1978   "Black Subordination and White Economic Well-Being: Comment on Szymanski." *American Sociological Review* 43 (October): 772–776.

Wachtel, Howard.

1971   "Looking at Poverty from a Radical Perspective." *Review of Radical Political Economics* 3 (Summer): 1–19.

1972   "Capitalism and Poverty in America: Paradox or Contradiction?" *Monthly Review* 24 (June): 51–64.

Wachtel, Howard, and Charles Betsy.

1972   "Employment at Low Wages." *Review of Economics and Statistics* 54 (May): 121–129.

Wallace, Michael, and Arne L. Kalleberg.

1982   "Industrial Transformation and the Decline of Craft: The Decomposition of Skill in the Printing Industry." *American Sociological Review* 47 (June): 307–324.

Wallerstein, Immanuel.

1974   *The Modern World System: Capitalist Agriculture and the Origins of the European World-Economy in the 16th Century.* New York: Academic Press.

Walsh, John.

1978   "Radicals and the Universities: 'Critical Mass' at U. Mass." *Science* 199 (6 January): 34–38.

Ware, Caroline T.

1931   *The Early New England Cotton Manufactures: A Study of Industrial Beginnings.* Boston: Houghton Mifflin.

Warren, Bill.

1973   "Imperialism and Capitalist Industrialization." *New Left Review* 81 (September/October): 3–44.

1980   *Imperialism: Pioneer of Capitalism.* London: New Left Books.

Weber, Max.

1954   *Law in Economy and Society.* Edited with an introduction by Max Rheinstein. New York: Simon and Schuster.

1958 *The Protestant Ethic and the Spirit of Capitalism*. Translated by Talcott Parsons. New York: Scribner's.

Weisskopf, Thomas E.
1978 "Marxist Perspectives on Cyclical Crisis." Pp. 241–260 in *U.S. Capitalism in Crisis*. New York: Union for Radical Political Economics.

Wolfe, Alan.
1971 "Thinking about the Unthinkable: Reflections on the Failure of the Caucus for a New Political Science." *Politics and Society* 1 (May): 393–406.
1977 *The Limits of Legitimacy: Political Consequences of Contemporary Capitalism*. New York: Free Press.

Wolpe, Harold.
1972 "Capitalism and Cheap Labour-Power in South Africa: From Segregation to Apartheid." *Economy and Society* 1, no. 4: 425–486.
——— (ed.).
1980 *The Articulation of Modes of Production: Essays from Economy and Society*. London: Routledge and Kegan Paul.

Women's Work Project.
1978 "Women in Today's Economic Crisis." Pp. 69–76 in *U.S. Capitalism in Crisis*. New York: Union of Radical Political Economics.

Woodward, Joan.
1965 *Industrial Organization: Theory and Practice*. London: Oxford University Press.

Wright, Erik O.
1975 "Alternative Perspectives in the Marxist Theory of Accumulation and Crisis." *The Insurgent Sociologist* 6 (Fall): 5–40.

Wright, Erik O., and Luca Perrone.
1977 "Marxist Class Categories and Income Inequality." *American Sociological Review* 42 (February): 32–55.

Wycko, Will.
1975 "The Work Shortage: Class Struggle and Capital Reproduction." *Review of Radical Political Economics* 7 (Summer): 11–30.

Yaffe, David.
1973 "The Marxian Theory of Crisis, Capital and the State." *Economy and Society* 2 (May): 186–232.

Zimbalist, Andrew.
1975 "The Limits of Work Humanization." *Review of Radical Political Economics* 7 (Summer): 50–58.
——— (ed.).
1979 *Case Studies in the Labor Process*. New York: Monthly Review Press.

Zucker, Lynne G., and Carolyn Rosenstein.
1981 "Taxonomies of Institutional Structure: Dual Economy Reconsidered." *American Sociological Review* 46 (December): 869–884.

INDEX

Greenwood, SC 29646